# Welfare Theory and Social Policy

# Welfare Theory and Social Policy

## Reform or Revolution?

Phil Lee and Colin Raban

Ⓢ SAGE Publications

London · Newbury Park · Beverly Hills · New Delhi

SAGE Publications Ltd
28 Banner Street
London EC1Y 8QE

SAGE Publications India Pvt Ltd
C-236 Defence Colony
New Delhi 110 024

SAGE Publications Inc
2111 West Hillcrest Street
Newbury Park, California 91320

SAGE Publications Inc
275 South Beverly Drive
Beverly Hills, California 90212

**British Library Cataloguing in Publication Data**

Lee, Phil
   Welfare theory and social policy: reform or revolution?
   1. Welfare state—Political aspects
   I. Title II. Raban, Colin
   361.6′5    HN28

   ISBN 0-8039-8130-9
   ISBN 0-8039-8131-7 Pbk

**Library of Congress catalog card number 87-051530**

Typeset and printed in Great Britain by The Alden Press, Oxford

# Contents

Preface and Acknowledgements     vii

Prologue     1

PART I    FABIAN REVISIONISM AND THE
WELFARE STATE
*Colin Raban*     9

**1   Legacies**     11
   Marxism and Fabianism     11
   Reform and revolution     14
   Scientific and utopian socialism     16
   The economic and the political     20
   The state and the transition to socialism     26
   The verdict of history     32

**2   Fabian Collectivism and the Welfare State**     38
   Fabian collectivism and the post-war settlement     39
   The ideology of an ending     44
   The mandarins of the welfare state     48
   The new left and the ideology of affluence     52

**3   Towards a Critical Social Policy**     60
   The Young Turks of the cultural revolution     61
   The pathology of welfare studies     63
   Fabian social criticism     70
   The social division of welfare     72
   The limitations of welfare statism     78
   Socialism and constitutional action     80

**Conclusion    Criticism and Crisis**     89

PART II    MARXISM AND WELFARE
*Phil Lee*     95

**4   A Cynical Gaze?**     100
   Marxist theory and welfare     100
   Accommodating capitalism: the unhelpful welfare state?     107
   Origins of Marxist fundamentalism     111

The politics of fundamentalism 114
Theoretical excesses of fundamentalism 122
The state revisited 128
Status of welfare reforms 132
Conclusion 137

**5 The Politics of Social Policy** 142
Moving beyond context 142
Traditional politics 144
Prefigurative politics 145
Realistic politics 153
Realism and the transition to socialism 159
Realism, welfare and Britain 164
Conclusion 166

**6 Marxist Theory, Welfare and Political Realism** 171
Beyond critique: towards the politically achievable 171
Dismissing the Fabian tradition? 176
Towards a critical policy analysis 180
Sensitising concepts 185
The state and policy formation 192
Living, breathing class struggle 199
A new view of power? 206
Conclusion 209

**Conclusion   Necessary Revisions: A Third Way?** 216
The crisis of socialism 216
The crisis of welfare 220

Index 228

# Preface and Acknowledgements

Teaching loads and administrative commitments in today's polytechnics are such that projects often have to be put down at the end of one vacation to be picked up at the beginning of the next. It was under these conditions, and over a period of six years, that this book was produced. We hope that the scars of its protracted birth are not too visible.

Many people have suffered over those six years – not least our students, who have been required to read various versions of our chapters and who have contributed in no small way to a better final product. Our colleagues in the Department of Applied Social Studies, Sheffield City Polytechnic, have also helped. The library staff have borne the brunt of our requests with great efficiency and politeness; and Angela Steel, Chris Roscoe and Marilyn Gregory must be thanked for typing sections of the manuscript.

Richard Kuper and Stephen Barr have suffered inordinately from our excuses and delays. We are indebted to them for their patient and helpful editing. We also thank Len Doyal, John Clarke and Ian Gough for their helpful comments on reading earlier drafts of the book. The *Critical Social Policy* collective has provided a creative and inspiring forum for one of the authors. Its many stimulating discussions, sometimes heated but always friendly, have helped clarify many ideas.

Particular thanks are due to friends who have provided the invaluable service of listening, arguing and helping us to see things differently. Last, but by no means least, our families and loved ones have suffered, and it is to them that this book is dedicated.

They say: you can't change horses in mid-stream.
True. But the old guard have drowned already.

You say: admitting our faults helps the enemy.
True. But who do our lies help?

Many say: in the long run socialism is inevitable.
True. But who's going to make it happen?

Wolf Bierman

# Prologue

This book has been written during a period of confusion and conflict in welfare politics, and at a time when the traditional verities and ground-rules of the post-war consensus are being decisively challenged by critics on the right and left. The welfare state has been condemned for its alleged contribution to economic decline, and for its failure to realise even some of the more modest aspirations of its architects. In Britain, Labour politicians have disowned the centralism and bureaucratic collectivism of public welfare services, and the one-nation Tory paternalists have been beaten into retreat by market liberals in their own party.

These are perplexing times for anyone concerned with the achievement of more democratic, egalitarian and cooperative forms of production and public administration. Whilst the radical right is making significant political and intellectual gains, socialists appear to be in a state of disarray and internal division. How is the welfare state to be defended, when so much left-wing analysis has been deeply critical of its purposes, effects and methods of administration? Are those on the left caught between the bankrupt orthodoxies of the Fabian tradition and the utopian recipes of the neo-Marxist approach?

In 1981 a new British journal for the study of social welfare was established – *Critical Social Policy*. Its principal aim was to offer alternatives to the inadequacies of Fabian socialism by drawing upon the resources provided by neo-Marxist perspectives on social policy. At the same time there was a growing interest in Fabian circles in the need to restate social democratic values, and to engage in a more critical analysis of the forms and objectives of the welfare state. This was seen as a precondition for the development of effective and electorally attractive social policies for future socialist governments. It appeared to us – of whom one is a member of the *CSP* collective and the other of the Fabian Society – that there was a need for a book that would explore the possible common ground between these new movements within Fabianism and Marxism.

This book represents an attempt to supply answers to three questions. First, what is Fabianism and why has it become such a target for the new left? Second, what exactly is different about neo-Marxist welfare theory? And, third, what policy and political inferences can be drawn from a critical evaluation of Marxist and Fabian ideas on the welfare state? As two people who have discussed these issues together at some length, and with initial loyalties firmly on either side of the Marxist–Fabian divide, we have come to the conclusion that the two traditions do possess certain complementary strengths. Our argument, simply stated, is for a fusion of the critical elements of Fabianism with a realistic version of Marxism.

It is revisionism that provides the meeting-point between the two traditions. The Fabian Society was founded more than a century ago in a revisionist spirit, and it is the sceptical way in which Fabians have continued to view political dogmas and theoretical orthodoxies that has kept that spirit alive. And the very attempt to adapt a nineteenth-century theoretical system for the purpose of analysing specifically twentieth-century phenomena places neo-Marxist approaches to the study of social policy in the revisionist camp. But this book is not only *about* revisionism, it is also intended as a contribution to a tradition whose style and intellectual method enables it to transcend sectarian political controversy. Our objective, ultimately, is to bring together elements from both sides of this sectarian divide. The purpose of this chapter is to prepare the ground by reviewing the ways in which the new (and neo-Marxist) and the more traditional (and Fabian) approaches to the subject of social policy have been brought into confrontation with one another.

It was in the early 1970s that influential figures within the discipline of social administration in Britain began to remark on an apparent polarisation of welfare debate and an outbreak of ideological warfare. These observations were made at a time of incipient economic and political crisis – the collapse of the long post-war boom, and the first significant departures from the Butskellite politics of the 1950s and 1960s. They were followed by the publication of several works which set out to reappraise the theoretical roots and political alignments of the discipline.[1]

Previously, the debate about welfare had been conducted largely on the basis of unacknowledged values and theoretical assumptions. The values had been derived from the Fabian tradition in British politics, and the assumptive base of welfare studies had been laid in the 1950s when it was widely believed that the fundamental structural problems of the capitalist order had been resolved. The basic premise was that the post-war welfare state had brought the 'real' into closer approximation to the 'ideal'; post-war Britain was seen as being, in every essential respect, 'the good society itself in operation'.[2] In these circumstances it is hardly surprising that academic commentaries on welfare had been largely conducted within a pragmatic, empirical and particularising idiom. This basically conservative idiom served, in turn, to mask the underlying assumptions of a consensus theory of welfare, politics and contemporary social problems.[3]

Since the early 1970s the position has changed quite dramatically. Several critical works on the problem of values in both social policy and policy analysis have appeared, and this development was followed by the emergence of a number of largely Marxist-inspired texts challenging the territorial claims and perspectives of orthodox social administration.[4] The new generation of writers and teachers that entered the field of social administration attacked not only the institutions of the welfare state, but also the vocational and theoretical stances of the old guard in the welfare intelligentsia. The Fabian heritage of traditional social administrators has been criticised for its parochial and pragmatic obsession with issues of administrative detail, and for its complacency in assuming that the welfare state embodied, at least potentially, the historical aspirations of the labour movement. Social administration has been described as 'the paper owl of the welfare state', as the ideological expression of an intelligentsia that is deeply compromised by its establishment connections.[5]

Social administration in Britain has certainly borne the imprint of Fabianism. Many of the standard works on the historical development of the welfare state advanced an implicitly Fabian defence of collectivism. The superiority of the collectivist welfare state over the institutions of the free market is asserted not only on ethical grounds, but also in terms of its greater efficiency. This theoretical commitment to collectivism also provides a mandate for the somewhat unusual blend of analysis and prescription that is found within the discipline. Social administration, a classic instance of the reformer's science, has set itself the task of providing the implements of rational government and efficient administration. In this respect its practical contributions to social development presuppose the tactics of persuasion framed within a broad strategy of incremental reform. This in fact is the outstanding characteristic of the discipline, and it could be argued that its conceptual formulations have been specifically tailored for the purpose of influencing social policy by placing a high premium on expert intervention in the decision-making processes that operate at various levels within the political system.

Some of the doyens of orthodox social administration were left in little doubt that their discipline had been the victim of an alien invasion, and they reacted in ways that indicated a less than positive attitude towards the new trend. Two early responses were provided by Robert

Pinker and David Donnison.[6] Pinker reserved a part of his attack for
the 'critical normative theory' of sociology. 'Marcuse's exhortation
that sociology is morally bound to adopt a critical stance towards its
subject matter is,' he suggested, 'only an exaggerated version of a
more general trend towards social misanthropy in theoretical
sociology.'[7] But the principal villain of the piece was, in Pinker's view,
*Marxist* theory:

> There comes a time when normative theories must . . . be judged in terms
> of their contribution to social progress, and that time has come for Marxist
> and neo-Marxist normative theory. So far these theories have helped to
> produce societies in which political brutality and incompetence have
> reached such dimensions that it is necessary to build brick walls and impose
> stringent controls on movement in order to preserve a social membership
> at all. The most charitable thing we can say about Lenin and Stalin is that
> had they each lived a little longer they might have grown bored with the
> slaughter.[8]

Donnison judged the issue in a way that was, perhaps, less harsh but
more telling. The relevance of a Marxist contribution to the welfare
debate was questioned on the grounds that, for Marxists, any consideration of social priorities is pointless and utopian. The irrelevance
of Marxism lies, for Donnison, in its failure to progress beyond mere
criticism. It furnishes its advocates with 'a very comfortable intellectual posture' since they are burdened 'neither by the philanthropic
duties of a conservative *noblesse oblige*, nor by the . . . compromises
of reformist politics'.[9]

There are some important differences between these two reactions.
Whilst Donnison appeared to be content to dismiss Marxism as
irrelevant to the practical concerns of social administrators, Pinker
seemed to be concerned with the political dangers inherent in utopian
thinking. In this respect, his argument was reminiscent of the conservative response to Enlightenment philosophy, and of the more recent
attacks on the ideologies of the extreme left and right. Thus, just as
Karl Popper constructed an invidious comparison between utopian
and piecemeal social engineering, absolutist and empiricist methodologies, Pinker's own account of the intellectual traditions of social
administration rested on the assertion that modern social and political
thought springs from two incompatible nineteenth-century sources:
one was a form of social enquiry that was empirical and sceptical,
whilst the other consisted of normative theories that were ideological
and authoritative in nature.[10] Pinker argued that, at a time when the
academic debate about social policy was becoming more imbued with
ideological imperatives, the discipline had to be preserved from 'the
wilder reaches of ideology'.[11] This Pinker did by locating social administration firmly within the empirical and sceptical traditions of

social enquiry. According to Pinker, the ethical preoccupations of social administrators have 'always been complemented by an equally strong commitment to democratic principles, rational discourse and a respect for evidence'. These qualities sharply distinguish the more revolutionary forms of social theory from the blend of pragmatism and moral conviction found within social administration. In the first case, the ideological abuse of reason and political freedom can only subvert the cause of social justice. Conversely, the empirical tradition, coupled with a willingness to compromise on issues of principle, should continue to enrich the subject and to ensure its future contributions to 'human betterment' and the 'maintenance of democratic values.'[12]

The same themes and preoccupations recur in Pinker's more recent work, which extended the attack to include not only the Marxist paradigm of welfare but also its counterpart in neo-classical economics.[13] Once again he reserved the term 'ideological' for any radical (or extreme) doctrine that seeks to transcend the present social order and extant political practices. The two opposed alternatives of classical economic theory and Marxism are portrayed as identical with respect to their political consequences (they tend, for example, to become 'instruments of oppression and diswelfare') and they are unfavourably compared with the pragmatic realism and open-minded eclecticism of the 'prudential philosophy' of the middle way.

Although Pinker's ostensible concern was to question the convention of locating competing welfare ideologies on a simple collectivism/anti-collectivism axis, it is clear that the rhetorical device that lay at the heart of his argument was, in fact, the old and familiar dichotomy between ideological dogmatism and free-thinking pragmatism. The impression that Pinker was merely substituting one dichotomy for another was confirmed when, at the 1981 conference of the Social Administration Association, he drew an invidious comparison between the 'middle range and piecemeal theory' of his discipline, and the 'abstract and millennial theories' of the new left and the new right ('the fifth horseman of the Apocalypse'). On this occasion Pinker was invoking empiricist canons of truth by arguing that the falsifiability of a theory is inversely related to its generality.

It would be easy to dismiss Pinker's rearguard defence of 'orthodox' social administration by simply pointing out that it constitutes little more than a latter-day version of the end-of-ideology thesis. Bell, Lipset and others, writing at a time when many intellectuals were renouncing their earlier commitments to leftist thinking in favour of a more full-blooded affirmation of Western ideals and achievements, tended to regard any kind of utopianism (or, in their terms, ideology) as a symptom of the pathological, destructive and malevolent facets of human conduct.[14] Pinker's defence has, however, become a part of the intellectual repertoire of the orthodox social administrator. Thus, the 1983 edition of *Issues in Social Policy* contains the accusation that the positions occupied by the detractors of the welfare state – whether they come from the 'extreme left' or the 'extreme right' – share the common characteristics of grandiosity, intellectual pretension, materialism, pitilessness, and a unidimensional view of mankind. In the words of the editors of that collection, *les extremes se touchent*.[15]

We seem, then, to be presented with two mutually antagonistic and equally entrenched intellectual stances. The confrontation between orthodox social administration and neo-Marxist critiques of the welfare state appears to exemplify Mannheim's original distinction between ideological and utopian thought. Ideologies are '"organically" and harmoniously integrated into the world-view characteristic of [a] period'; ideologists are those 'whose thought and feelings are bound up with an order of existence in which they have a definite position'. Utopias, on the other hand, offer 'revolutionary possibilities' and 'orient conduct towards elements which the situation, in so far as it is realised at the time, does not contain'.[16]

Thus the orthodox social administrator stands accused of ideological thinking, whilst neo-Marxists have the charge of utopianism levelled against them. Intellectually, the contest is between a parochial and particularised empiricism on the one hand, and abstractly theoretical, over-generalised and totalitarian methodologies on the other. The former implies a reformist political style: it is conservative, pragmatic and deeply compromised by its commitment to public service and incremental change. The latter appear to be intrinsically revolutionary – oppositional, utopian and wedded to an uncompromising and apocalyptic conception of the transition to socialism.

We have already noted the tendency for some orthodox social administrators, like those pronouncing the 'end of ideology', to assert the rationality, authority and objectivity of their own statements whilst treating the views of their opponents as symptoms of 'a diseased nature', calling for 'medical examination' rather than reasoned argument.[17] This claim to epistemological excellence is, for the utopian (and the neo-Marxist), a masquerade. Thus, just as C. Wright Mills maintained that the 'fetishised empiricism' of the 'end-of-ideology' school cloaked a partisan identification with the status quo, orthodox social administration has been attacked for its 'arthritic empiricism' and on the grounds that it renders the subject incapable of achieving 'an independent and critical standpoint'.[18] This kind of argument has provoked the retort that the critical standpoint of the new social administration (or, for that matter, the new left) is, in Mannheim's terms, 'absolutely' rather than 'relatively' utopian – that is, it embodies 'conceptions of existence which . . . can in principle never be realised'.[19] The basis for this charge is provided by the claim to value *eu*topian ideals whilst rejecting as dangerously impractical the *u*topian fantasies of one's critics. In this respect Pinker's arguments echo Daniel Bell's concluding comments in *The End of Ideology*. Bell called for the end of rhetoric, and of rhetoricians whose beliefs are 'suffused by apocalyptic fervour' and in whose hands 'ideas become weapons . . . with dreadful results'. The ladder to the city of heaven must be empirical, not founded on faith; passion must, Bell wrote, be fused with intelligence.[20]

In preparing this book we have taken the view that the contrast between Fabian and critical approaches to social policy has been overdrawn. This is, as we have seen, partly a consequence of misconceptions on both sides of the argument, exaggerating both the complacency and optimism of Fabian attitudes to the welfare state and the nihilism of the Marxist critique. And it is also the result of a common tendency to employ absolutist epistemologies in condemning the ideological (or utopian) qualities of their opponents' thought.[21] But there is now some evidence to indicate that the protagonists are adopting less entrenched positions and that a mutually productive dialogue is developing. These days, many orthodox social administrators acknowledge that the crisis in the welfare state demands a greater attention to conceptual issues and a 'radical rethinking' of the philosophy of Beveridge and the Webbs.[22] And many of those writers who are engaged in the development of a 'critical' social policy have come to concede that there is a need to build upon the empirical strengths and practical relevance of the social administration tradition. The point was made by Paul Wilding when he wrote that, if the new social administration is not to degenerate into 'wild and windy rhetoric', it must marry the detailed empirical study of the operation of particular services with the more theoretical concerns that have developed in recent years.[23]

Although we do not take the view that dialogue will be facilitated by obscuring the real differences between the two traditions and their associated intellectual styles, we do believe that the one can complement the other. This book is intended as a contribution to such a dialogue, and it seeks to achieve this purpose in two ways. First, we have tried to emphasise the intrinsic complexity and diversity of both the Fabian and the Marxist traditions. We feel that it is essential to distinguish the one from its more complacent and uncritical forms, and the other from its 'fundamentalist' variants, if we are to escape from the fruitless image of two monolithic and incompatible traditions locked in mortal struggle. This act of rehabilitation should reveal the critical potential of the Fabian tradition as well as the practical relevance of Marxism for those engaged in professional practice and constitutional political action in the welfare state. Second, we have set out to interpret the development of both traditions — in both the long and the short term – against the background of contemporary socio-economic and political circumstances. By emphasising the historical contingency of, say, Fabian optimism and the neo-Marxist revival we should avoid the idealism and epistemological absolutism that has been implicit in so many of the past encounters between the new left and the academic establishment. This means that both Fabianism and Marxism will be regarded as living traditions, capable in certain circumstances of acquiring both 'ideological' and 'utopian' characteristics, rather than as timeless doctrines whose essential character is embodied in a particular set of written texts.

## Notes

1   For example, R. Pinker, *Social Theory and Social Policy* (Heinemann, 1971); V. George and P. Wilding, *Ideology and Social Welfare* (Routledge and Kegan Paul, 1976).
2   S.M. Lipset, *Political Man* (Heinemann, 1963).
3   V. George and P. Wilding, *Ideology*, chapter 1.
4   I. Gough, *The Political Economy of the Welfare State* (Macmillan, 1979); P. Taylor-Gooby and J. Dale, *Social Theory and Social Welfare* (Edward Arnold, 1981).
5   Taylor-Gooby and Dale, *Social Theory*, chapter 1.
6   Pinker, *Social Theory*; D. Donnison, *Social Policy and Administration Revisited* (George Allen and Unwin, 1975).
7   Pinker, *Social Theory*, p. 132.
8   Ibid., pp. 132–3.
9   Donnison, *Social Policy*, p. 35.
10   Pinker, *Social Theory*, p. 50.
11   Ibid., pp. 97, 133.
12   Ibid., p. 133.
13   R. Pinker, *The Idea of Welfare* (Heinemann, 1979).
14   Lipset, *Political Man*, chapter 13; D. Bell, *The End of Ideology* (Free Press, 1960).
15   K. Jones, J. Brown and J. Bradshaw (eds), *Issues in Social Policy* (Routledge and Kegan Paul, 1983), p. 10.
16   K. Mannheim, *Ideology and Utopia* (Routledge and Kegan Paul, 1960), p. 174.
17   N. Harris, *Beliefs in Society* (Penguin, 1971), p. 19.
18   C.W. Mills, 'The new left', in I.L. Horowitz (ed.), *Power, Politics and People* (Oxford University Press, 1963); Taylor-Gooby and Dale, *Social Theory*, p. 21.
19   Mannheim, *Ideology*, pp. 176–7.
20   Bell, *The End of Ideology*, pp. 405–6.
21   P. Lee and C. Raban 'Ideology and welfare', in M. Loney, D. Boswell, and J. Clarke (eds), *Social Policy and Social Welfare* (Oxford University Press, 1983).
22   Jones et al., *Issues in Social Policy*, p. xi.
23   P. Wilding, 'The evolution of social administration', in P. Bean and S. MacPherson (eds), *Approaches to Welfare* (Routledge and Kegan Paul, 1983), p. 13.

# PART I

# FABIAN REVISIONISM AND THE WELFARE STATE

## Colin Raban

Although our general concern here is with the part of the socialist tradition that might be broadly termed 'revisionist', most of the discussion will focus specifically on British Fabianism. Chapter 1 will also make some reference to the ideas of Eduard Bernstein (1850–1932) – a leading proponent of revisionist theory and an important figure in the history of the German Social Democratic Party. During the 1890s Bernstein was compelled to seek exile in England, and it was there that he came to be influenced by Fabian thinking. The Fabian Society itself was founded in 1885 by, amongst others, George Bernard Shaw, H.G. Wells and Sidney and Beatrice Webb. In the course of the past century the Society has exerted a considerable influence on the British Labour Party. Most significantly for our purposes, members of the Fabian Society have played a major part in the formulation of Labour social policy and – mainly through the agency of the London School of Economics – in the development in Britain of the disciplines of sociology and social administration.

We distinguish between three broad phases in the development of Fabian thought, arguing that the character of each phase must be understood in the context of the historical circumstances in which it occurred. Chapter 1 is mainly concerned with what might be described as the 'classical' period in which the early Fabians set out to formulate practical 'revisions' and alternatives to Marxist theory and politics. Chapter 2 reviews the character of Fabian writing at a time when, in the late 1940s and 1950s, most social commentators took a broadly optimistic view of the achievements of the welfare state and of Fabian collectivism. (This was also a period in which many leading Labour intellectuals admitted, more or less enthusiastically, to the charge of 'revisionism'.) Discussion of the early post-war period is followed, in chapter 3, by an assessment of the Fabian contribution to the relatively recent development of a more critical literature on the welfare state and post-war society.

The general purpose of part I is to dissociate the Fabian tradition from some of the features that its detractors have ascribed to it. We emphasise the variegated nature of the Fabian tradition and the dangers inherent in the attempt to reduce it to any one of its many forms (collectivism, reformism etc.). We have already begun to explore aspects of Fabian notoriety in the prologue, and we shall continue to do so. Thus, in chapter 1, we start by restating the conventional opposition between Fabian and Marxist thought, but this is followed by the suggestion that both Fabians and Marxists have tended to overstate the differences that divide them. Chapter 2 argues that the reputation that Fabianism has had in the eyes of its critics should be seen as the specific product of the intellectual mood and political circumstances of the early post-war period. Chapter 3 then proceeds to critically re-examine the charges levelled against Fabianism by its critics in the new left and the 'new' social administration.

Our ultimate concern is to identify and explain the nature of the revisionist contribution to *current* welfare debate. It is with this end in view that we shall refer to the earlier development of Fabianism, and to certain other traditions of social thought. Our treatment of these earlier developments and other traditions is therefore selective. We have not attempted to provide a history of the Fabian Society, still less a history of British socialism. Nor have we attempted to supply a comprehensive discussion of classical Marxist thinking. Our objectives have been more modest. History has been used as a *resource* – as a means by which some of the cardinal and perennial features of Fabian thinking can be defined, and as a device for emphasising the need to understand the character and quality of the Fabian contribution in the context of contemporary circumstances. Equally, our references to Marxism are designed to achieve the limited purpose of explaining what it was that the early Fabians and revisionists felt was distinctive about their contribution to socialist analysis and politics.

# 1

# Legacies

Fabian socialism can be presented as the antithesis of Marxism and, indeed, it was originally conceived as an intellectual and political alternative to Marxism. Polemicists on both sides have tended to stress the differences between the two traditions. Thus, if Marxist politics are essentially revolutionary and proletarian, Fabian socialism can be defined as universal and reformist. If Marxist theory rests on materialist premises, Fabian theory incorporates elements of idealism. Whilst Marx tended to regard the capitalist state as an instrument of class rule, then, presumably, Fabians would be more inclined to see the state as a relatively neutral agency. And, where Marxists employed a 'catastrophic' theory of history, Fabians resorted to the notion of unilinear but gradual progress to explain and predict its course.

This chapter takes as its starting point the opposition, as it is conventionally drawn, between Marxism and Fabianism. The purpose of the present discussion is not to provide an introduction to classical Marxism, but to establish the central features of Fabian thought as they were defined by its early proponents. Thus, to the extent that this chapter provides a discussion of Marxist ideas, it does so selectively and as they have appeared from the vantage point of the Fabian and revisionist critic. Certain aspects of Fabian thinking are also introduced by referring to their counterparts in Marxist theory. Propagandists and polemicists – whether of Marxist or Fabian persuasion – will tend to advertise the novelty of their own position by emphasising its differences from that of their opponents. In this chapter, however, we shall be concerned to highlight the continuities as well as the contrasts between Marxism and Fabianism.

## Marxism and Fabianism

Many of the early Fabians were, in fact, ambivalent in their attitudes to Marxist ideas. Several of the founder members of the Fabian Society were also involved in the Social Democratic Federation and, partly for this reason, Marxism exerted an important influence on early Fabian thinking. The subsequent break with the SDF occurred once the Fabians had definitely abandoned the revolutionary idea and advocated instead the principle of 'evolutionary' socialism through constructive legislation.[1] Subsequently, and for some Fabians, the breach seemed more tactical than theoretical. G.D.H. Cole, for example, felt able to reject the doctrine of proletarian revolution without denying his intellectual commitment to a certain kind of Marxism.[2] His kind of Marxism was unashamedly revisionist and it was justified by the argument that the essence of Marxism lay in its methods rather than its doctrines.

We should recognise that the classical concerns of Marxism were, in certain basic respects, identical with the preoccupations of the early socialists (including the founder members of the Fabian Society). Marx shared with other socialists a primordial concern with what might be defined as 'problems of welfare'. Classical Marxism, like other socialist philosophies, provided both a critique of bourgeois society and a normative theory which was ultimately concerned with its transcendence.

In *Capital* we are presented with the 'epic vision' of the remorseless spread of an economic system, converting human beings into mere commodities, and driven by 'the basest and the most abominable' of the passions 'of which the human breast is capable' – the 'furies of personal interest'.[3] This indictment of the competitive market system echoes other (and earlier) critical responses to the new industrial age – the 'mechanical age' as Carlyle had called it, a civilisation that was epitomised by Dickens in his description of the 'melancholy madness' of the machines of Coketown.[4] At this level, then, it can hardly be claimed that Marx's work possessed any great novelty. To the extent that his writings expressed 'the moral point of view of the prophet', they employed a language that had already become the distinctive hallmark of nineteenth-century social criticism – a language that formed the common heritage of both Marx and the Fabians.[5]

Beyond the indictment of capitalism one can also find in Marx all the classical elements of socialist normative theory – a distinctive ethical outlook. Here one might emphasise the 'humanistic' qualities of Marx's writings: his concern, for example, with what Erich Fromm has described as 'the spiritual emancipation of man'; his ideal of a needs-based distribution; and his conception of a future society based on the values of solidarity and cooperation.[6] Marx's *analysis* was inspired by his *aim* to eliminate the alienated condition of man, and establish a communist society:

> Communism is . . . the return of man himself as a social, i.e. really human, being, a complete and conscious return which assimilates all the wealth of previous development. Communism as a fully developed naturalism is humanism and a fully developed humanism is naturalism. It is the definitive

resolution of the antagonism between man and nature, and between man and man.[7]

The references in this passage to 'naturalism' and to the 'return of man' to his original condition of integrated wholeness are reminiscent of the restorationist and romantic strains of the early socialism of Proudhon and others. There would also appear to be no inherent incompatibility between Marxist humanism and the implicitly Fabian values of equality and fellowship. These values will, of course, be subject to differences of interpretation. It also has to be acknowledged that the ideals of fellowship and equality were more fully articulated in the writings of Morris, Tawney and Cole than in the writings of Marx and in the work of such 'mainstream' Fabians as the Webbs. The former took it as self-evident that they should establish a clear moral case for socialism, and it can certainly be argued that one weakness that the Fabian tradition has shared with Marxism is its failure to specify its core values. As Bernard Crick has argued, both Marxism and Fabianism have either dismissed values as 'empty idealism' or 'failed to define them precisely'.[8]

This brings us to the fundamental point that it is at the level of analysis rather than of aims that Marxism can be distinguished from other forms of socialism. Marx denounced his socialist contemporaries for their philosophical idealism and he himself refused to speculate on the precise form of any communist society of the future. The problem for Marx was to derive a strategy for revolutionary practice from an analysis of the underlying realities of present-day capitalism, rather than to superimpose on those realities one or another 'utopian' vision of man's future. This, the essential difference between Marxism and other forms of socialism, is outlined in two important documents – the *Manifesto of the Communist Party*, and Engels's essay *Socialism: utopian and scientific*.

These texts provide a useful starting point for our discussion, given that the objective of this chapter is to identify some of the major points of agreement and disagreement between Marxist and Fabian thought. We shall first consider the distinction between Marxism as a 'revolutionary' doctrine and the 'reformist' practices advocated by Fabian and other social democratic movements. We shall then discuss the claim that Marxist political strategies are uniquely based on a scientific understanding of the real material forces at work in society and history. This is a claim that we shall try to qualify. We shall argue that the differences between Marxism and Fabianism should not be interpreted in terms of the invidious contrast between 'scientific' and 'utopian' socialism: rather, their true identities are more accurately revealed by the distinction between materialist and idealist approaches to the understanding of history and social change. This point will lead us into a discussion of the place accorded by Marx and the Fabians to the economic and political factors, the parts played respectively by the working class and 'enlightened' sections of the bourgeoisie, and the significance given in each case to the state in effecting (or retarding) the transition to socialism. Our comparison of the two political traditions will be concluded with a brief outline of the Fabian and revisionist claim that Marxist politics and analysis had been superseded by historical events.

## Reform and revolution

In the *Communist Manifesto* Marx and Engels distinguish between three main types of socialism – 'bourgeois', 'critical utopian' and 'reactionary'.[9] What they had to say about bourgeois socialism is of particular interest to us because the comments they made foreshadow the modern neo-Marxist critique of the Fabian and revisionist traditions. Bourgeois socialists were indicted by Marx and Engels on the charge that all they offered was the mere panacea of social reform, leaving intact the capital–labour relation. Their aim, according to Marx and Engels, was not to return to former conditions; nor was it to institute a fundamental change in the productive system. Bourgeois socialism was, they argued, intended as a means of ensuring the continuation of capitalist society by correcting its worst abuses through a process of administrative reform.

Marx and Engels clearly reserved their approval for movements that were revolutionary rather than reformist and, in this connection, social democratic parties are commonly identified as having substituted parliamentary and constitutional strategies for the allegedly revolutionary doctrines of Marxism. This is something of an oversimplification – partly because 'revolutionary' in the sense of violent or forced change is not essential to Marxism, and partly because the revolutionary option has not always been entirely alien to the social democratic tradition. Nevertheless, it must be conceded that liberal-socialist movements have generally based their strategies on 'gradualist' principles. Whilst these principles may not, in themselves, be incompatible with the notion of revolutionary change, their strategic implications do run counter to orthodox Marxist politics.

For a founder member of the Fabian Society, George Bernard Shaw, 'the necessity for cautious and gradual change' was obvious: 'Demolishing a Bastille with seven prisoners in it is one thing; demolishing one with fourteen million is quite another.'[10] In later years, however, Shaw conceded that the Russian Revolution had 'changed the world more in four years than Fabian constitutional action seems likely to do in four hundred'. Bernstein, too, acknowledged that 'violence and conspiracy might be necessary tactics for a labour movement shackled by a controlled press and crippling police regulations.'[11] It is important that we recognise that these statements only appear to provide evidence of equivocation, self-contradiction or, in Shaw's case, of a late conversion to insurgency if it is assumed that revolution and gradualism are logically incompatible. The fact that they are not was clearly stated on the title page of the first collection of *Fabian Essays*:

> For the right moment you must wait, as Fabius did most patiently, when warring against Hannibal, though many censured his delays; but when the time comes you must strike hard, as Fabius did, or your waiting will be in vain, and fruitless.

The divergence between Marxism and Fabianism becomes more apparent if we examine the tactical inferences that have been drawn from the principle of gradual or incremental change. These are expressed in the doctrines of 'permeation' and 'persuasion' which, in both cases, presuppose *constitutional* action as the means of effecting the transition to socialism. Permeation could mean one of two things. It could refer, first, to the interim establishment of social institutions – the municipalities, publicly owned amenities, nationalised industries and so on – in an otherwise capitalist society. It was envisaged that local and institutionally focused campaigns for socialist organisation would provide the 'bridgeheads' from which socialism could be constructed on a larger scale. Permeation also meant, particularly for the Fabians, the infiltration and capture of existing political parties and other decision-making bodies. The objective was to 'join all organisations where useful socialist work could be done, and influence them'.[12]

The last phrase contains an important point, because permeation in either sense of the term only promises the advance of socialism if the socialist uses 'persuasion' to exploit his strategic advantage. Again the term has a double meaning, referring either to the persuasive *example* of successful socialist administration, or to the direct persuasion of politicians, bureaucrats and workers to induce them to accept the unanswerability of the socialist case. The principle of persuasion rests, therefore, on the optimistic belief that the future of socialism can be secured by the force of reason, the potency of factual documentation and the ethical compunction of socialist ideals. In the words of Shaw, the Fabian Society used 'the collection and publication of authentic and impartial statistical tracts' in order to make 'the public conscious of the evil condition of society under the present system'.[13]

## Scientific and utopian socialism

Apart from the strategic issues, the *Communist Manifesto* also criticised contemporary socialist movements for their failure to develop a sound political and economic analysis of the conditions of production, distribution and exchange – an analysis that should (from the point of view of later Marxists) reveal the ultimate futility of the Fabian faith in the power of reason. Marxist materialism implies a fundamental objection to the 'idealist' and (allegedly) 'utopian' premises of Fabian socialism and offers, in its place, a view of history that would seem to contradict the strategy of persuasion. For the Marxist, the expectant attitude is vindicated by the groundswell of history and not by some mystical belief in the absolute truth (and thus the inevitable realisation) of socialist ideals.

The issue is raised in the *Manifesto*, particularly in Marx and Engels's comments on utopian socialism. This term was used to refer to the work of Saint-Simon, Owen and Fourier. These individuals stood as representatives of a larger group of socialist thinkers and movements who were united by the common aspiration to construct a new science of social and human nature for the purpose of directing the course of social change. One suspects that the utopian socialists had a special significance for Marx and Engels because they, too, shared this basic aspiration. Where they differed, of course, was in the particular character of their 'scientific' analyses, and over the political significance they gave to socialist values and theory.

The utopian socialists were damned only with faint praise in the *Manifesto*. It was not until the later publication of Engels's *Anti Duhring* and *Socialism: utopian and scientific* that a full-blooded attack was mobilised on the grounds that utopian socialism constituted the very antithesis of its Marxist (scientific) counterpart. The theoretical systems of the utopian socialists were found to be rationalist: they presupposed the power of absolute truth, they assumed that persuasion and example would be sufficient to the task of transforming society, and they attributed messianic properties to 'the individual man of genius' – a seer or prophet who proclaims the absolute and universal truths of the socialist ethic. Scientific socialism, by contrast, was founded upon a 'real basis': it was historical and materialist. Its theoretical and practical achievements sprang, it was claimed, from the realisation that 'the final causes of all social changes and political revolutions are to be sought, not in men's brains . . . but in changes in the modes of production and exchange. They are to be sought not in the *philosophy* but in the *economics* of each particular epoch.'[14] By the same token, the failure of utopian socialism was retraced to the paucity of its analysis: 'The socialism of earlier days certainly *criticised* the existing capitalistic mode of production and its consequences. But it could not *explain* them and, therefore, could not get *mastery* of them.'[15]

The point that Engels was making was that, whilst the utopians found the socialist imperative in ethics, Marxism turned to the economic processes inherent in capitalism itself. Socialism was, for the Marxist, the '*necessary* outcome of the struggle between two historically developed classes', and this struggle is in turn orchestrated by the economic contradictions of the capitalist mode of production. In the words of the revisionist and founder member of the German Social Democratic Party, Eduard Bernstein, Marx had drawn socialism 'out of the clouds of fantasy to the firm soil of the actualities of social existence' and had thus provided the labour movement with its greatest impetus and its solid foundation.[16] Marx's life work was dedicated to the task of demonstrating that 'contemporary social and economic relations were necessary, and that the better life could not be achieved through the building of model communities and the condemnation of the rapacious capitalist, but through *the mighty movements of history*.'[17]

Marx and Engels were not alone in claiming that their socialism was 'scientifically' based. Similar claims had been made before Marx by the utopian socialists, and against him by Proudhon. The later schemes of revisionist and Fabian socialists were also based on 'scientific' premises, even though it is arguable that their systems possessed a more explicit ethical component. What distinguished the Marxist venture into the field of scientific socialism was the view of the historical process that was implied by Marx's materialism and by the use he made of the concept of surplus value.

Engels claimed that Marxist theory had placed socialism on a 'real basis'. Marxist materialism could penetrate the level of 'appearances': it could cut through the merely formal equalities and freedoms of the capitalist market and the superficial stabilities of the system of commodity exchange, to discern the 'contradictions' inherent in the capitalist mode of production. The concept of surplus value was essential in demonstrating the coercive and exploitative nature of the relationship between capital and labour. This concept also underlined the point that capitalist production is subject to the imperative of accumulation, and that this process is itself limited by certain constraints.

The constraints on capitalist accumulation precipitate a succession of crises. Marx regarded these periodic crises as being simultaneously a manifestation of the internal contradictions endemic to the capitalist system, and as the means by which the impediments to accumulation could be resolved and equilibrium could be restored. But the resolution can only be temporary and, as one crisis follows another, capitalism must move inexorably towards its final collapse. As Giddens has explained:

> A crisis is simply an expansion of production beyond what the market can absorb and still return an adequate rate of profit. Once overproduction occurs . . . it can set into motion a vicious circle of reactions. As the rate of profit falls, investment declines, part of the labour force has to be laid off, which further diminishes consumer purchasing power, producing another decline in the rate of profit, and so on. The spiral continues until unemployment has increased to such a degree . . . that there exist new conditions for the creation of an increased rate of surplus value, and thereby a stimulus to the resumption of investment. During the crisis, some of the less efficient enterprises will have gone out of business; those remaining can therefore take over their share of the market, and are in a position to begin a new period of expansion. Thus the cycle is renewed, and another upward phase gets under way.[18]

The stage-by-stage elimination of unprofitable enterprises, and the consequent concentration and centralisation of capital leads, ultimately and inevitably, to the destruction of the central institutions of capitalism – the competitive market and the private ownership of the means of production. Thus 'the imminent trend of movement of the capitalist system generates the social conditions which provide for its dialectical transcendence' – the socialisation of production and the transition, through the 'dictatorship of the proletariat', to the first stage of socialism.

Marx's concept of history as subject to an economically orchestrated 'logic of becoming' is commonly regarded as the apotheosis of scientific socialism and the antithesis of its utopian counterpart. But the charge of utopianism is all too often used as a blanket condemnation of each and every variety of (non-Marxist) socialism. On closer inspection, though, Marx and Engels used the term in two loosely connected senses. The first describes those movements which owed their inspiration to historically groundless and practically unrealisable visions of some future society ('fantasies'). Karl Mannheim later described these as 'absolute utopias'. The second refers to a particular conception of the historical process – one that attributes a primary causal role to ideas, ideals and, possibly, intellectuals.

The early Fabians could hardly be accused of 'utopianism' of the first type. As Jeffrey Weeks has argued, they were acutely aware of the dangers of entertaining socialist dreams that were 'out of kilter with the real, "objective" possibilities of the age'.[19] The Fabian Society was itself founded in a conscious break from the romantically utopian Fellowship of the New Life and, if anything, its leaders erred in the opposite direction. Thus, in 1913, G.D.H. Cole remarked that 'in endeavouring to persuade the world that socialism was a "business proposition", [the Society] forgot that it must be a "human" proposition also: it found definiteness and collectivism and lost idealism, which is essential for real socialism.' In the same year the Webbs seemed to be almost embracing the charge when they wrote that 'it is from the actual facts and coldly impassive arguments that socialism draws its irresistible cogency.'

It is when we examine the *nature* of these 'coldly impassive arguments' that we may be forced to concede the accusation on the second count. It was not that the Fabians failed to provide a coherent and 'scientifically' based theoretical analysis, or that they were impelled by an irrational 'dread of violence' or an emotional need to rationalise a 'cowardly "parliamentarism at any price"'.[20] Fabian tactical doctrines were, instead, based on an idealist theory of history which asserted the inevitability of socialism whilst disputing the particular historical course that had been charted by Marxists. Against what they saw as the 'materialistic reductionism' of Marx, Graham Wallas and the Webbs propounded an approach to historical understanding which, despite frequent recourse to the theoretically agnostic device of 'multi-factorial' explanation, tended to give priority to intellectual factors.[21] This tendency is particularly apparent in Sidney Webb's contribution to *Fabian Essays* where the political advances of the past were depicted as having been borne on the intellectual currents of European social thought.[22] For Webb, though, it was public opinion rather than 'philosophical notions' that was the agency through which ideas were translated into political and social realities: 'it is through the slow and gradual turning of the popular mind to new principles that social reorganisation bit by bit comes.'[23]

However, the quality of idealism found in the work of the Webbs and their contemporaries does not necessarily expose them to the charge of 'utopianism' in Engels's sense of the term.[24] Sidney Webb was himself no less critical of those socialists 'who took no account of the blind social forces which they could not control, and which went on inexorably working out social salvation in ways unsuspected by the utopian'.[25] Webb, like Marx, contended that there was a historical inevitability about the transition to socialism (although the arguments he deployed emphasised the evolutionary character of the passage, giving no role to class conflict and the struggle for power). Socialism, the rebirth of community and of the collective, would be brought about through society's spontaneous recovery from the anarchy and 'unrestrained licence' of the market. The socialist imperative was to be found not in the conscious motives of individual actors or in the ethical programmes of parties or classes, but in the historical process itself, 'the grandiloquent sweep of social tendencies'. The advent of the 'new synthesis' could be accelerated or delayed but never wholly produced or prevented by the actions of individuals. This, for Webb, was where socialist ideas and a scientific appreciation of history could play their part:

> Though our decisions are moulded by the circumstances of the time . . . it still rests with the individual to resist or promote the social evolution, consciously or unconsciously, according to his character or information. The importance of complete consciousness of the social tendencies of the age lies in the fact that its existence and comprehensiveness often determine the expediency of our particular action: we move with less resistance with the stream than against it.[26]

Webb took the argument one stage further. Apart from the catalytic role he assigned to knowledge, he also sought a historical justification for his own idealism in the changing circumstances of his time – circumstances which allowed man to 'assume more and more, not only the mastery of "things", but also a conscious control over social destiny itself'.[27]

This notion was more fully developed by Bernstein when he argued the case for his own brand of 'voluntaristic', ethical socialism. He contended that growing human control of the social environment had meant that the materialist's 'iron laws of history' would give way to 'independent activity' and 'ethical factors'.[28] This kind of argument was pressed even further in the work of the liberal sociologist, L.T. Hobhouse. Hobhouse's idealism was developed as the result of an attempt to provide a scientifically argued alternative to the 'materialist' implications of Spencer's sociology. Where Spencer had treated the human mind as 'a sort of glorified reflex action', with man's existence being determined by 'the internecine struggle' for physical survival, Hobhouse set out to demonstrate that mind was 'an empirical fact in the world of time' in which the 'higher self-consciousness' (of positivism) would develop to the point where humanity could regulate its own life and control its own destiny.[29] According to Hobhouse, man was subject to the process of 'orthogenic evolution', culminating in the final stage when he could, through his own efforts, work intelligently towards his own perfection.[30]

## The economic and the political

The case against Marxist materialism can be constructed in two ways. The first takes issue with Marx's prognostications on the economic future of capitalism. This was certainly an argument that was advanced by the early Fabians and others who, like Bernstein, were struck by the long-term potential for growth in the capitalist system. The second objection is more a matter of perspective and methodology and involves a repudiation of the economic determinism associated with the Marxist tradition.

At first sight it would seem to be possible to describe the positions occupied by Marxists and Fabians in terms of the conventional opposition between voluntarism and determinism. On closer inspection, however, this proves to be another over-simplification. In attributing an independent and important role to ideas and political factors, some Fabians took the view that this was not necessarily incompatible with a 'loose economic determinism'.[31] This concession was reinforced (in Cole's case) by a singularly apologetic treatment of Marx's theory of history and was complemented (more generally) by a distinctly Fabian conception of history which, whilst emphasising the contingency of future developments on political and intellectual factors, was not in any meaningful sense 'voluntarist'.[32]

In this section we shall argue that, although the Fabian arguments for the 'inevitability of socialism' were constructed on political rather than economic grounds, Marxism should not be equated with a narrow economic determinism. An examination of the 'political' arguments advanced by both Fabians and Marxists suggests that the crucial differences lie in the *nature* of these arguments and, in particular, in the roles they assign to the proletariat and the middle class as agents of socialist transition.

One could read Marx's materialism as entailing an essentially mechanistic interpretation of the determining role of economic forces. However, to do so would be to gloss over some of the ambiguities that are essential to the materialist interpretation of history and to Marx's conception of the relationship between the 'economic' and the 'political'. These ambiguities are rooted in his treatment of the relationships between the basic elements of his theoretical system: the forces and relations of production; the economic base and the political and ideological superstructure; and the respective roles, in the historical process, of class struggle and economic crisis. Towards the end of his life Engels felt impelled to repudiate the 'rare kind of balderdash' that issued from 'many of the recent "Marxists"' who had insisted on the interpretation that 'the economic situation is the sole active cause and everything else only a passive effect.'[33] And Engels's apologia would seem to be vindicated by those passages in *Grundrisse* in which the relations of production are invested with the capacity to shape productive forces, and by various discussions of the relative autonomy of the superstructure.

Engels's disclaimer is important because Marxism – despite its seemingly reassuring predictions of the inevitability of socialism – is also often regarded as a sociology of revolution, a praxis for revolutionary struggle and an inspiration for political activism. What, then, is the place of class struggle in a theory which would seem to emphasise the inevitable breakdown of the capitalist mode of production owing to the impersonal logic of its own internal economic contradictions? How is one to reconcile the *contingent* with the *necessary* aspects of the transcendence of capitalism? And, if the breakdown of capitalism is inevitable, what role is left for Marx's revolutionary proletariat and what part, if any, is played by the state in averting or facilitating the transition to socialism?

These issues are, as we shall see in part II, crucial for any student wishing to apply Marxist insights to the field of social policy. But, for the moment, let us stay with the more general issue concerning Marx's view of history. The outstanding insight of historical materialism is that history is not the result of accident or of the actions of great men, but the largely unconscious creation of men subject to observable laws. Thus Marx wrote that 'men make their own history, but not just as they please. They do not choose the circumstances for themselves, but have to work upon circumstances as they find them, have to fashion the material handed down by the past.'[34] The significance of this passage is that it left the way open for later interpretations that would differ in terms of the balance accorded to the contingent and necessary aspects of the historical process, the degree of emphasis to be given to the impersonal and predictable economic forces (on the one hand) and the more indeterminate development of class struggle (on the other) in effecting the transition to socialism. The one argument, stressing the historical inevitability of the collapse of capitalism, struck a sympathetic chord with those of Marx's contemporaries who were familiar with evolutionary ideas, was subsequently adopted by Kautsky and now provides the basis for 'structuralist' and 'capital-logic' theory. The other viewpoint has inspired various and not always compatible developments – including the work of Korsch and Lukacs in the 1920s, and the post-war publications of the Frankfurt school. Pressed to its logical conclusion, and combined with major revisions of Marx's economic theories, it served as the key tenet of Fabian and revisionist socialism; and, in the hands of G.D.H. Cole (the most influential English populariser of Marx's ideas in the pre-war period), it produced a version of Marxism that was 'activist, idealist, voluntarist . . . [and] minimally determinist'.[35]

We might resolve this issue (or, rather, hold it in abeyance) by insisting on a strict reading of the passage from the *Eighteenth Brumaire*: men make history, but they do so by working within the circumstances provided principally by the economic development of the capitalist mode of production with its tendency to centralisation and concentration. This, presumably, is what Marx and Engels meant in the *Manifesto* by the metaphor of the bourgeoisie having produced its own gravediggers: the structural development of capitalism produces the agents who, at the propitious moment, act to convert necessary into sufficient conditions. As Giddens has put it: 'The question of the "inevitability" of the revolution poses no "epistemological" (as opposed to "practical") problems. The process of development of capitalism engenders the objective social changes which, in interrelationship with the growing class-awareness of the proletariat, creates the active consciousness necessary to transform society through revolutionary praxis.'[36] The 'objective social changes' which were thought to foster the 'active consciousness' of the workers were: first, the development of the system of free wage labour; second, the creation (through residential 'congregation' and the centralisation of capital) of a homogeneous industrial proletariat; third, the periodic crises of the capitalist mode of production, which would have the effect of demonstrating the common class situation of the proletariat; and, finally, the disruption of the informal agencies of social control that had so effectively restrained workers in pre-capitalist society. Once the earlier sentimental ties between master and servant had been replaced by the bond of pecuniary profit the worker, according to Engels, 'begins to recognise his own interests and develop independently'.[37]

The last phrase points to a developmental process whereby the class of workers is transformed from a mere 'class in itself' to a 'class for itself', a revolutionary proletariat. They cease to be the creatures of their creators, the bourgeoisie, and become the masters of their own destiny and that of humanity in its entirety. In *The Condition of the Working Class* Engels claimed to discern the beginnings of this process and here, as elsewhere, the developmental stages are mapped out in some detail.[38] The critical phase is that in which the historical initiative passes from the hands of the bourgeoisie into the hands of the proletariat. At first, the unification of the proletariat 'is not yet the consequence of their own active union, but of the union of the bourgeoisie'. But 'with the development of industry', the strength of the proletariat grows 'and it feels that strength more'. Thereafter, 'the workers begin to *form* combinations against the bourgeoisie; they club together . . . ; they found permanent *associations*.'[39]

This juxtaposition of the two terms 'combination' and 'association' describes the beginning and end of the process where the revolutionary proletariat, labour as a class *for* itself, develops. As the economic contradictions of capitalism lead inexorably to a situation where the state is obliged to undertake the direction of production, they provide the *opportunity* for a politically mature proletariat to take decisive action – to seize power and turn the means of production into state property. In so doing, according to Engels, the proletariat abolishes itself, abolishes all class distinctions, and abolishes the state: 'The government of persons is replaced by the administration of things.'[40]

Thus, for Marx and Engels, the agents of socialist transition were to be the working class. The question of agency and class allegiance represents one of the three grounds on which Marx and Engels criticised bourgeois socialism. In the *Manifesto* this was described as a 'mere figure of speech', with the bourgeois – philanthropist, intellectual or reformer – acting *as* a bourgeois 'for the benefit of the working class'.

In the late 1930s G.D.H. Cole wrote that although the recent history of Western Europe appeared to vindicate Marx's *philosophy* of history, the practical implications of his doctrine needed to be revised 'in the light of the present class structure of Western society'.[41] In this respect Cole was echoing the earlier arguments of Eduard Bernstein. Both writers found a special significance in the changing structural configuration of late capitalist societies, focusing in particular on the evolution of the joint stock enterprise and the growth of a new middle class. Their reading of contemporary structural changes entailed a pessimistic assessment of the prospects for a proletarian revolution:

> The proletariat by itself is not strong enough or technically well enough equipped . . . to win and hold a parliamentary majority, or to carry through the construction of a new industrial system by constitutional means. If it has to fight alone, it can win only by revolution, accompanied by a forcible destruction of all the opposing forces. Such a victory can be achieved only by the accident of a highly favourable conjuncture . . . and the winning of it will leave the constructive task of building socialism far harder than it need be [partly] because of the proletariat's inevitable lack of adequate resources of trained knowledge and administrative experience.[42]

This, combined with a correspondingly optimistic view of the attitudes and significance of the 'salariat' – 'many more of them have been prepared to entertain the notion of socialism, if not positively throw in their lot with the socialist movement'[43] – led Cole to the following conclusion:

> There is at least . . . the possibility of an alliance . . . between the proletariat and a substantial section of the salaried intermediate class against the large capitalists and the more reactionary *petit bourgeois* groups. An alliance of this sort offers the only possible prospect of achieving socialism by peaceful and constitutional means.[44]

The Fabians, like Marx, recognised that working-class awareness would be a key factor in the transition to socialism. Where they differed, perhaps, was in the stress they placed on the contingency of the development of working-class consciousness on the good offices of the enlightened (and principally middle-class) sections of society. This, together with the Fabian analysis of the changing class structure of capitalist society, was why they rejected 'the crude Marxist melodrama of "the class war"':

> In view of the fact that the socialist movement has been hitherto inspired, instructed and led by members of the middle class or 'bourgeoisie', the Fabian Society . . . protests against the absurdity of socialists, denouncing the very class from which socialism has sprung as specially hostile to it.[45]

One might also distinguish Bernstein's insistence on the importance of building a mass party by forging alliances with the radical bourgeoisie from the role that the Fabians assigned to the middle class. The Fabian argument seems to have been that the middle classes would act as the progenitors and guardians of socialism, and not merely as the allies of a proletarian movement. This, of course, was perfectly consistent with the fact that the Fabian Society was overwhelmingly middle class in composition, and stands even today as the only British socialist organisation to appeal specifically to intellectuals. Hobsbawm argues that the more significant section of the Society's membership was composed of 'self-made professionals', *la nouvelle couche sociale*, and that it was their interests and experiences which gave Fabian theory its distinctive hue:

> The Webbs' entire structure of socialism pivots on such professionals. They are the trained, impartial and scientific administrators and expert advisers who have created an alternative court of appeal to profit . . . .. [In] the ethos of such professions . . . [the Webbs] saw a working alternative to a system in which men worked in proportion only to their financial incentive, a sort of anticipation of the ethos of communism.[46]

As we shall see in the next chapter, it was the socialist adaptation of the 'professional ideal'[47] that was such an important feature of the Society's influence on the modern discipline of social administration. Post-war sociologists and social administrators have, in effect, inherited the Fabian idea that man might 'intelligently work towards his own perfection'. Not only were they inclined to the gratifying view that the growth of social scientific knowledge had prompted the advance of British collectivism, but they also tended to appoint themselves to the role of the 'intelligence officers' of the welfare state, with the task of consolidating its achievements and guiding its future development. In so doing they would have found substantial support in the ideas of both Sidney Webb and L.T. Hobhouse. Webb argued that our control over social destiny was associated with the 'advance in sociological knowledge', and Hobhouse maintained that the social sciences represented the systematisation of humanity's higher self-consciousness. Sociology, according to Hobhouse, could be a 'reformer's science' providing evidence 'of the line of "natural" human development, and, thereby, guidance in which branches to prune and which to encourage'.[48] This combination of an idealist philosophy of history and the special role assigned to middle-class intellectuals is traceable to the positivist influence on both the Fabians and the new liberals. For example, in Saint-Simon's writings the purpose of science was the realisation of man's destiny: the objective of the scientist was to facilitate the transition to the next and final 'organic' epoch, industrial society. The same point was made by Auguste Comte, both in his dictum *prévoir pour pouvoir*, and in his declaration concerning the aims of sociology: 'The aim of every science is foresight [*prévoyance*]. . . . it is clear that knowledge of what social system the elite of mankind *is called to* by the progress of civilisation . . . involves a general *determination* of the next social future as it results from the past'.[49] Once accomplished, the task of the scientists was to exercise 'spiritual power' in the new society – a power based on their combined knowledge and experience, and a power that was to be used for the collective good.

**The state and the transition to socialism**

Marx's writings display a fundamental, perhaps necessary ambiguity on the question of the nature of the state and of its role in the transition to socialism. The collapse of the capitalist order has been commonly seen as a sudden and explosive event, a catastrophic reversal of fortunes. Yet the implication, at least, of many of Marx's economic writings is that the transition to socialism is as likely to be gradual and cumulative – a series of quantitative steps as each successive crisis temporarily resolves the contradictions of capitalism, leading ultimately to the qualitative transformation of social, economic and political relations. The very phrase 'revolutionary proletariat' suggests a forcible overthrow of the state and the seizure of economic power by worker cadres. Yet it is well known that Marx abhorred violence, that the term 'revolution' had other equally strong connotations in his writings and, of course, that Marx never did produce a strategic or tactical blueprint for the proletarian vanguard. The *Manifesto* may have scoffed at the reformist aspirations of the bourgeois socialists, but elsewhere serious attention was given to the prospects for initiating, through the state, reforms that might significantly modify the social system in a socialist direction. As for the state itself, here too one can find passages which suggest that it could become a relatively autonomous entity capable of responding to considerations other than the immediate interests of capital, together with others which express the view that it merely serves as the instrument of the dominant class.

It is certainly possible to find in the writings of Marx and Engels some support for the view that constitutional action can secure incremental concessions which lead, ultimately, to the transcendence of capitalism. Ramesh Mishra cites Marx's treatment of the Factory Acts as evidence that this possibility was not discounted.[50] As Mishra acknowledges, this argument rests on a view of the state which, although present in Marx's work, is not commonly associated with a 'Marxist' position. This is a view which holds that the state can achieve a degree of autonomy *vis-à-vis* the economically dominant class, thereby achieving the capacity for universalist action.[51] Mishra claimed that Marx raised this possibility in his comments on the professionalism of the British civil service, and further support might be obtained from his comments on the Bonapartist state in the *Eighteenth Brumaire*. Here, and in Engels's *Origin of the Family*, it is conceded that in certain circumstances the state may perform a more complex role than simply that of an instrument of the dominant class: 'By way of exception . . . there are periods when the warring classes so nearly attain equilibrium that the state power, ostensibly appearing as a mediator, assumes for the moment a certain independence in relation to both.'[52]

The other view, more commonly associated with Marxism, regards reform as a means of 'prolonging the life of the capitalist social order and blunting the edge of the revolutionary propensities of the working class'.[53] Certainly, it was on these lines that Marx and Engels attacked the administrative reforms proposed by the 'bourgeois socialists', and it was in these terms that Engels discussed the Ten Hours Bill (1847) and other reforms leading to the apparent 'moralisation' of manufacturing industry.[54] In relation to these examples Engels argued that, although these administrative measures were inimical to the spirit of free trade and unbridled competition, they served to accelerate the concentration of capital and thus secured the interests of the 'giant capitalists'. Elsewhere in the *Condition of the Working Classes* Engels attacked contemporary educational provision: '[The bourgeoisie] bestows upon [the workers] only so much education as lies in the interests of [the bourgeoisie].'[55] However, here it must be said that Engels was writing at a time when state-sponsored education was overshadowed by the 'private' efforts of the Church, charitable bodies and employers. Towards the end of that book Engels makes the general pronouncement that 'all legislation is calculated to protect those that possess property against those who do not', and this general principle is, of course, consistent with the view that the state, far from being a 'neutral agency', is merely the instrument of its bourgeois masters.

To the extent that Marxism is associated with the presumed *incorrigibility* of the capitalist state, the transition to socialism must entail its overthrow and replacement by a state of a quite different sort (a 'proletarian' state). In his response to this view, G.D.H. Cole argued that Marx had been greatly influenced by the states of which he had, in his formative years, direct experience. These were not based on 'representative democracy', nor were they engaged in any significant sense in 'welfare activities'. In these circumstances 'there was . . . nothing surprising in the fact that Marx, in 1848, regarded the state as incapable of being used as the instrument of a voteless proletariat, and set out to devise a method of compassing its destruction rather than its reform.'[56] Cole retraces his own position to the 'bitter controversy' between Lenin and Kautsky. Where Lenin merely echoed the views of the master, Kautsky and the German Social Democrats 'had come to think in terms of the capture and democratisation of the existing state'.[57] The position adopted by Kautsky, Bernstein and the early Fabians found a special significance in what they took to be the inexorable and irresistible progress of democracy. This long-term trend towards democratisation provided the historical mandate for their idealist philosophy of change, it justified their attitude towards the modern state, and it created opportunities for socialists to advance their cause by means of propaganda, persuasion and education.[58]

McBriar has argued that the Fabians stood on the watershed between modern and nineteenth-century liberal-radical attitudes towards the state.[59] Where the latter either sought to reduce state activity to a minimum, or envisaged the ultimate 'withering away' of 'central, organised, coercive power', the modern and Fabian view was altogether more sanguine. Shaw, in particular, denounced the anarchists on the Saint-Simonian or Comtean grounds that socialism requires an extension rather than a diminution of state powers, and he attacked the Marxist theory of the state as an 'organ of class oppression' by arguing that it had been superseded by the advent of democracy.[60] In contradistinction to both the Marxist and anarchist traditions, Fabian reformism and gradualism rested on the view that the state was a relatively neutral agency and administrative apparatus whose powers were at the disposal of any group that commanded the legislature.

Fabian socialism has conventionally been equated with 'collectivism' despite the fact that the founder members of the Society were initially opposed to the equation. In 1886 Sidney Webb argued that 'it would be no more fair to identify socialism with collectivism than to identify Christianity with Primitive Methodism' and Shaw 'regarded collectivists as the "Tories" of socialism and collectivism as a doctrine incompatible with his libertarian beliefs'.[61] Collectivism did, nevertheless, become the touchstone of orthodox Fabianism, setting it apart from such other 'native' traditions as syndicalism and guild socialism. The transformation occurred with the formation and growing influence within the Society of the Fabian Parliamentary League. This organisation, formed for the purpose of bringing 'socialism to bear on current politics, and organising the socialist vote', published a statement in 1887 which was to become the virtual manifesto of subsequent Fabian politics:

> Now that the doctrine of *laissez-faire* has fallen into disrepute, and the right of the state to compete with private enterprise is admitted and acted upon . . . , the Fabian Parliamentary League sees a peaceful and expeditious path to socialism, through such measures as nationalisation of railways, municipalisation of ground rents and of industries connected with local transit, and with supply of gas and water in the towns.[62]

This statement placed the Fabian Society in the vanguard of history as they saw it. By allying socialism with collectivism the Fabians were able to argue that their cause transcended the partisan ideologies and interests of particular individuals, parties or classes. Collectivism represented, to the Fabian, an irresistible force that was already at work even in the actions of those 'practical' men who 'believed socialism to be the most foolish of dreams'.[63] The assumption, by the state, of progressively more responsibility for registering, inspecting and controlling industrial functions, together with the expansion of state provision for the welfare of the people, were seen as evidence of an 'unconscious socialism' which, by force of practical necessity, 'compelled' England 'to put forth her hand to succour and protect her weaker members'.[64] It was also argued that parallel changes in the character of business management – the 'elimination of the purely personal element', management by 'salaried officers', and the growth of the joint stock company – promised, at some point in the future, a unique opportunity for the socialist capture of industry. The more socialised the organisation of production became, the greater were the possibilities for 'the community' to 'expropriate' the shareholders with a minimum 'dislocation' to the daily running of their industries.

Collectivism, 'gas and water socialism', was seen by the early Fabians as more than simply a strategy for transcending capitalism; it became instead the essential feature of their vision of the socialist society of the future, the end as well as the means of both socialism and history itself. Sidney Webb, in particular, regarded collectivism – the subordination of individuals to the higher needs and purposes of society – as a moral and historical imperative, and he argued his case by drawing upon the theoretical resources of idealism, positivism and social Darwinism.[65] Not only did he equate socialism with collectivism on ethical grounds, he also succeeded in reducing the equation to a matter of logic or definition. Socialism was defined as the antithesis of *laissez-faire* individualism, and the former thus came to be identified, necessarily, with collectivism: 'The best government,' according to Webb, 'is that which can safely and successfully administer most.'[66] The formula was completed by the demonstration that socialism and collectivism were not just the logical opposites of individualism, but also its historical successors. Here Webb, like Hobhouse, used a form of social Darwinism as a weapon against its greatest populariser, Herbert Spencer. He argued that the process of 'natural selection' applied, at the higher stages of evolution, to the struggle between entire societies for their survival. Since the outcome of this struggle would rest, ultimately, on the 'social fitness' of each nation – its health, industrial efficiency, and moral solidarity – and since history had demonstrated that these qualities could only be secured through state intervention, then only collectivism could ensure that England took her place at the highest stage of social development.[67]

There is some irony in the fact that the historical advance of democracy should be cited as an empirical justification for a political theory that entailed a less than completely sanguine view of democracy itself. On the one hand, Fabianism shared with revisionism a commitment to the two values of socialism and democracy, and in both cases the emphasis was placed on representative and parliamentary rather than direct and plebiscitary democracy.[68] In this respect the Fabian Society's repudiation of 'extreme forms' of democracy – of mass meetings, the popular election of officials, the referendum and the initiative – was entirely consistent with the general principles of social democracy. But, on the other hand, Fabianism often entailed a more radical solution to the deficiencies of direct democracy, and it was a solution that followed logically from its collectivist ideals. Its extreme form was presented in the writings of Shaw, in which democracy was attacked for substituting 'election by the incompetent many for appointment by the corrupt few'[69] and in which he held that the main hindrance to socialism was the 'stupidity of the working class'.[70] Shaw's somewhat eccentric solution was for government by a selected breed of 'supermen' distinguished by their higher intelligence, altruism, energy and organising ability. There is evidence of a similar development from libertarian to parliamentary and, finally, authoritarian socialism in the later work of the Webbs. On their return from the Soviet Union in 1931, Sidney and Beatrice Webb expressed a new faith in the 'vocation of leadership', declaring that Stalin's regime was nothing more (or less) than applied Fabianism. This was not, as Eric Hobsbawm has pointed out, a product of senile decay; nor, we might add, was it merely a question of the Soviet system having 'touched deep rooted elements in . . . their *personalities*'.[71] What Norman and Jeanne MacKenzie have described as 'the streak of elitism and authoritarianism . . . the desire for a planned and efficient order, the belief in the rightness of the expert' and the 'distrust of the people's capacity to govern themselves' were also deeply rooted in their theoretical system.[72]

As heirs to the positivist tradition, the Webbs propounded a view of the future that, in effect, updated the original visions of Saint-Simon and Auguste Comte. In contrast to the humanist, libertarian socialism of Marx, the socialist tradition that was inaugurated by Saint-Simon and so fully developed by the Webbs emphasised 'the rational, scientific and efficient organisation of society and its natural environment'.[73] The collectivist Webb world of the future was a truly Saint-Simonian utopia, a society that was 'collectivist' not only in the narrow sense of the state and civil society becoming virtually indistinguishable, but also in the deeper sense of a society in which the individual habitually subordinates his 'personal interest' to the 'common good'. In the 'socialist commonwealth' envisaged by the Webbs, efficient organisation would be complemented by such an 'advance in personal morality' that the very notion of *private* interests would become redundant.[74] The commonwealth would rest on an entirely new 'conception of government', a conception that was only possible in the 'organic' society originally conceived by Saint-Simon. Government, in a community that was 'so variously organised and so highly differentiated in function' could dispense with 'centralised authority' because government itself would entail 'the widest possible variety in the forms of socialisation', cooperation in all spheres of social activity. 'Authority' would, in fact, rest on consensus, and the viability of the organic commonwealth would depend on the success of collectivised industry in producing 'enough commodities and services . . . to keep the community in health and efficiency, [and to provide] a decent mental and physical environment for the whole people'. In both respects the role of science and of scientists would be crucial. 'The whole body of citizens,' according to the Webbs, must be *induced* 'to realise the imperative need for a rapid development of science in its widest sense.' The social sciences, in particular, would supplement our 'knowledge of things' with a 'greater knowledge of men: of the conditions of the successful working of social institutions'. This knowledge would perform the dual service of rendering 'more effective every form of social organisation' and of making 'more socially fertile the relations among men'. Thus the Webbs, like the positivists before them, elevated the sciences to the status of a religion – a religion of humanity – with the scientists, its priesthood, providing both the moral creed and the rational basis for efficient organisation in the socialist commonwealth. It was the apparent success of Stalinist Russia in achieving this object that appealed so strongly to Beatrice

Webb: 'It is the invention of the religious order as the determining factor in the life of a great nation that is the magnet that attracts me to Russia. . . . Practically that religion is Comteism – the religion of humanism. Auguste Comte comes to his own.'[75]

## The verdict of history

> No thinker thinks beyond his time, in the sense that his thought can be adequate for any generation later than his own. He may lay lasting foundations, good for later generations to build upon; but woe betide those who seek to save themselves the pain of mental building by inhabiting dead men's minds.[76]

The Marxist-Leninist view of the state has a number of attractions for anyone seeking to offer a commentary on the activities ('welfare' or otherwise) of the nineteenth-century state. Theoretically, it allows us to 'read off' the significance of state activities from our prior analysis of the internal contradictions and constraints on accumulation. The activities of the state can be analysed in simple 'functionalist' terms as subserving the long-term interests of capital in two ways: by facilitating the re-equilibrating effects of the capitalist mode of production; and by forestalling the development of a class-conscious and politically mature proletariat. Thus the 1834 Poor Law Reform Act, together with the repeal of the Master and Servant Laws and the activities of what Marx described as the 'flesh agents', can be seen as attempts to facilitate the extraction of labour power and the production of surplus value.[77] The expansion of state-sponsored welfare provisions and of charitable activity can be regarded as having been instrumental in promoting the realisation of surplus value and the longer-term reproduction of labour power. Equally, nineteenth-century street clearance schemes and 'dishousing' policies could be interpreted as serving the function of dispersing the potentially 'dangerous classes'.[78] And the reforming activities of the state in general, and its interventions in the field of education in particular, could be taken as examples of an attempt to confer legitimacy on the capitalist order and to establish forms of social control that were appropriate to the conditions of a market society.

The value of Marxist ideas for the purpose of understanding the social policies and other activities of nineteenth-century governments should not, therefore, be under-estimated. It should also be stressed that the apparent 'simplicity' of a 'functionalist' analysis would be belied by any account that attempted to comprehend the conflicting and complex requirements of the capitalist system. Such an account must be capable of calculating the effects of state activity on both the long-term interests of capital *and* the particular and immediate demands of individual capitalists, the extraction *and* reproduction of surplus value, the imperatives of accumulation *and* legitimation. The very fact that Marxist analysis is capable of revealing the limits and paradoxes of state action is in itself a strong testimony to its value for historians. However, it is not self-evident that the same analysis is equally valuable for the purposes of understanding the 'welfare activities' of the modern twentieth-century state: it is one thing to argue that the 'tutelary' state of the nineteenth century subserved at least the long-term interests of capital, but quite another to attribute the same 'functions' to the 'democratic' and 'collectivist' state of the modern period. It is this problem, amongst others, that has provided the basis for the Fabian and revisionist challenge to Marxian thought.

The Fabians, according to Eric Hobsbawm, have always been strong on public relations, pressing with some success the claim that their system is politically relevant to and strategically useful in the changing conditions of late capitalism. The claim to relevance was based on the ostensible 'realism' of Fabian principles, and of the principle of collectivism in particular. The Webbs' theoretical formulations rested on the premise that social and political theory must be derived inductively – derived, that is, from empirical observation of actual social conditions. This led the Webbs to take an iconoclastic attitude towards both liberal and Marxist political economy. Bernstein, too, invested his energies in 'the attempt to corrode dogmatic encrustations and test the apparently eternal truths of orthodoxy in an empirical fashion'.[79] Their claim to attention was based on the assertion that orthodox socialist theory had been superseded by historical events: the 'crises' of capitalism were showing signs of abatement, the franchise was being extended, the 'bourgeois' state had taken up the cause of social reform, and working-class living standards were undergoing a significant improvement.

The credibility of the Fabian case rested, above all else, on its commitment to collectivism. We have seen how, for the Fabians, socialism was identified positively with 'state action' or collectivism, and negatively with *laissez-faire* individualism. This device allowed the early Fabians to attach a special significance to any evidence that the powers of the state were being extended – particularly when the state intervened in the provision of basic welfare amenities, and especially when the exercise of these new powers was matched by a corresponding improvement in the condition of the people. Such evidence would lend strong support to the 'evolutionary' view of the transition to socialism, and it would also legitimate the Fabians' tactical and theoretical mission to *revise* socialist doctrines in the light of fresh empirical evidence and new political opportunities. By claiming to have taken account of these events, Fabian and revisionist theory could be represented as flexible, empirical, non-dogmatic and, above all, as a realistic guide to political action – a system that had been especially tuned to changing economic and political circumstances. Its reputation and thus its influence stood or fell according to the nature of the wider political context. In Britain, until recently and with the possible exception of the 1930s, this context has developed in a way that has become progressively more favourable to the Fabian case.

The circumstances of late Victorian and Edwardian Britain were particularly favourable to the revisionist enterprise. Fabian theory was conceived in the 'golden age' of Victorian capitalism and was developed in the wake of an 'administrative revolution'. From the 1870s working-class incomes rose in real terms, and death rates – which are a reliable index of social well-being – started the accelerating decline that has continued through to the present day.[80] Labour unrest came to assume a different form, with the 'new unionism' being interpreted by the middle class as 'a means towards the socialisation of the poor' and as evidence of the growing responsibility of unskilled labour.[81] Even the latest revelations of the poverty researchers seemed to provide cause for growing optimism. Charles Booth's investigations into the condition of the London poor carried the reassuring message that chronic poverty was less extensive than had been commonly supposed, and that the 'demoralised' and 'degenerate' residuum of casual labour presented little or no threat to the established order.[82] All in all, the condition of labour appeared to be undergoing a marked improvement; the modern worker, according to Alfred Marshall, was possessed of 'more firmness and elasticity of character', his 'mental horizons' were wider and his character was more 'rational' by comparison with his proletarian predecessor.[83] And the future of capitalism itself, albeit in a 'moralised form', seemed to have achieved a new security. As H.G. Wells wrote in 1902: 'Everything seems pointing to the belief that we are entering upon a progress that will go on with an ever widening and ever more confident stride for ever. . . . We are in the beginning of the greatest change that humanity has ever undergone'.[84]

The Edwardian period presents a somewhat different picture, with the decline in real wages up to 1914 and the great 'labour unrest' of 1911–13. There is a stark contrast to be drawn between the rosy optimism of the last decades of the nineteenth century, and the sense of foreboding communicated by Sir George Askwith to his audience at the Cavendish Club in Bristol in 1913: he repudiated any suggestion that the 'present unrest will cease', and went on to predict that 'within a comparatively short time there may be movements in this country coming to a head of which recent events have been a small foreshadowing.'[85] Nevertheless, the activities of the state – the succession of social reforms which culminated in the welfare legislation of the 1906–14 Asquith and Lloyd George administrations – seemed to promise a more peaceful route to a rather different kind of 'socialism', the socialism of active and responsible government. From the late 1880s any form of state protection for the poor and the weak, and any kind of governmental 'interference' in the workings of the market, were popularly equated with socialism. In this respect the Fabians merely echoed an assumption that was shared by such unlikely bedfellows as the Liberty and Property Defence League. But contemporary events also seemed to confirm the central tenets of Fabian collectivism. The steady accumulation of social reforms over some decades served to indicate the apparent inevitability of 'collectivism'. The success of the Labour Representation Committee in establishing an electoral pact with Liberal governments could be taken as a vindication of the political tactics recommended by the Fabian Society. The claim of leading politicians like Lloyd George to have been persuaded to act for the poor by the evidence of social investigation and by the compunctions of their own consciences could be regarded as living proof of the effectiveness of propaganda and persuasion. And the willingness of some industrialists and non-socialist politicians to concede that social reform could be justified in the interests of national economic efficiency, gave greater credibility to the Fabian conviction that the common interest would ultimately triumph over selfish egoism.

## Notes

1 A. McBriar, *Fabian Socialism and English Politics* (Cambridge University Press, 1966), pp. 6f.
2 G.D.H. Cole, *The Meaning of Marxism* (University of Michigan Press, 1966), pp. 11–14.
3 E. Wilson, *To the Finland Station* (Fontana, 1960), p. 293.
4 C. Dickens, *Hard Times* (Penguin, 1969).
5 Cf. P. Keating, *The Victorian Prophets* (Fontana, 1981).
6 E. Fromm, *Marx's Concept of Man* (Frederick Ungar, 1961), p. 3. Cf. also A. Collier, 'Scientific socialism and the question of socialist values' and A. Wood, 'Marx and equality', in J. Mepham and D.-H. Ruben (eds), *Issues in Marxist Philosophy*, vol. IV (Harvester, 1981).
7 K. Marx, *Economic and Philosophical Manuscripts*, tr. T. Bottomore, in Fromm, *Marx's Concept of Man*, p. 127.
8 B. Crick, 'Equality', in B. Pimlott (ed.), *Fabian Essays in Socialist Thought* (Heinemann, 1984), p. 11.
9 K. Marx and F. Engels, *Selected Works* (Lawrence and Wishart, 1968), pp. 53–62.
10 G.B. Shaw, 'The transition to socialism', in *Essays in Fabian Socialism* (Constable, 1932).

11    P. Gay, *The Dilemma of Democratic Socialism* (Octagon, 1979), p. 104.
12    A. McBriar, *Fabian Socialism and English Politics* (Cambridge University Press, 1966), p. 9.
13    *Report on Fabian Policy*, Fabian tract no. 70, 1896, p. 7.
14    Marx and Engels, *Selected Works*, p. 411.
15    Ibid., p. 410 (our emphasis).
16    Quoted in Gay, *The Dilemma*, pp. 146–7.
17    Ibid., p. 86.
18    A. Giddens, *Capitalism and Modern Social Theory* (Cambridge University Press, 1971), p. 55.
19    Pimlott, *Fabian Essays*, p. 68.
20    Gay, *The Dilemma*, p. 220.
21    McBriar, *Fabian Socialism*, pp. 63–4.
22    S. Webb, 'Historic', in *Fabian Essays* (George Allen and Unwin, 1962).
23    Ibid., p. 66.
24    F. Engels, 'Socialism: utopian and scientific', in Marx and Engels, *Selected Works*.
25    Webb, 'Historic', p. 66.
26    Ibid., p. 82.
27    Ibid., p. 90.
28    Gay, *The Dilemma*, p. 149.
29    S. Collini, *Liberalism and Sociology* (Cambridge University Press, 1979), pp. 150–2; cf. J. Owen, *L.T. Hobhouse: sociologist* (Nelson, 1974), chapter 6.
30    Collini, *Liberalism*, p. 183.
31    A.W. Wright, *G.D.H. Cole and Socialist Democracy* (Oxford University Press, 1979), p. 210.
32    Cole, *The Meaning of Marxism*, pp. 27–9.
33    Wilson, *To the Finland Station*, p. 183.
34    K. Marx, 'The eighteenth brumaire of Louis Bonaparte', in Marx and Engels, *Selected Works*.
35    Wright, *Cole*, p. 211.
36    Giddens, *Capitalism*, pp. 59–60.
37    Engels, 'Socialism', pp. 161–2
38    Ibid., pp. 250 f; K. Marx and F. Engels, *The Manifesto of the Communist Party*, pp. 42–4.
39    Marx and Engels, *The Manifesto*, pp. 42–3.
40    Engels, 'Socialism', pp. 421–4.
41    Wright, *Cole*, p. 212.
42    Cole, *The Meaning of Marxism*, p. 133.
43    Ibid., p. 132.
44    Ibid., p. 133.
45    *Report on Fabian Policy*, p. 7.
46    E. Hobsbawm, 'The Fabians reconsidered', in *Labouring Men* (Weidenfeld and Nicholson, 1964), pp. 258–9; cf. S. Webb and B. Webb, *The Decay of Capitalist Civilisation* (George Allen and Unwin, 1923), pp. 123–5.
47    For a discussion of the professional ideal see H. Perkin, *The Origins of Modern English Society* (Routledge and Kegan Paul, 1969).
48    Webb, *Fabian Essays*, p. 90; Collini, *Liberalism*, p. 184.
49    K. Kumar, *Prophecy and Progress* (Penguin, 1978), pp. 23–4 (our emphasis).
50    R. Mishra, 'Marx and welfare', *Sociological Review*, 23(3), 1975, pp. 293–5.
51    Ibid., p. 296.

52 Wilson, *To the Finland Station*, p. 188.
53 Mishra, 'Marx and welfare', p. 294.
54 F. Engels, *The Condition of the Working Class in England*, p. 27.
55 Ibid., p. 143.
56 Cole, *The Meaning of Marxism*, p. 185.
57 Ibid., p. 183.
58 Webb, *Fabian Essays*, pp. 63–7.
59 McBriar, *Fabian Socialism*, p. 73.
60 G.B. Shaw, *The Impossibility of Anarchism*, Fabian tract, 1893; cf. W. Wolfe, *From Radicalism to Socialism* (Yale University Press, 1975), pp. 266–70.
61 Wolfe, *From Radicalism*, pp. 281–2.
62 Ibid., pp. 260–1.
63 Webb, *Fabian Essays*, p. 81.
64 Ibid., p. 78.
65 Wolfe, *From Radicalism*, pp. 275–84; cf. *The Moral Aspects of Socialism*, Fabian tract no. 72, 1896.
66 S. Webb, *Socialism in England* (1908), quoted by S. Lukes, *Individualism* (Basil Blackwell, 1973), pp. 36–7; cf. *The Difficulties of Individualism*, Fabian tract, 1896.
67 Wolfe, *From Radicalism*, pp. 279–80; cf. Webb, *Fabian Essays*, pp. 88–93, and *Twentieth Century Politics: a policy for national efficiency*, Fabian tract, 1901. A short but useful discussion of the Fabian appeal to Darwinian theory is provided by D. Oldroyd in *Darwinian Impacts* (Open University Press, 1980), pp. 234–6.
68 Cf. Gay, *The Dilemma*, pp. 244–6.
69 G.B. Shaw, *Man and Superman* (Penguin, 1946), p. 252.
70 Quoted by McBriar, *Fabian Socialism*, p. 84.
71 N. MacKenzie and J. MacKenzie, *The First Fabians* (Weidenfeld and Nicolson, 1977), p. 408 (our emphasis).
72 Ibid., p. 408.
73 Kumar, *Prophecy*, p. 40.
74 This and the following quotations are taken from S. Webb and B. Webb, *A Constitution for the Socialist Commonwealth of Great Britain* (Longman, Green, 1920), pp. 350–6.
75 S. Webb and B. Webb, *Soviet Communism* (Victor Gollancz, 1937), pp. 1215–16.
76 Cole, *The Meaning of Marxism*, p. 13.
77 K. Marx, *Capital*, vol. I, pp. 254–5; Engels, *The Condition of the Working Class*, pp. 320f.
78 Cf. G.S. Jones, *Outcast London* (Penguin, 1971).
79 Quoted by Gay, *The Dilemma*, p. 162.
80 E. Hobsbawm, *Industry and Empire* (Penguin, 1969), pp. 159f.; cf. G.D.H. Cole and R. Postgate, *The British Common People* (Methuen, 1961), chapter 36.
81 Jones, *Outcast London*, chapter 17.
82 E. Hennock, 'Poverty and social theory in England', *Social History* 1(1), 1976.
83 A. Marshall 'The future of the working classes' (1873), in A.C. Pigou, *Memorials of Alfred Marshall* (Macmillan, 1925), p. 117.
84 Quoted in Kumar, *Prophecy*, p. 165.
85 Quoted in W. Runciman, *Relative Deprivation and Social Justice* (Penguin, 1972), p. 67.

# 2

# Fabian Collectivism and the Welfare State

Permeation has more than done its job. Today we are all incipient bureaucrats and practical administrators. We have all, so to speak, been trained at the LSE, are familiar with Blue Books and White Papers, and know our way round Whitehall. We realise that we must guard against romantic or Utopian notions: that hard work and research are virtues: that we must do nothing foolish or impulsive: and that Fabian pamphlets must be diligently studied. We know these things too well. Posthumously, the Webbs have won their battle, and converted a generation to their standards.[1]

The first generation of Fabians advanced a specifically socialist interpretation of the popular 'illusion' of automatic progress by drawing theoretical and tactical inferences from contemporary events. Their 'realism' was the realism of a progressive movement standing expectantly in the vanguard of history. When we turn to examine the intellectual contribution of the post-war generation of Fabians, another kind of 'realism' is revealed – the conservative realism of a movement which placed itself and its 'achievements' at the acme of the historical process. A similar point has been made by Nigel Harris in connection with the transformation of Marxism-Leninism in the Soviet Union. What began as a group of beliefs that were 'radical, profoundly opposed to the existing status quo' ended 'as conservatism, in defence of the Soviet status quo'. The 'practical impact' of Western conservatism and Marxism-Leninism has, he argues, become the same: 'The contrast between the ideal and the real narrows; operative aims become inoperative, "utopian"; the given national framework replaces the postulated international.'[2] In this chapter we shall argue that the same processes were apparent in the development of the Labour Party and in the mainstream of British intellectual life in the early post-war period.

In less than ten years the British Labour Party was transformed, first triumphantly from the party of the future into the party of the moment; and then, less happily, from the midwife (if not the parent) of the welfare state into what many feared would become a party that had been stranded by the historical tide that it had itself initiated. The fear was that 'socialist dogma' and irrational 'political neurosis' – the failure to adjust the political language of the Party to new realities, and the dogged adherence to nationalisation and clause 4 – would result in the electoral impotence of the Party. However, after some fourteen years in opposition, the Labour Party re-emerged armed with Harold Wilson's programme for a 'new Britain'. The Labour platform in the 1960s was unashamedly pragmatic in style and technocratic in content. This, as we shall see, complemented the empiricist and technical preoccupations of the contemporary academic establishment – preoccupations that were justified by the presumed 'end of ideology', and by the belief that Marxism, in particular, had no relevance in the modern age.

As it turned out, Marx's ghost was not to be so easily exorcised. When in 1964 a Labour government was returned the intellectual mood, together with Britain's economic fortunes, was already beginning to change. The 'ideology of affluence', the 'political empiricism' of the Labour Party and the 'quietistic' attitude of Western intellectuals were challenged by a revival of left-wing and libertarian thought. The later development of British intellectual culture and the welfare debate owed a great deal to the 'new left' of the early 1960s, and to the subsequent split between those who found radical inspiration in European Marxist theory and those rooted in native political traditions (the 'new' and the 'old' new left). For this reason we shall conclude this chapter with a brief review of the changing temper of that period.

## Fabian collectivism and the post-war settlement

> The political actions of the labour movement as a recognisable body have, in general, been under Fabian direction; we now live, in certain evident respects, in a Webb world. The identification of socialism with state action is the clear result of this.[3]

Although Raymond Williams may not be entirely correct in his assertion that the political wing of the labour movement has been under Fabian *direction*, there can be little doubt that individual members of the Fabian Society have, at times, exerted a strong influence on the Labour Party. Certainly the doctrines, beliefs and values of at least a powerful faction within the movement have acquired a distinctly Fabian hue. And there is, in the post-war period, some evidence of 'Fabian direction'. By 1945 the Society had played a key role in the reconstruction of the Party after the debacle of 1931; it had made a major contribution to the drafting of the post-war settlement; and, after the 1945 election, it could count amongst its membership the premier, nine cabinet ministers and more than half of the new Labour Members of Parliament. The legislative programme of the first post-war Labour government, with its emphasis on nationalisation, centralisation and state intervention, testifies perhaps to the potency of the Fabian influence.

Viewed in retrospect, the Labour victory of 1945 was not exactly a revolutionary moment in the history of British parliamentary politics. The Labour manifesto – *Let Us Face the Future* – did not represent a significant break with the coalition government's plans for social reconstruction; and the electoral landslide which brought the Attlee government into power was the predictable outcome of the popular radicalism of the early 1940s.[4] Nevertheless, the return of a Labour government with a large parliamentary majority did take many by surprise, and the battle cries of the new Labour parliamentarians appeared to promise an imminent social revolution of unprecedented proportions.

Labour, it seemed, was at the dawn of its 'heroic age'. 'We have before us,' declared the Member for Watford, 'a battle for peace no less arduous and no less momentous than the battle we have lived through in the past six years. Today the strategy begins to unfold itself, today we go into action. Today might rightly be regarded as D-day in the battle for the New Britain.'[5] And the purpose of the campaign was, as the 1945 manifesto reminded the electorate, 'the establishment of the socialist commonwealth of Great Britain – free, democratic, efficient, progressive, public-spirited, its material resources organised in the service of the British people'. The strategy, like its objective, had a distinctively Fabian flavour: 'Socialism cannot come overnight, as the product of a week-end revolution. The members of the Labour Party, like the British people, are practical-minded men and women.'[6]

What is striking about the life of this Parliament is how the rhetoric of the Labour Party leadership changed in the course of some three or four years. Socialism may not have come overnight, but it seemed as if much had been achieved by 1948. By then the foundations of the 'welfare state' had been laid, and the government had completed its nationalisation programme. Following the enactment of the 1944 Education Bill the Attlee government had moved quickly to implement the new family allowances scheme, higher pensions, and the National Insurance, Industrial Injuries, National Assistance and National Health Service Acts. Over the same period the government had also introduced legislation to nationalise the Bank of England, coal, electricity, gas and inland transport. If, as Hugh Dalton has recalled, the new Members had entered Parliament in 1945 exhilarated by the belief that they were 'walking with destiny', by 1948 they could join with Aneurin Bevan in congratulating themselves for having regained 'the moral leadership of the world'. 'The eyes of the world are turning to Great Britain,' he said, 'and before many years we shall have people coming here as to a modern Mecca, learning from us in the twentieth century as they learned from us in the seventeenth century.'[7] Collectivism, it appeared, had achieved the traditional socialist aspirations for improved human welfare. In the words of the chairman of the 1950 Party conference: 'Poverty has been abolished. Hunger is unknown. The sick are tended.'[8] The 'Fabian blueprints for social welfare, redistributive taxation, nationalisation and national minima' now formed 'part of the law of the land'; 'the familiar landmarks on the road to socialism had been left behind.'[9]

This appraisal of the 'achievements' of the Attlee administration was broadly supported by the conventional wisdom of the day. Academics and journalists, supporters and opponents were, for the most part, agreed on the impact of the government's policies. Rowntree and Lavers in the third and final York poverty survey concluded that the combined effect of full employment and welfare provision had been to secure the virtual abolition of poverty.[10] As early as 1946 the editorial writer of *The Economist* complained of the 'forceful transfer' of income and wealth from the middle classes and the rich to the wage earners. A similar point was made nearly ten years later by Professor Robbins when he asserted that 'relentlessly, year by year, the tax structure is pushing us towards collectivism and propertyless uniformity.' And Lewis and Maude, the post-war obituarists of the middle class, were in little doubt that they were witnessing the 'dawn of a classless society' and the fulfilment of Attlee's dictum that the 'abolition of social classes is fundamental to the socialist conception of society.' For Lewis and Maude the signs were unmistakable:

> Today the class structure of the nation is changing. . . . The upper levels of the working class have overtaken and in respect of income are now indistinguishable from a very deep sector at the lower end of the middle class. . . . The change is profound, and has indeed been described as a social revolution, the last act in the long drama of middle-class domination.[11]

This was, of course, only one view of the 'achievements' of the 1945 government. It is a view that has been justly criticised by more recent writers, whose assessment of the political will and actions of the Labour government is altogether less sanguine.[12] And it was a view that was not fully shared by all sections of the post-war Labour Party. The period between 1948 and 1955 was one of the more critical phases in the Party's post-war history. The run-up to the 1950 general election, the defeat at the polls in 1951 and the struggle for the leadership which culminated in the election of Hugh Gaitskell in 1955 fuelled a long-running debate on the Party's achievements and future prospects. The very nature of the Labour Party's political identity was called into question. Success in the legislature and failure at the hustings forced the Party to redefine its general outlook:

> Did it still claim to be a socialist party and, if so, what did that word mean? How many features of the new society had been truly established; how many more were needed to secure the fundamental change which Labour had traditionally demanded; how long was to be the period of transition; and did the leaders wish to travel this road at all?[13]

On one level the Party seemed to be deeply split by these controversies: loyalists were pitted against the left, leaders against activists. One faction, symbolically represented in the press by Bevan, the 'revolutionist', was opposed by the electoral pragmatists who, like Morrison, were prepared to sacrifice the Party's traditional commitment to public ownership for the sake of retaining the moderate and middle-class vote.

The contest was, in fact, less fundamental than it seemed at the time, and the contestants turned out to be ill-matched. The early dispute between leaders and activists centred not on the question of what the Party had achieved in office – few questioned the claim that the government's welfare and economic policies had transformed the social landscape – but on whether these 'achievements' signified the long-awaited advent of socialism. The question was whether the social revolution had been *completed* by 1948, or whether it had been merely *initiated*.[14] Also, as David Howell has pointed out, the loyalist analysis achieved a greater coherence than anything that was formulated by the left, leaving them vulnerable to the claim that poverty had virtually disappeared, and that the government had secured economic efficiency without resorting to wholesale nationalisation.[15] In the optimistic climate of post-war Britain, and in the context of the anti-communistic paranoia of the Cold War, the case of the left was all too easily discredited. Pleas for further nationalisation could be represented as symptoms of an irrational 'political neurosis' which, if it were to spread, could endanger the viability of the Party as an electoral force.[16] Calls for a further extension of state controls could also be impugned by recalling the newly revealed horrors of the Stalinist regime. If the Conservative Party had achieved its political advances by surrendering its traditional commitment to a social market economy, then it was equally incumbent on the Labour Party to demonstrate that it, too, was capable of adapting its traditional principles to new political realities. Economic growth, mass consumption, full employment and the growing electoral security of a Conservative Party that was dominated by its 'progressive' wing, combined to ensure the eventual supremacy of the Labour Party loyalists, the ascendency of the 'realists' over the 'ideologists'.

Thus by 1955 the Labour Party was dominated by a new generation of political 'realists'. For the rest of the decade the debate within the Party was overshadowed by two kinds of realism. The first, more complacent form was represented by the 'consolidationists', who defended the status quo at a time when, in view of the Conservative government's apparent acceptance of the welfare state and the mixed economy, no defence was necessary.[17] And the second was represented by the 'revisionist intelligentsia', who set about the task of rethinking traditional socialist aspirations in the light of changed social, economic and political circumstances. Although the revisionists reformulated traditional doctrine in a way that appeared to contravene some of the more basic principles of Fabian socialism (the question of nationalisation would be a case in point), they did so because they believed that the aspirations of full employment and the elimination of 'want' had been achieved by other means. The revisionist enterprise was conceived in an essentially Fabian spirit, reaffirming the pragmatic Fabian case for a gradualism that was to be dictated by the democratically monitored pulse of the electorate.

political expediency'.[19] His 'empirical approach to democracy' was based upon the supposition that since America had already achieved the status of the good society, the traditional 'grand warfare of rival ideologies', the 'political labels and ideological approaches' of the past, could no longer be relevant to the problems that do remain.[20] Politics, for the Kennedy administration, had become merely a tactical matter of success at the polls, and a technical exercise in the practical and efficient management of social and economic affairs. The same judgement applies with equal force to the political style of Labour and Conservative governments in Britain during the 1950s and 1960s. The primordial characteristic of the 'Butskellite consensus' was its 'political empiricism'. Labour *and* Conservative politicians appeared to welcome the 'generous development of social welfare', the 'humanisation of industry', and 'the bridging of the chasm between the two nations' that had been brought by the post-war settlement. This perception of the condition of post-war society meant that where the intellectuals now vied with one another to present themselves as 'common-sense fellows with no time for theorising', the two major parties tempered their traditional political philosophies so as to maximise their electoral advantages in competing for the 'middle ground', the votes of middle England, the support of the affluent worker and the new middle class.[21] It was in these circumstances that the Labour Party, having stripped socialism of its ideology, set out to

achieve a 'modernised' society that was to be governed by a technocratic elite of scientific experts and professional administrators. In
1964 the Labour Party, under the leadership of Harold Wilson,
returned to government. His vision of a new Britain, forged in the
white heat of the technological revolution, appeared to fulfil Saint-
Simon's original conception of a society governed without political
power and under the intelligent and benevolent guidance of scientists:

> The social agency was to be the experts, the men of knowledge, the
> scientists, engineers, mathematicians and economists, with a leavening of
> those – bankers and industrialists – who could claim to be honest men of
> affairs with no political axes to grind and with special skills to offer. Theory,
> scientific theory, was to govern social practice, thereby eliminating much of
> the human and material waste caused by the old order of political debate
> and political conflict. Society would then have completed its long-drawn-
> out transition to a new organic stage which would be its final one; the
> revolution would have been terminated at last.[22]

### The ideology of an ending

> The planned, full employment welfare state, which has been the outcome
> of the first successful spell of Labour government, is a society of exceptional
> merit by historical standards.[23]

For Saint-Simon, man's future lay in a society that would be fully
industrialised, meritocratic and harmoniously integrated, a society
that would be *managed* (not governed) by a state that acted in
accordance with scientific principles to secure the common interest
and the welfare of all.[24] Politics would be the province of the
technician, and central planning by experts would ensure that social
and economic affairs were administered with a maximum of efficiency
and justice.[25]

   By the 1950s a number of social commentators were prepared to
declare, in effect, that Saint-Simon's prophecy had been fulfilled. They
argued that industrial society had, in the case of the 'advanced
nations', progressed beyond its transitional, free-market phase to
become 'the good society itself in operation'.[26] The case rested on
three basic assertions. It was argued, first, that a comparison between
pre-war and post-war Western societies revealed a significant
abatement of class conflict and an 'end of ideology'. On the industrial
front, harmony rather than conflict seemed to rule the day, and
consensus seemed to be the predominant feature of our political life.
Second, there had been – or so it was argued – a significant narrowing
of 'class' inequalities, and this had been secured by state intervention

in the economy and by state welfare provision. The point was made by the English sociologist T.H. Marshall when he wrote that post-war social policies were remodelling 'the whole building of society' and that they would end by 'converting a skyscraper into a bungalow'.[27] It was assumed that the planned redistribution of material resources and the extension of social opportunities would result in a weakening of traditional status attitudes, a convergence of lifestyles, and the eventual embourgeoisement of the working class. This was a development that had been anticipated by Harold Beales in 1946 when he wrote that 'the social policy of today leads towards social classlessness . . . we grow more alike, and privilege now wears the pallid look of impending superannuation.'[28] And, finally, these changes were thought to have been dictated by a deep-seated and ineluctable historical process, by a long-term transformation in the very infrastructure of society. They were not merely the result of some partisan adventure on the part of ideologically inspired politicians, but the natural and inevitable result of the 'logic of industrialism' and the imperatives of political democracy.

Britain, then, in company with the other advanced industrial nations, had undergone a 'social revolution'. In the words of Tony Crosland, a leading member of the 'revisionist intelligentsia' of the British Labour Party, 'the most characteristic features of capitalism have all disappeared. . . . This is no minor modification; it is a major historical change.'[29] Crosland's contemporaries were similarly impressed by the changes that had brought post-war Western societies into being, and they devised new labels to distinguish present-day society from the capitalist order of the nineteenth century. Modern Britain and America were variously described as 'post-capitalist', 'post-industrial' and 'post-maturity' societies,[30] and these epithets were employed for the express purpose of stressing the extent to which the advanced industrial nations had broken with their 'capitalistic' past. The question of nomenclature is important. Its immediate significance was fully appreciated by Crosland himself when he wrote that he believed that 'our present society is sufficiently defined, and distinct from classical capitalism, to require a different name.'[31] Crosland went on to argue that there is 'some powerful evidence to support the view' that our society is one in which 'capitalist features and attitudes no longer predominate, and that a change in degree has become a change in kind'.[32]

In each case state intervention – collectivism – was cited as an important distinguishing feature of the new age. For Tony Crosland, post-war Britain was above all else a *statist* society in which the practice of Keynesian economic management, combined with the assumption of state responsibility for welfare, provided an almost complete contrast with the *laissez-faire* capitalism of the nineteenth century.[33] Crosland, having assumed a basic incompatibility between capitalism and collectivism, equates collectivism with socialism, and is thus led to the inescapable conclusion that post-war Britain had become a 'nearly socialist' society. The 'welfare state' and the 'affluent society' would, Crosland believed, have 'seemed a paradise to many early socialist pioneers'.[34]

If this view could be sustained it would seem to challenge any claim that Marxism has a continuing relevance in the twentieth century. If it can be shown that nineteenth-century capitalism has evolved more or less in the direction that was predicted by Saint-Simon, then classical Marxist analysis could be locked safely away in the cupboard of history: Marx, the child of Victorian culture and society, could not speak in relevant terms about our experience in the collectivist and 'nearly socialist' world of the twentieth century. This point did not escape the post-war theorists of industrial society who took the systematic 'refutation' of Marxist analysis as their principal purpose.[35] 'It is a commonplace today,' wrote Dahrendorf, 'that many of Marx's predictions have been refuted by the social development of industrial societies over the past century.'[36]

The experience of the West seemed to demonstrate that progress was to be achieved by evolution rather than revolution: in this sense, therefore, Marx had misjudged the future of capitalism. There was, as Edward Shils observed, a lesson here for 'the economically under-developed countries': they, too, 'would have to go through an industrial revolution which . . . would not be less painful than the industrial revolution in the West'. They should not, for this reason, think that 'they will be able to make more rapid and better economic progress' by renouncing their political liberties and turning to a communist solution.[37] It was also supposed that the same example had been equally instructive for 'the intellectuals'. Marxism, it was claimed, had 'lost its appeal' partly because of the 'very triumph of the democratic social revolution in the West':[38]

> [The] change in Western political life reflects the fact that the fundamental political problems of the industrial revolution have been solved: the workers have achieved industrial and political citizenship; the conservatives have accepted the welfare state; and the democratic left has recognised that an increase in overall state power carries with it more dangers to freedom than solutions for economic problems.[39]

We had at last achieved the optimal correspondence between social, political and economic realities on the one hand, and humanitarian ideals on the other.

This is not the place to defend Marx against his post-war critics, or to reassert the continuing vitality and relevance of Marxist analysis in the modern world. This task will be tackled initially in the next chapter and in considerably more detail in part II of the book. For the moment it is necessary only to state that the Marxist 'counter-attack' has been launched on three related fronts. In the first place it might be argued that those post-war social commentators who so triumphantly consigned Marx to the shelf of history had done so by setting up a vulgarised version of Marx's analysis of capitalist development. Second, a number of authors have pointed out that Marx did, in fact, anticipate many of the changes that occurred in the first half of the twentieth century. These include the apparent embourgeoisement of the British worker, the payment of 'surplus wages' (and consequent rise in living standards), and the socialisation of industry.[40] It is this aspect of Marx's work that has prompted a number of recent attempts to 'periodise' the development of capitalism in a way that explains the development of the 'mixed economy', and of the corporatist welfare state, without departing from the basic principles of Marxist economic analysis.[41] Third, it has been argued that post-war social commentators misconstrued these changes and that by propagating the 'ideology of affluence' they obscured the fact that the industrial nations of the West remained essentially 'capitalist' and were no less subject to the 'periodic crises' that only temporarily resolved the basic 'internal contradictions'.[42] The 1950s represented merely a period of respite, not a new era in the historic development of industrial society.

The dispute resolves ultimately into two contrasting philosophies of history. Bell, Lipset and the 'end-of-ideology' school of the mid 1950s claimed, in effect, to have turned Marx on his head one more time. Their thesis was an ideological justification for the status quo, not only because it celebrated the present, but also because the present was instated as the touchstone for measuring the past and the future. Their argument was that all the nations of the world are

> racing toward a static state of equilibrium; only some countries have a head start. A few have already achieved the good society. Others are fast approaching it. And still others, the underdeveloped countries, have only just begun their ascent. In time, all will have arrived, but until such time it will be the responsibility of those already at the pinnacle to reach down and help the others up. In all this, it would seem, dynamic change is a transitory phenomenon, and all of human history, in all its turmoil and in all its travail, has been moving, inexorably, towards this supreme goal of universal peace.[43]

This argument brings the Marxian dialectic to a halt in 'the final synthesis of the modern, non-ideological, democratic welfare state' by adopting a two-stage model of history.[44] This is a device that had been adopted in the past by liberal writers who were convinced of the superiority of their own age: Spencer in the nineteenth century, Bell and Lipset in the twentieth, have 'tended to see the present as simply the polar opposite of the past, with the future being the prolongation of present tendencies'.[45] Their critics have responded by reasserting a model of history in which the present appears as the penultimate stage. Thus, just as Fabian historiography challenged Spencerian apologetics by representing the capitalist epoch as the 'period of anarchy' intervening between the 'old' and the 'new synthesis',[46] modern Marxist writers have questioned the epochal significance of the collectivist, welfare state by describing it as one more stage of *capitalist* development – the stage, perhaps, of advanced or state-directed monopoly capital.[47] From the perspective of the new left the end of ideology was, in fact, the 'ideology of an ending', a 'weary know-it-all justification . . . of the cultural and political default of the NATO intellectuals'.[48] This complacent celebration of the affluent society rested on the provincial illusion of 'the prematurely middle-aged' that history had been brought to rest in the rich Western societies.

## The mandarins of the welfare state

> The new Elizabethan age is an age of very notable talent but it is a talent of fine lineaments, of delicate but not deep voice, of restraint which binds no passion, of subtlety without grandeur. Outside the China of the Mandarins no great society has ever had a body of intellectuals so integrated with and congenial to its ruling class, and so combining civility and refinement. . . . Never has an intellectual class found its society and its culture so much to its satisfaction.[49]

As we have seen, the welfare state and the affluent society were regarded by many leading Labour politicians as fair approximations to their collectivist ideals. Their task, as they saw it, was to consolidate and defend the historic gains achieved by the Attlee administration. The conservative analysis of the condition of modern Britain and of the future role of the Labour Party was shared by at least one section of the post-war intelligentsia – the 'welfare intelligentsia', the policy scientists and social administrators. Although its origins are retraceable to the last century, academic policy science is very much the product of the post-war period. In all its essential features – its preoccupation with administration, its empiricism, its theoretical assumptions, and its vocational dedication – it has displayed that quality of 'civility' that Shils attributed to the British intelligentsia as a whole in the post-war period.

The first and primordial intellectual characteristic of the policy sciences in post-war Britain was their subservience to the state. They exhibit, according to Taylor-Gooby, a 'perennial tendency to analyse social needs, and arrangements for meeting them, from the standpoint of the modern welfare state'.[50] Their methods and conceptual formulations were specifically tailored for the purpose of influencing social policy. The second outstanding feature of the British policy sciences was their 'empiricist' reputation. The empirical or pragmatic attitude, the rejection of general theoretical analysis is, as Nigel Harris has pointed out, a common feature of conservative thinking. It was also, according to Shils, a general attribute of post-war intellectual life. Shils, like so many of his contemporaries, announced that the modern age was witnessing the end of visionary, 'ideological' thinking.[51] In the specific case of the policy sciences, what first appears to be a virtue – the Fabian distrust of *a priori* reasoning, their iconoclastic attitude towards the received wisdoms of political economy, their insistence on the importance of empirical observation of actual social conditions – became something of a vice: an inability to penetrate the level of 'appearances', a failure to see society as anything other than a world of individuals with problems, a neglect of the underlying structures of power and domination, and an inability to engage in a critical discussion of the objects of policy science. Thus, in the words of Peter Taylor-Gooby: 'An uncritical empiricism has led to a persistent tendency to analyse social problems and social needs in a way that takes the limitations of state intervention in a capitalist society for granted.'[52]

The fact that the policy sciences have tended to adopt a pragmatic, empirical and technical idiom may have resulted in a certain 'theoretical naivety' but it does not mean that the policy scientist's practice has been entirely atheoretical. It has to be admitted, of course, that explicit theoretical analysis has only become a pronounced feature of British welfare debate within the last ten years. It was not until 1971 that a major review of the theoretical and political roots of the discipline of social administration was published[53] and, in the following year, George and Wilding were still able to remark on the fact that the first issue of the *Journal of Social Policy*, even though it was billed as a special number on 'values in social policy', offered very little in the way of an explicit and critical theoretical discussion on the influence of social values and conflict on the development of social policy.[54] This failure to engage in theoretical analysis has meant that underlying theoretical assumptions – tacit theories and values – have been obscured. Social administrators have been so anxious to justify their empiricism by 'debunking' the pretensions of social theorists[55] that they have remained largely unconscious of the extent to which their own work is constructed within the terms of a consensus theory of welfare, politics and contemporary social problems.[56]

This becomes apparent when we examine the themes that were developed in the post-war literature of social administration. First, social administrators have both assumed and advanced the classical nineteenth-century indictments of market society, drawing for this purpose on the earlier work of Fabian and liberal historians – Polanyi, the Webbs, the Hammonds and Toynbee.[57] Second, they adopted 'progressivist' and 'idealist' interpretations of the historical development of the welfare state, with the result that many of the basic texts described and explained the process of policy development in terms that were reminiscent of the old Whig interpretation of history.[58] And, third, the subject of social administration was premised on a definition of its subject matter – of social policy – that prejudiced any serious attempt to engage in critical theoretical debate, and made it inconceivable that social policy could be anything other than beneficent and redistributive in both its intentions and, at least potentially, in its effects. These three themes combined to reinforce the general assumption that the welfare state, acting in concert with Keynesian economic policies, had resolved the structural problems of capitalist society. All that remained were the technical problems of ensuring that social policies were efficiently administered and that the 'beneficiaries' adapted their lifestyles and expectations to the new opportunities afforded by the welfare state. It is in the resolution of these 'technical' problems that the professional skills of the empirically and practically minded social administrator were regarded as so important. Social administration has adopted a prescriptive and interventionist approach to its subject matter. This is a quality that it shares with Marxism, and it is one of the features of the subject that distinguishes it from the avowedly 'value-free' academic social sciences. The vocation of the social administrator has been to serve two constituencies – policy-makers on the one hand, and the growing army of workers in the 'personal service professions' on the other.

The presumption that the technical services of the social administrator could contribute to the resolution of social problems has rested on two basic assumptions. The first is that any shortfall between the 'aims' and the 'achievements' of the welfare state can be explained in essentially non-structural terms. Thus the 'persistence' of poverty and social deprivation might be attributed to the intransigence of certain 'lower-class' families and individuals who, by failing to utilise and exploit the services, benefits and opportunities afforded by the welfare state, remain entrapped in a self-perpetuating cycle of deprivation. Alternatively, the same problems might be explained in terms of the technical inefficiency of some public agencies which are failing to translate national policy provisions into effective local services. Both explanations emphasise the amenability of such problems to skilled, professional intervention by circumventing the suggestion that the persistence of social deprivation is, at root, a problem of political will and practicability.

The second basic assumption concerns the process of policy development itself. Intervention, not just at the level of welfare delivery but also at the level of political decision-making, presupposes a rationalist explanation of policy development and a consensus theory of welfare politics.[59] It assumes that the behaviour of the modern if not the historical state conforms to the model of 'rational action' – that government, having committed itself to certain agreed welfare goals, will employ the available social scientific intelligence to identify and resolve whatever obstacles stand in its path. One of the clearest and earliest statements of this position was provided by Thomas Marshall in 1939:

> The social services have lost . . . their class character. They are inspired by the spirit of professionalism, in the sense that they do not design their work to meet an articulate and effective demand only, but plan it in the light of expert knowledge of the social arts and sciences and of fundamental principles of social welfare formulated on the basis of accumulated human experience.[60]

'The British social services,' he concluded, 'are not yet above or beyond politics, but they are moving in that direction.' Wide areas of social action are now left to the administrators and the professions: here 'the voice of the politician is but dimly heard as the distant ineffectual bleating of a wandering sheep.'

This notion of the increasingly 'rational' character of state action can also be found in the more recent writings of British policy scientists. Paul Halmos, for example, argued that 'social science intelligence' has become 'a pervading factor in the social process'.[61] Similarly, Mark Abrams and the Simeys contended that developments in the modern state, together with the cumulative improvement in the techniques of sociological research, had produced a situation in which the offices of the social scientist had become an indispensable 'instrument of government'. The social survey had developed as 'a method by which society could obtain precise information about itself and thus achieve social change in a peaceful and coherent manner' and, thus, 'no amendment of social policy' is now possible 'without a carefully tested appeal to experience and the evaluation of proposals in the light of the relevant evidence'.[62]

The social scientist's claim to occupy a strategic role in the policy-making process was not the plaintive plea of the disenfranchised intellectual. The 'professionalisation' of government had been adopted as a prominent feature of the political style of both Labour and Conservative administrations in the 1960s. The Wilson government, in particular, having espoused the ideals of pragmatic reform and technocracy, formally incorporated social scientists into the civil service and into a variety of positions close to the cabinet and prime minister's office.[63] Social administrators and sociologists with a close interest in policy issues played an increasingly active part in the framing and evaluation of government policy, occupying seats on official committees and royal commissions, staffing the new ministries and 'think tanks' and sometimes exerting a direct informal influence on senior members of the government.[64] In the age of 'modernisation' the mandarins of the new establishment constituted a truly 'civil' branch of the British intelligentsia.

## The new left and the ideology of affluence

We began this chapter by reviewing some of the ideas of writers who regarded the welfare state as the culmination of history, as 'the good society itself in operation'. For these writers the 'end of ideology' was the inevitable outcome of the triumph of democracy and advanced technology over the 'problems' of industrial society. The welfare state and the affluent society were living testimony to the success of pragmatic reform and constitutional action, and to the corresponding redundancy of 'ideological' solutions and 'catastrophic' theories of change. It should also be apparent that the work of these academic writers provided a natural complement to the 'socialist realism' of the Labour Party's revisionist intelligentsia. The strategic thinking of Crosland and his associates, like the politics of John F. Kennedy, had stripped politics of the 'ethics of conscience' and reduced it to the 'art of compromise and technical manipulation'.[65] Their participation in consensus politics, their advocacy of piecemeal social engineering in the welfare state and of Keynesian management techniques in the mixed economy, were based on an equally sanguine assessment of the achievements of the post-war settlement. The practice of political empiricism should also be recognised as an important if implicit contribution to the defence of 'Western values' against the threat of Eastern totalitarianism. Thus academics and politicians renounced their respective ideological heritages and combined forces to mobilise a final pragmatic assault on the surviving adherents of the outmoded dogmas of pre-war and classical Marxism.

By 1960, however, the British left was beginning to regroup. It was during that year that the *New Left Review* was inaugurated, bringing together disillusioned ex-communists and a younger, more amorphous group of radical intellectuals. The 'new left', according to David Howell, emancipated left-wing thought 'from the stultifying choice between Stalinism and acceptance of NATO and the mixed economy'.[66] Its preoccupations initially reflected its diverse and contradictory origins: 'Attempts to develop Marxist analyses after the frozen years of Stalinism rubbed along with appeals to traditional English radicalism, or variants of existentialism.'[67] Nevertheless it was supported by a genuine undercurrent of radical feeling. In 1960 Edward Thompson, one of the 'midwives' of the new left, wrote that 'beneath the polarisation of power and ideology in the Cold War period, a new, rebellious human nature was being formed.' A 'new critical temper' was emerging 'just as the new grass springs up beneath the snow'.[68] In its unformed and original state this new rebellious impulse was intrinsically anti-political. Its sentiments were accurately reflected by Colin Wilson's *Outsiders* which, together with the publications of various other members of the 'angry young men' movement, portrayed the malaise of our civilisation in spiritual terms – as a problem of man's consciousness (or lack of it).[69]

The problem for the new left was to define, to shape, 'the new human nature' so that it could express itself in 'positive rebellion'. At the same time its work had to be addressed to the needs of the traditional constituency of the left-wing intelligentsia by relieving 'the poverty of ideas in the labour movement'. Thus 'the task of socialism' was, on the one hand, to 'meet people where they *are*, where they are touched, bitten, moved, frustrated, nauseated – to develop discontent' whilst, on the other hand, it sought 'to give the socialist movement some *direct* sense of the times and ways in which we live'.[70] The new left must work for socialism 'as the old missionaries worked'. But, if the work of 'socialist propaganda' is to be effectively accomplished, the new left must acknowledge the bankruptcy of the old left (which 'could only speak in the language of power, not of socialised humanity'), and it must give credence to the popular experience of and concern with bureaucracy and over-centralisation. Thus the new left set out to bridge the gulf between intellectual and industrial workers by respecting the experiences of the latter without discarding the 'proper role' of the former. The role of a left intelligentsia, and thus the editorial policy of the *New Left Review*, was to develop and clarify ideas, to inform and educate the labour movement.

Throughout the 1960s, and particularly during the first few years of its life, the pages of the *New Left Review* were filled with post-mortem dissections of the corpse of the old left. These retrospectives on the condition of the post-war intelligentsia largely concurred with the idea that the 1950s had witnessed an 'end of ideology' although, in their case, the phenomenon was evaluated in entirely negative terms. In 1960, for example, Alasdair MacIntyre delivered a savage indictment of the contemporary intellectual mood. 'There is,' he said, 'not much enthusiasm abroad . . . for the day when the last king will be strangled with the entrails of the last priest.' Most 'present-day British intellectuals . . . are on the whole content with what they have'. In the age of conformism the intellectuals conformed as hard as anyone else: 'The writers elevate Western values in *Encounter*. The scientists play their part at Harwell, Aldermaston and Porton. The teachers and the journalists purvey second-hand versions of the dominant ideas.'[71] And what the sociologists had to say seemed, to MacIntyre, 'as devoid of immediate political significance as the study of butterflies or Buddhism'.[72] Elsewhere in the same year Bernard Crick celebrated the tenth anniversary of Laski's death by declaring that his passing had marked the demise of socialist literature – of a literature that had been distinguished by its vision and commitment:

> The days of the giants seem over. Even a handful of young angries and a quorum of old Marxists boiled together in an anthology do not emerge as one giant. Most socialist writers in the last decade have been content to be all too human dwellers on a middle earth inhabited by particular, not general truths.[73]

The point was, as Thompson has reminded us, that the state of the post-war intellectuals had amply confirmed Orwell's prophecy that 'the passive attitude will come back'. In 1940 Orwell had written: 'Seemingly there is nothing left but quietism – robbing reality of its terrors by simply submitting to it. Get inside the whale . . . give yourself over to the world process, stop fighting against it or pretending that you control it; simply accept it, endure it, record it.'[74] And this, of course, is precisely what the post-war Jonahs did. Post-war social and political scientists diligently recorded the world process, whilst other intellectuals employed their visionary talents to justify their 'flight from pre-war socialism'. On the one hand, Fabian empiricism – 'factualism' – 'inevitably became the ideology of [the] existing system', divorced as it was from 'any even tentative general theory'.[75] Those, on the other hand, who were possessed of a larger, often literary vision contributed to the conservative mood by elaborating *Brave New World* images of the only conceivable alternative to welfare capitalism – a regimented, Stalinist utopia.

The task of explaining the moribund condition of the post-war intelligentsia was crucial to the project of regenerating socialist theory and politics in the future. What was it about the economic, social or political circumstances of the time that enables us to account for the remarkable quiescence of the post-war intellectuals? Once again there are similarities as well as differences between the ways in which the 'integrated' intelligentsia and the 'alienated' new left answered this question. Edward Shils, for example, argued that the intellectual mood of the period had been a more or less rational response to 'real' social changes that were initiated during the Second World War. The common front against fascism, the incorporation of the intellectuals into the wartime administration, the promise of social improvement in the post-war settlement – all contributed, according to Shils, to a final re-establishment of amicable and harmonious relations between the intellectuals and British society. Other exponents of the end of ideology were inclined to attribute this phenomenon to the fundamental structural changes that accompanied, or so they argued, the long-term and irreversible evolution of industrial societies.

On the other hand, Edward Thompson and his associates tended to see the passivity of the post-war intelligentsia as a temporary and historically contingent *abdication* from their true responsibilities as critical and visionary thinkers. C. Wright Mills, an American sociologist and contributor to the *New Left Review*, argued that those American intellectuals whom he described as 'the Old Futilitarians' – the remnants of the left circles of the 1930s – having discovered that in the Soviet Union communism had become the reactionary instrument of a national elite, reacted by rejecting all traditions of the left. According to Mills these ex-communists had come to display 'a kind of weariness with any politics of moral concern, for which they . . . substituted the nationalist celebration': they were transformed, rather suddenly, into patriots.[76] Implicit in these interpretations is the charge of defeatism, to which Ralph Miliband added the accusation of betrayal. Miliband suggested that the leaders of the labour movement had failed, in 1948, to grasp the opportunity of 'going forward with a programme which, by necessity, would have transcended the traditional categories of labourism'. They opted, instead, for 'a programme of tinkering empiricism within the framework of capitalist society' and thus they contributed to 'the contemporary trivialisation of politics and to the creation of an image of socialism as a mean little experiment in bureaucratic piecemeal social engineering'.[77]

As they stand, these explanations present the quietistic attitude of the 1950s as the historically unique product of a fortuitous combination of circumstances: the passive attitude begins to look like a historical accident that resulted from exceptional events and contingencies. It might however be preferable to see this attitude as a regular, recurring feature of our intellectual life, one that is rooted in the changing economic fortunes of capitalist democracies, the swing between growth and recession, the periodic alternation of crisis and stability. Hobsbawm has provided what could be taken as a starting point for this kind of analysis when he wrote that 'reformist' strategies, 'political empiricism' and intellectual quiescence seem to be 'natural' or plausible in 'conditions of stable or flourishing capitalism and of official recognition of labour movements'.[78] Thompson, too, has argued that the viability of the reformist tradition had depended on three factors – imperialism; the experience of the Russian Revolution (which had discredited the concept of a revolutionary transition to socialism); and the fact that 'war, post-war recovery and next-war preparations' had given the capitalist economy a 'fresh lease of life'.[79] What was crucial, then, was the presence of economic factors which made it 'possible for liberal reformism . . . to continue to win substantial benefits for the people', and of political factors which foreclosed on the alternative socialist options.

From this point of view, the ideology of affluence appears to be the finite product of a specific era in the history of British capitalism. Its survival and potency are clearly seen as being contingent on the continued presence of certain economic, social and political conditions. This means that attention is drawn away from specific movements or individuals and towards the wider intellectual milieu on which they may or may not exert an influence. This milieu or mood appears to alternate in concert with the periodic crises of a capitalist economy. Thus, if the 1920s and the 1950s were marked by intellectual 'passivity' and 'quietism', the 1930s and, presumably, the 1980s represent periods in which the intellectual mood is less receptive to reformist thinking. According to this argument economic crisis and the evaporation of the growth-generated surplus tend to result in a reassertion of the fundamental contradictions of the capitalist order – contradictions which can only be temporarily and partially obscured by welfare provision and consumer affluence. It is during times of economic crisis that the need for a critical socialist theory is redis-covered.

## Notes

1　C.A.R. Crosland, *The Future of Socialism* (Jonathan Cape, 1956), pp. 235–7.
2　N. Harris, *Beliefs in Society* (Penguin, 1971), p. 131.
3　R. Williams, *Culture and Society* (Penguin, 1961), p. 187.
4　R. Miliband, *Parliamentary Socialism* (Merlin, 1973), pp. 272–4. Cf. K.O. Morgan, *Labour in Power 1945–1951* (Oxford University Press, 1984) and P. Addison, *The Road to 1945* (Jonathan Cape, 1975).
5　Major John Freeman, 15 August 1945, quoted by A. Howard, 'We are the masters now', in M. Sissons and P. French (eds), *Age of Austerity* (Penguin, 1964).
6　*Let Us Face the Future*, Labour Party Manifesto 1945.
7　Quoted in M. Foot, *Aneurin Bevan 1945–60* (Granada, 1975), p. 234.
8　Quoted in D. Howell, *British Social Democracy* (Croom Helm, 1976), p. 50.
9　R.H.S. Crossman, *New Fabian Essays* (Turnstile Press, 1952), pp. x, 1–2.
10　B. Rowntree and G. Lavers, *Poverty and the Welfare State* (Longman, 1951).

11  R. Lewis and A. Maude, *The English Middle Classes* (Penguin, 1953), p. 23.
12  For example Howell, *British Social Democracy*, chapter 5, and Miliband, *Parliamentary Socialism*, chapter 9. See also K. Morgan, *Labour in Power*.
13  Foot, *Bevan*, p. 254.
14  Miliband, *Parliamentary Socialism*, p. 307.
15  Howell, *British Social Democracy*, pp. 189–90.
16  R.H.S. Crossman, 'On political neurosis', *Encounter*, 2(5), 1954.
17  V. Bogdanor and R. Skidelsky (eds), *The Age of Affluence* (Macmillan, 1970), p. 81.
18  Examples of their work can be found in Crossman, *New Fabian Essays*, and Crosland, *The Future of Socialism*.
19  S. Rousseas and J. Farganis, 'American politics and the end of ideology', in I. Horowitz (ed.), *The New Sociology* (Oxford University Press, 1964), p. 281.
20  Kennedy's commencement address at Yale University, 1962, quoted in ibid., p. 284.
21  R.H.S. Crossman, 'Towards a philosophy of socialism', in Crossman, *New Fabian Essays*.
22  K. Kumar, *Prophecy and Progress* (Penguin, 1978), p. 44.
23  Crosland, *The Future*, p. 79.
24  Kumar, *Prophecy*, pp. 38–44.
25  F. Markham, *Saint-Simon: selected work* (Basil Blackwell, 1952).
26  S.M. Lipset, *Political Man* (Heinemann, 1960), p. 403.
27  T.H. Marshall, 'Citizenship and social class', in *Class, Citizenship and Social Development* (University of Chicago Press, 1977), p. 114.
28  H. Beales, *The Making of Social Policy* (L.T. Hobhouse memorial lecture) (Oxford University Press, 1946), p. 24.
29  Crosland, *The Future*.
30  By Dahrendorf, Bell and Rostow, respectively.
31  Crosland, *The Future*, p. 34.
32  Ibid., p. 35.
33  C.A.R. Crosland, 'The transition from capitalism', in Crossman, *New Fabian Essays*.
34  Crosland, *The Future*, p. 79.
35  See C. Kerr, *Industrialism and Industrial Man* (Penguin, 1973); W.W. Rostow, *The Stages of Economic Growth* (Cambridge University Press, 1960); R. Aron, 'Development theory and the ideological problems of our time', in *The Industrial Society* (Frederick A. Prager, 1967); R. Dahrendorf, *Class and Class Conflict in an Industrial Society* (Routledge and Kegan Paul, 1959).
36  Dahrendorf, *Class*, p. 36.
37  E. Shils, 'The end of ideology?' *Encounter*, 5(5), 1955, p. 55.
38  Ibid., p. 57.
39  Lipset, *Political Man*, p. 406.
40  The point about the embourgeoisement of the British worker was made by Engels in a letter to Marx, dated 7 October 1858: K. Marx and F. Engels, *Selected Correspondence* (Moscow, 1956), p. 133.
41  See E.O. Wright, *Class, Crisis and the State* (Verso, 1979), chapter 3.
42  See S. Hall, C. Critcher, T. Jefferson, J. Clarke and B. Roberts, *Policing the Crisis* (Macmillan, 1978).
43  Rousseas and Farganis, 'American politics', p. 286.
44  Ibid., p. 286.

58    *Fabian revisionism and the welfare state*

45   Kumar, *Prophecy*, p. 60.
46   S. Webb, 'Historic', in *Fabian Essays* (George Allen and Unwin, 1962).
47   Wright, *Class Crisis*, pp. 163ff.
48   C.W. Mills, 'The new left', in I.L. Horowitz (ed.), *Power, Politics and People* (Oxford University Press, 1967), pp. 248–9.
49   E. Shils, 'The intellectuals: Britain', *Encounter*, 4(4), 1955, pp. 16, 6.
50   P. Taylor-Gooby and J. Dale, *Social Theory and Social Welfare* (Edward Arnold, 1981), p. 10.
51   E. Shils, 'Ideology and civility' (1958), in *The Intellectuals and the Powers* (University of Chicago Press, 1972). Shils and the other members of the 'end of ideology' school used the term 'ideology' to refer, in fact, to what Mannheim described as utopian thinking.
52   Ibid., p. 10.
53   R. Pinker, *Social Theory and Social Policy* (Heinemann, 1971).
54   V. George and P. Wilding, 'Social values, social class and social policy', *Social and Economic Administration*, 6(3), 1971, p. 236.
55   Taylor-Gooby and Dale, *Social Theory*, pp. 26–7; cf. Pinker's attack on the 'normative theories' of Marxism and critical sociology.
56   This point is developed by R. Mishra in *Society and Social Policy* (Macmillan, 1977), chapters 3 and 4; and by V. George and P. Wilding, *Ideology and Social Welfare* (Routledge and Kegan Paul, 1976), chapter 1.
57   For example, R. Titmuss, *The Gift Relationship* (George Allen and Unwin, 1970).
58   Cf. J. Baker, 'Social conscience and social policy', *Journal of Social Policy*, 8(2), 1979; M. Gettelman, 'The Whig interpretation of social welfare history', *Smith College Studies in Social Work*, 44 (June), 1974; T.H. Marshall, *Social Policy* (Hutchinson, 1965); D.C. Marsh, *The Future of the Welfare State* (Penguin, 1964); Beales, *The Making of Social Policy*.
59   Cf. D. Donnison, 'Research for policy', in M. Bulmer (ed.), *Social Policy Research* (Macmillan, 1978); J. Coleman, 'Sociological analysis and social policy', in T. Bottomore and R. Nisbet, *A History of Sociological Analysis* (Heinemann, 1978); M. Rein, *Social Science and Public Policy* (Penguin, 1976), chapter 3; G. Payne et al., *Sociology and Social Research* (Routledge and Kegan Paul, 1981), chapter 7.
60   T.H. Marshall, 'A recent history of professionalism in relation to social structure and social policy', in Marshall, *Class, Citizenship and Social Development*.
61   P. Halmos, *The Personal Service Society* (Constable, 1970), p. 68.
62   M. Abrams, *Social Surveys and Social Action* (Heinemann, 1951), p. 124.
63   Cf. articles by Barnes and Kegan in D. McKie and C. Cook (eds), *The Decade of Disillusion* (Macmillan, 1972).
64   See Donnison, 'Research for policy'; M. Bulmer, *Social Research and Royal Commissions* (George Allen and Unwin, 1980).
65   Rousseas and Farganis, 'American politics', pp. 284–5.
66   Howell, *British Social Democracy*, p. 215.
67   Ibid., p. 215.
68   E.P. Thompson, 'Outside the whale', in *The Poverty of Theory* (Merlin, 1978), pp. 30–1.
69   D.E. Cooper, 'Looking back in anger', in Bogdanor and Skidelsky, *The Age of Affluence*.
70   Editorial, *New Left Review*, I(Jan./Feb.), 1960, p. 1.
71   A. MacIntyre, 'Breaking the chains of reason', in E. Thompson (ed.), *Out of Apathy* (New Left Books, 1960), p. 197.
72   Ibid., p. 199.

73 B. Crick, 'Socialist literature in the 1950s', *Political Quarterly*, 31, 1960, p. 361.
74 George Orwell, quoted by Thompson, 'Outside the whale'.
75 Crick, 'Socialist literature', p. 364.
76 Mills, 'The new left'.
77 R. Miliband, 'The sickness of labourism', *New Left Review*, 1, 1960, pp. 7–8.
78 E. Hobsbawm, *Labouring Men* (Weidenfeld and Nicolson, 1964), p. 341.
79 Thompson, *Out of Apathy*, pp. 10–11.

# 3

# Towards a Critical Social Policy

In the early 1960s Edward Thompson looked forward to a rediscovery (or restoration) of socialist ideals and, in doing so, he tended to place a positive evaluation on the historic traditions and achievements of British socialism and the labour movement. Thus Thompson wrote of the 'incomparable fortitude' of the English working class, and of the reforms of 1945 as having embodied 'a socialist *potentia*' that was 'fleshed by actually existent socialist values and practices within the working-class community'. These notions were challenged by the 'new' new left of the late 1960s, and it is their contrasting response to the 'ideology of affluence' that we discuss in the next section.

This response was founded on a much more dismissive account of English working-class culture and of the past 'achievements' of the labour movement. As Perry Anderson put it, they doubted whether 'any working-class movement' had 'produced as many "traitors"' . . . as had labourism'. The 'dominant ethos' of labourism 'was timorous, curmudgeonly and funereal moralism, sunk in hopelessly dusty routines and indescribably boring rhetoric'. For Anderson and the other members of the 'new' new left, the 'origins of the present crisis' were to be found in a cultural malaise that had long since struck at the roots of working-class culture and the labour movement. The remedy that they proposed consisted of a break with past, native traditions and the dissemination of foreign, 'marxisante' theory.

The ultimate purpose of this chapter is to assess the criticisms that have been levelled by the 'new' social administration against 'orthodox' policy science. We shall approach this task by using the distinction between the 'old' new left and the new and rising generation of 'marxisante intellectuals' whose writings dominated the pages of the *New Left Review* from the late 1960s onwards. The significance of this distinction is to be found in the attitudes displayed by the two groups towards the Fabian and British socialist traditions. In the discussion that follows we shall suggest that criticisms of orthodox social administration tend to derive from the ideas initially advanced by the later group of new left intellectuals and that, in both cases, one finds a prematurely dismissive attitude towards the Fabian tradition. This chapter will be concluded, therefore, with a more positive assessment of the recent contributions of Fabian commentators, and with an emphasis on the importance of Fabian critiques of the welfare state for the development of a new and more radical social administration.

## The Young Turks of the cultural revolution

When, in 1967, Herbert Marcuse addressed the 'dialectics of liberation' congress he argued that socialism represents 'a definite negation of the established society', and that the transition to socialism must take the form of a 'rupture of history', a 'radical break', a 'leap into the realm of freedom'.[1] Marcuse went on to illustrate this point by referring to the events of 1848:

> Walter Benjamin quotes reports that during the Paris Commune, in all corners of the city of Paris there were people shooting at the clocks on the towers of the churches, palaces and so on, thereby consciously or half-consciously expressing the need that somehow time has to be arrested; that at least the prevailing, the established time continuum has to be arrested, and that a new time has to begin.

The point of this example was that it emphasised the 'qualitative difference' and the 'totality of the rupture' between the new society and the old. Liberation from the 'affluent society' would require no less of a 'radical break' from the established order, the 'time of the others'. Marcuse concluded his address on an optimistic note. 'We can already see the signs,' he said, 'not only that *they* are getting frightened and worried but that there are far more concrete, far more tangible manifestations of the essential weakness of the system.'[2] His audience was left with the impression that they were standing on a historical threshold, surrounded by the wreckage of broken clocks, preparing for the advent of the 'new time'.

If, from one perspective, the 1960s offered the first real prospects for realising the aspirations of those social scientists who saw their role as the priesthood of a rational society, the same decade also witnessed the emergence of a new generation of radical, disaffected intellectuals. Their style was impious, prophetic and apocalyptic. They looked forward, not to the prospect of 'undreamed-of living standards' and unbounded leisure in a planned society forged by the 'white heat' of the technological revolution, but to a world threatened by imperialism and thermonuclear war. They, too, might have followed *The Economist*'s injunction to 'look up at the TV aerials sprouting above working-class homes' and 'down on the housewives in tight slacks on the summer road to Brighton': but where the editorial writer found 'a great poetry', they would have seen the cultural wasteland of the affluent society. And the welfare state – for some, 'the good society itself in operation' – was, to the new generation, the home of one-dimensional thought, repressive tolerance and disguised exploitation.

George Woodcock has described the politics of the children of affluence as 'anarchic rather than anarchist, bred of frustration rather than of thought'.[3] The libertarian movements of the 1960s reflected the contemporary 'climate of rebellion', the 'insurrectionary state of mind', rather than any new and coherent 'revolutionary ideology'. In this respect the term 'counter-culture' was particularly appropriate: it described the various attempts to achieve a total, qualitative and ruptural break with the past. On the negative side this entailed a general antagonism to 'structured thinking', a hostility towards any kind of intellectual orthodoxy, and a rejection not only of the existing political structures but also of the old parties and traditions of the left. More positively, the apocalypticism of the radical generation was symbolically affirmed by its *style*. The style of radical youth, the style of popular music, and even the peculiar verbal style of the Young Turks in the sociological establishment seemed, in each case, to signify a revolutionary transcendence of the social, lyrical and academic conventions of the affluent society and the welfare state.

The apocalyptic mood was equally characteristic of the new left in the mid to late 1960s and of the critical and committed sociology that developed in the following decade. In these cases the sense of a ruptural break with the past was achieved, not by a 'revolt into style', but by the construction of reasoned critiques of their parent traditions. The new left intelligentsia asserted their radical credentials by attacking the 'labourist' traditions of the 'old' left; and the new reflexive, humanist, radical sociology of the underdog attacked the positivistic, functionalist and 'correctional' sociology of the establishment. The new was presented as the antithesis of the old, and criticism was seen as an act of liberation from past traditions.

These features are also to be found in the later work of 'critical' policy analysts. There can be little doubt that the field of welfare studies has experienced something like a 'scientific revolution'.[4] The 'normal science paradigm' which had, during the 1950s and early 1960s, promised a cumulative progress towards the mature development of social administration as 'the reformers' science', was challenged by a new revolutionary 'problematic' which called into question both the conventional wisdom of the discipline and its historical vocation.[5] It has been a somewhat belated revolution. The fact that radical texts in social policy only appeared in the late 1970s, and the fact that their presence is still barely acknowledged in some university and polytechnic courses, testifies perhaps to the arrested and uneven development of the discipline. Nevertheless, the publication of avowedly Marxist texts on questions of social policy has become something of a boom industry, and the major incursions into the field have been accomplished by that generation of sociologists that had been weaned, during the 1960s, from Parsonian functionalism and Lazarsfeldian empiricism on to the more solid diet of foreign Marxist theory. Armed with these weapons, critical policy analysts have sometimes represented their cause as the very antithesis of the 'orthodox' social administration approach – as constituting a 'ruptural break' with a discipline that had been tainted by reformist compromise.

In part II we shall return to examine the results of this 'scientific revolution'. The conclusion to part I attempts to prepare the ground by outlining some of the tasks confronting the new, radical and 'critical' social policy. But the issue that recurs throughout the book concerns the question of how a critical social policy might be best distinguished from the approach commonly attributed to 'orthodox' social administration. Since it is our impression that critical policy analysis has inherited something of the apocalypticism of the radical political and intellectual movements of the 1960s, we would suggest that there has been a tendency to exaggerate the contrast between the 'old' and the 'new', between orthodox welfare debate and current neo-Marxist approaches to the study of welfare. It is for this reason that we turn, now, to re-examine the alleged 'pathology' of welfare studies in their 'traditional' form.[6] Once this task has been completed it should be possible to re-evaluate earlier critical perspectives on the welfare state, and to set the current 'revival' of Marxist theory and its application to welfare issues in their historical and intellectual context.

## The pathology of welfare studies

The traditional social administration approach is irrevocably committed to a piecemeal and uncritical empiricism that has value as a watchdog and buttress for the welfare state. It encounters difficulty in theorising social arrangements to meet need adequately because it takes a particular form of society for granted.[7]

In this section we shall argue that there are two currently fashionable explanations for the limitations of traditional policy science and the associated 'civility' of the old guard within the welfare intelligentsia. The first attributes the 'pathology' of welfare studies to the existence of direct institutional links between academic policy science and the British state. The second treats the sterility of conventional perspectives on welfare issues as symptoms of a condition that is endemic to the totality of English intellectual culture. In the course of the ensuing discussion it will be apparent that each of these two arguments assigns an important role to Fabianism and the Fabian Society, although they differ in terms of where they locate the Fabian incubus and of the influence and identity they ascribe to it.

### The compromises of establishment politics

Social administration, according to Peter Taylor-Gooby, is 'the paper owl of the British welfare state'. Its 'intellectual liaison' with the welfare state has resulted in 'an inability to construct a critical standpoint' and a failure to give an account of 'popular values'.[8] It takes, in short, 'the perspective of the state'. This fatal weakness is also, apparently, a prominent feature of the 'old' sociology of education. In one study, educational policy research was described as having been connected with a 'high-political and statist kind' of formal politics. The political involvements of educational sociologists have revolved around the 'private salon' rather than 'the party branch'. Their work therefore reflects and reinforces an 'orientation towards reform via the state' rather than to change through 'popular agitation'.[9]

The professional ideology of British policy scientists has certainly placed a high premium on *expert* intervention in the decision-making processes that operate in the upper reaches of the political system. Its basic doctrines include an expectation of continued economic expansion, the belief that the main function of the social services is to redistribute the fruits of growth in favour of those in need, the supposition that government (supported by a popular 'welfarist' consensus) represents the natural vehicle of progress towards the good society, and the belief that the public service professions could and should act as front-line troops in the struggle against injustice and inefficiency.[10] Donnison argues that the possession of this ideology has guaranteed the policy scientist a hearing in the corridors of power because there are many among the leaders of the professions, bureaucracies and political movements who have shared their ideas.[11]

Although this philosophy had been endorsed by progressive Conservatives, Labour governments seem to have been particularly receptive to the overtures of the policy scientist. The ideology of British policy science is entirely consistent with the emphasis in post-war Labour policy on 'centralism' and expert administration and, for this reason alone, one might expect to find a strong rapport between senior Labour politicians and leading policy scientists.[12] The fact that the connections were even stronger, resulting in the formation of closely knit circles of intimates composed of academics and cabinet ministers, is revealed by Crosland's accounts of some of the private meetings held at his home, Boyd-Carpenter's description of Titmuss,

Townsend, Abel-Smith and Crossman as the Labour Party 'skiffle group', and by Donnison's reference to the existence of a 'radical-liberal establishment' straddling the worlds of academia, administration and policy-making.[13] It was through the Fabian Society that these close personal ties had been forged and cemented. The first chair in social administration was established in 1950 at the London School of Economics, an institution which had provided many of the leaders of the post-war Labour Party with a university education, and which had been created and staffed by founder members of the Fabian Society. Through the agency of these two institutions – the Labour Party and the London School of Economics – the Fabian Society exerted a powerful influence on post-war welfare debate.

The strength of this influence was also a product of the extent to which social policy research and teaching was insulated from the wider intellectual environment. The primary reference group of the social administrator was to be found not in the groves of academe, but outside in the everyday practical world of the practitioner and policy-maker. By continuing to emphasise its commitment to professional training and public service, social administration remained true to the traditions of its mother department in the London School of Economics: the Department of Social Science had been set up in 1912 to cater specifically for those students who wished 'to prepare themselves to engage in the many forms of social and charitable effort'.[14] The academic isolation of departments of social administration was, in effect, the price that they paid for their continued commitment to the vocational and interventionist traditions of their discipline. This kind of 'relevance' carried little academic credibility at a time when one group of social scientists was staking its claim to professional status on its 'detachment' and 'value-neutrality', and another, younger generation was beginning to decry any form of involvement with the political establishment and the agents of social control. Perhaps it was for this reason that the new generation of radical sociologists in the 1960s sought to dissociate their discipline from the practical study of social problems. The task for the Young Turks of the British Sociological Association was, as Hilary Rose has put it, 'to drive out the do-gooders and to delegitimise the claims of the ameliorists to be doing sociology'.[15]

### The poverty of English intellectual culture

Critiques of 'orthodox' social administration and of the 'old' sociology of education have been largely preoccupied with these direct institutional and personal links between academic policy science and the 'liberal-left' establishment. At one stage, however, Peter Taylor-Gooby's discussion is conducted on a larger canvas. Social administration's 'arthritic empiricism' is also, he suggests, a consequence of the labour movement's failure to act both as a revolutionary force and as a stimulus to radical theoretical development.[16] This point introduces an argument which attributes the pathology of welfare studies to forces and circumstances which historically precede the birth of social administration as a discipline, and whose influence is felt throughout the entirety of English culture and politics. The general terms of this argument were originally advanced by Perry Anderson and Tom Nairn in the pages of the *New Left Review*. Its implications for a socialist reassessment of our native academic traditions were also spelt out in some detail by Gareth Stedman Jones and Perry Anderson.[17]

In its original form the Anderson–Nairn thesis was concerned less with the specific weaknesses of the labour movement than with the stultifying effect of 'English bourgeois culture' on the development of both the intelligentsia and the working class. Nairn and Anderson argued that our 'native intellectual traditions' had been infected by a particular form of 'hegemonic culture'. This bourgeois culture had also imprinted itself on the forms of 'British' socialism, and it had even permeated the consciousness of the English working class. Our intellectual traditions are described as being inveterately complacent, backward, moralistic, philistine and empiricist. British socialism is represented by Tom Nairn as merely a 'moderate' and 'timid' form of corporate action, imitating bourgeois evolution by 'behaving as if the workers could, in their turn, transform society in their own image by a gradual extension of their influence, by an accumulation of reforms corresponding to the bourgeois accumulation of capital'. And English working-class culture is presented as a mere 'carapace of dead matter', the static and vegetative culture of a people who have become a docile and 'consciously subordinate part of bourgeois society'.[18]

According to this line of argument the Fabian Society provides a direct link between the current state of the policy sciences, the retarded condition of the labour movement, and the deadening forces of English bourgeois culture. The significance of Fabianism lies in its role as an intervening variable; it acts, according to this argument, as both the prime symptom and the principal carrier of a long-standing national disease. Thus, in his essay 'Origins of the present crisis', Perry Anderson has described 'the Webbs and their companions' as 'the direct successors of Jeremy Bentham and James Mill and the positivist ideologues of the mid nineteenth century'. Since the Fabians were, he argues, the first sizeable group of intellectuals to join the English proletariat,

> no more poisoned legacy could have been left the working-class movement.
> . . . Complacent confusion of influence with power, bovine admiration of

bureaucracy, ill-concealed contempt for equality, bottomless philistinism – all the characteristic narrowness of the Webbs and their associates became imprinted on the dominant ideology of the Labour Party thereafter.[19]

Anderson's arguments were echoed by Tom Nairn when he asserted that Fabian theories had 'adapted and transformed third-rate bourgeois traditions into fourth-rate socialist traditions'. Fabianism, for Nairn, is merely an 'ideology of minor functionaries' – or, as Peter Taylor-Gooby has put it, 'reformism writ small'.[20]

In fairness to Nairn and Anderson – or, perhaps, in fairness to their predecessors – this characterisation of British socialism and of the intellectual culture of which it is a part could hardly have been 'news' to the pre-war generation of left-wing intellectuals. The early Fabians had, quite explicitly, sought to adapt socialist ideas and methods in ways that would be congenial to 'the English temperament'. Thus Cole and Postgate could argue that the formation of the Independent Labour Party and of the Fabian Society marked the emergence of 'a socialism of distinctively British type': 'It envisaged socialism as a heap of reforms to be built up by the droppings of a host of successive swallows who would, in the end, make a socialist summer.'[21] And, in the opening pages of *The Acquisitive Society*, Richard Tawney describes, more generally, the 'characteristic vice' of Englishmen as their 'reluctance to test the quality' of their ideas 'by reference to principles':

> They are incurious as to theory, take fundamentals for granted, and are more interested in the state of the roads than in their place on the map. . . . The blinkers worn by Englishmen enable them to trot all the more steadily along the beaten road, without being disturbed by curiosity as to their destination.[22]

What Tawney had to say about the vices of the English is important because it returns us directly to the criticisms of 'the social administration approach' that one finds in the work of Mishra, Taylor-Gooby and others. Prior to *their* intervention, social administrators had remained 'incurious as to theory'; their interest in 'the state of the roads', their preoccupation with the technical problems of the welfare state, had led them to 'take fundamentals for granted' and to maintain a studied indifference as to 'their destination' – their 'place on the map'. One might conclude, then, that the inadequacy of 'the social administration approach' has to do less with its Fabianism than with its Englishness.

*Exorcising the Fabian incubus*
Despite the differences between these two diagnoses of the pathology of welfare studies, they do share some common shortcomings. The

first stems from the way in which they portray the influence of Fabianism on the British welfare debate. In both cases there is a tendency to underwrite the recent 'revolution' in welfare studies by constructing Manichaean contrasts between the old and the new, the forces of light and darkness. The intellectual revolution in socialist and sociological thinking is sometimes presented as the product of some cosmic drama in which Fabianism is cast as an agent of reaction, as an Antichrist, that must be vanquished if the new dispensation is to be established. This implies, in turn, a contempt for native radical traditions of which a certain kind of Fabianism is taken to be representative. The point has already been made by Edward Thompson in his references to the 'inverted Podsnappery' of the Nairn–Anderson thesis, as well as in his later allegation that the intellectuals of the new left 'have consistently presented images of French life and politics which are little more than fairy-tales derived from Parisian cafe gossip'.[23] Whatever the truth of these allegations it seems at least probable that Anderson and his associates have been premature in their dismissal of English radical traditions. Nineteenth-century social criticism is passed over on the grounds that its inspiration was literary rather than 'scientific', and the Marxist revival of the 1930s has been discounted as 'a passing product of a political conjuncture' expressing nothing more than 'the adolescent fervour of the public school *enragé*'.[24] Neglect rather than criticism has ensured that a similar fate has befallen the Fabian critics of the post-war settlement. In the next section of this chapter we shall attempt a partial rehabilitation of the Fabian tradition. Our concern will be to demonstrate that Fabian criticism of the welfare state and its supporting ideologies has preceded and provided invaluable resources for recent neo-Marxist policy analysis.

The second problem arising from these arguments concerns their implied explanations for the revival of radical and critical theories of welfare. Our first argument might lead us to suppose that the 'revolution' in welfare studies has been the successful outcome of some kind of intervention on the part of a new and rising generation of radical sociologists, economists, political scientists and historians. Particular emphasis might be given to the contribution of radical sociologists for whom Marcuse's discussion of the concept of social control provided a way of revealing the hidden agendas, or rationales, lurking behind the seemingly benign provisions of the welfare state and the avowedly humane practices of the 'caring' professions.[25] The new sociology also had a marked impact on the younger generation of radical social workers and teachers and so, in the pages of *Case Con* and *Rank and File Teacher*, as well as in the various publications of the National Deviancy Conference, the welfare activities of the state came to be associated with the functional requirements of 'the system'.

The second argument rests on the assertion that an intellectual revolution could only be accomplished by breaking down the insularity and empiricism of the English. Hitherto the British intellectual had been so screened by the blinkers imposed by our bourgeois civilisation as to be utterly unreceptive to 'the ideas of Marx'. His or her thinking has been impervious to the theory, the 'intellectual force' that is, according to Nairn, the 'necessary prerequisite of revolution'.[26] It is only the intellectual force of 'theory' that will enable us all to 'throw off the immense, mystifying burden of false and stultifying consciousness imposed upon us by English bourgeois civilisation'. This 'prodigious cultural task' must, Nairn argues, be accomplished by 'a radical and disaffected intelligentsia' – one that has been serviced, presumably, by a journal such as the *New Left Review*, which after 1966 and under Perry Anderson's editorship imported and translated 'the key texts of Western Marxism'.

Radical sociology and theoretical Marxism have, undoubtedly, made important contributions to the intellectual revolution in welfare studies, but to attribute this development in the literature of social policy solely to their influence would be to construct an argument that is vulnerable to the charge of 'idealism'. Our first explanation is idealist by default because it fails to move beyond the realm of the intellect in seeking to explain why the Fabians should have succeeded in capturing and dominating the field of welfare studies. Admittedly Taylor-Gooby does attempt to explain what he calls 'the tenacity of an overly atheoretical practice in the study of social welfare' by referring to the close association of social administration with government and the intimate links that it has had with the profession of social work.[27] But this, rather than resolving the problem, merely restates and enlarges it. The only occasion on which he looks beyond the confines of the discipline and its supportive institutional nexus is when he refers to the work of Nairn and Anderson. This is, by their own admission, idealist. Perry Anderson has defended his own work against Thompson's allegation of 'economic reductionism' by aligning himself with 'the idealist dimension' of modern Marxist scholarship: he concedes James Hinton's point that he and Tom Nairn have asserted 'the primacy of the political and ideological forces'.[28]

This quality of idealism would be less of a problem if it were not accompanied by a view of the relationship between 'popular', 'mass' and 'high' culture which produced an image of the working class as a bovine mass dependent – for good or ill – upon the intellectual leadership of *either* the 'bourgeoisie' *or* a vanguard of theoreticians versed in the latest products of European Marxist scholarship. The implications of this line of argument might be unacceptable if it were to be generalised to form the basis of a radical political strategy and, in any case, it leaves its exponents vulnerable to the charge that their 'natural constituency' is not the working class – 'the class that really matters' – but 'the massed ranks of undergraduates and postgraduate students in the social sciences'. The danger is that the Marxism of the new left comes to resemble what Frank Parkin has described as 'professorial Marxism', carrying out its discourse 'through the medium of an arcane language not readily accessible to the uninstructed'.[29] Professorial Marxism might thus share a part of the responsibility for the alleged 'imperviousness to theory' of the British working class. At this stage, however, the more important objection is that the argument ignores the possibility that intellectual developments might be contingent on the material circumstances in which they are conceived. Thus it will be one of the concerns of the next section to argue that the development of both Marxist *and* Fabian critiques of the welfare state has to be understood in the context of the economic and political developments that have occurred in Britain during the past fifteen to twenty years.

### Fabian social criticism

> The assumptions of the Titmuss years – the Butskellite years they might be called – are disintegrating. We cannot rely on economic or on demographic growth . . . . We cannot assume that the social wage or the taxes which finance it will grow – least of all that they will grow in egalitarian ways. 'Middle England' is not ready to be convinced by research and blue books that benign public services will – or should – create a more humane and a more equal society. Yet the old evils of capitalism . . . for which Crosland pronounced a requiem are still very much alive.[30]

So far we have treated Fabianism as if it were a monolithic and homogeneous intellectual tradition whose exponents all shared a wholehearted commitment to, if not the responsibility for, the 'errors' of social administration and the 'orthodoxies' of post-war labourism. Fabianism, however, is more fluid and variegated than some of its critics would allow.[31] This is a point that has been made by Taylor-Gooby and, although it was originally advanced as a rejoinder to Trotsky's unkind observation that Fabianism was 'the most boring form of intellectual creation', it serves equally well as the basis upon which one might defend the movement against the tendency to equate it with its more panglossian and collectivist forms.

In this section we intend to examine the role played by Fabian commentators in questioning some of the basic tenets of post-war welfare ideology, and in criticising the actions and policies of successive Labour governments. In the course of this examination we shall argue against the detractors of the Fabian tradition by stressing the continued vitality and critical potential of its contributions to welfare debate. At the same time, however, we shall set out to explore the *limits* of Fabian criticism, its intellectual 'blind spots' and the apparent bankruptcy of its political prescriptions. We shall conclude by arguing that economic recession and the crisis in the British Labour Party have contributed to the diminishing plausibility of the Fabian tradition and its consequent vulnerability to radical attack.

Before we embark on this exercise we must first specify the main targets of Fabian criticism. For this purpose we have distilled four basic propositions from our earlier discussion of revisionist thinking within the Labour Party, the intellectual characteristics of social administration, and the 'professional ideology' of British policy scientists. Together these four propositions form the basic elements of a welfare ideology that was shared by the intellectuals, politicians, administrators and professional workers of the 'liberal left'. They are as follows:

1  That the institutional framework of the social services represents the appropriate focus of social policy intervention and research. The domain of social policy is thus formally separated from other areas of state activity (including economic policy).

2  That the social services were instituted for such purposes as meeting 'social needs', compensating socially caused 'diswelfares' and promoting broadly socialist principles of social justice. They operate in ways that are generally benevolent, at least at the level of intentions if not always in terms of their effects. Their underlying functions are, therefore, ameliorative, integrative and redistributive.

3  That social progress has and will continue to be achieved through the agency of state and professional intervention. Increased public expenditure, the cumulative extension of statutory welfare provision and the proliferation of government regulations, backed by expert administration, represent the main guarantors of equity and efficiency.

These three propositions were supported by a particular view of the development of the welfare state and, *pari passu*, of the 'welfare society'. Collectivisation, the historical evolution of a statist society and of an 'institutional-redistributive' welfare system, was equated with a fundamental change in the relationship between the state and civil society. The period of the *laissez-faire*, liberal state was presented as one in which there is a near-complete separation of the economic from the political, or where the latter is subordinated to the former. State activity and individual welfare were said to be governed in this period by market criteria, by the laws of supply and demand, by 'market performances'. The age of collectivism, on the other hand, was represented as a period in which the economic and the political were 'recoupled', with the state occupying the role of senior partner. In this, the 'neo-mercantilist' welfare state, government activities were said to be framed according to welfare criteria so that resources were reallocated and redistributed in accordance with the principle of social need.[32] This brings us, then, to the fourth, 'core' proposition:

4    That the modern state not only is a relatively autonomous agency, with a capacity for independent action, but also can and has acted against the interests of the economically dominant class. Having assumed the separability of economic and political power, it is thus possible to argue that the state stands in a *generative* relationship with civil society and the economy, and that social policy creates and sustains progressive social change.

Taking these statements as our starting point, we shall distinguish three types of Fabian criticism. The first might be described as an 'empirical' critique of post-war social policy in that it set out to challenge on factual grounds what Titmuss referred to as the myth of 'an all-pervasive welfare state for the working classes' – a myth that centres on the 'supposedly egalitarian aims or effects of the social services'.[33] Thus it is proposition 2 that comes under scrutiny here although, as we shall see, this criticism also calls proposition 1 into question. The second type of criticism is targeted on proposition 3 – a proposition that identifies socialism with statism. Third, Fabian commentary has also cast doubt on our 'core' proposition 4 by demonstrating the failure of successive Labour governments to pursue their social objectives at a time of economic crisis and in the face of opposing business interests.

## The social division of welfare

Empirical criticisms of the welfare state are rooted in what Halsey has called the 'political arithmetic' tradition of investigative social research. Its exponents have included William Petty in the seventeenth century; Charles Booth, the Webbs and Seebohm Rowntree in the late nineteenth and early twentieth centuries; and Richard Titmuss, Brian Abel-Smith, Peter Townsend and Halsey himself in the post-war period. In each case:

> They were concerned to describe accurately and in detail the social conditions of their society, particularly of the more disadvantaged sections, but their interest in these matters was never a disinterested one. Description of social conditions was a preliminary to political reform. They exposed the inequalities of society in order to change them.[34]

The modern, post-war political arithmeticians of the Fabian Society set out, like their predecessors, to expose the gap between political ideology and social reality – the shortfall between the imputed or avowed aims of the welfare state and its actual 'achievements'. In the past the main object of attack had been classical liberalism. Fabian investigators like the Webbs and ethical socialists like Richard Tawney had set out to expose the mendacity of the claim that capitalist society had secured equality of opportunity for all its citizens. In the post-war period modern Fabian critics have subjected the claims of avowedly 'socialist' governments to the same empirical test. They have, in effect, hoisted successive Labour governments with their own petard – the petard of minimum standards, equal opportunities and, most important of all, equality of circumstance.[35]

Peter Townsend's introduction to a Fabian study of the last Labour government's social policies provides a good example of this strategy. His discussion, and the book as a whole, is prefaced by a reminder of the Party's egalitarian commitments: 'In the history of the Labour Party, equality has always been a dominant preoccupation (expressed in clause 4 of the Party's constitution, as well as in its literature and manifestos). In fact allusions and direct references (to equality) are so frequent as to amount in opponents' minds to an obsession.'[36] Townsend goes on to itemise six aims that were expressed in the 1974 manifesto, all of which drew upon the 'complex idea of equality'. These aims he suggests, 'provide a standard by which to judge [Labour's] performance in office' and against which the record of the Wilson and Callaghan governments must be counted a dismal failure. Cuts in public expenditure, the use of traditional forms of pay restraint, the abandonment of wealth tax proposals, increased poverty and rising unemployment rates did not, according to Townsend, constitute 'a record of success in establishing socialism'.

Townsend and Bosanquet's book is one example of what has become a very large and growing literature. It includes Titmuss's *Income Distribution and Social Change*, Townsend's *Poverty in the UK*, Frank Field's *Wealth Report* and his *Inequality in Britain*, Le Grand's *Strategy of Equality*, the Black report on *Inequality in Health*, Halsey's *Origins and Destinations*, Goldthorpe's *Social Mobility and Class Structure in Britain*, a host of pamphlets and research studies published by the Fabian Society and the CPAG and, perhaps most important of all, a series of government-sponsored enquiries (mainly in the field of education, although the Black report is another example) whose findings have been incorporated into the reports of royal commissions and government committees.

Fabian studies of the effects of social policy employ two further strategies, both of which are of a technical nature. The first represents an attempt to translate the egalitarian and humanitarian objectives or ideals of the labour movement into *operational* standards or criteria for the evaluation of social policies. This, in turn, has resulted in three further innovations in the study of social deprivation, each contributing to the substitution of the general concept of social inequality for Beveridge's original concept of minimum standards.[37] The first innovation transformed the study of poverty into the study of inequality by replacing Booth and Rowntree's absolute definition of poverty with the concept of relative deprivation.[38] The second innovative feature of these studies was their attempt to relate inequalities of income to a range of non-material 'life chance' privileges and deprivations – inequalities of educational opportunity, health, mobility chances and so on.[39] And the third major contribution lay in the attempt to compare the resources at the disposal of various groups within the population during the course of their entire lifespan.[40] The research that has been conducted on the basis of these methodological innovations has broadly confirmed Abel-Smith's judgement that

> the particular changes in the social services (over the past twenty or thirty years) did not consist in lavishing gifts upon the working classes. The major beneficiaries of these changes were middle income groups. . . . When one remembers that these groups probably make more use of nationally financed social services than the lower income groups, and also that the tax system does not always hit the rich harder than the poor, it becomes far from easy to say who is helping whom.[41]

The second strategy has entailed a direct attack on the first of our four propositions, an attempt to 'escape the traditional disciplinary and professional blinkers which have functioned to advance a particular social construction of "the welfare state"'.[42] The illusion that the development of the social services represents a 'unilinear progression in collective benevolence' for the working classes is undermined by the expedient of extending the scope of analysis beyond the traditional domain of the social services. This strategy was pioneered by Titmuss in his seminal essay 'The social division of welfare', and it has now become an indispensable feature of modern Fabian policy analysis.[43] For example, Bosanquet and Townsend's *Labour and Equality* 'deliberately treats employment, income, wealth and fiscal policies as well as health, education, welfare, housing and social security as part of social policy': 'Its authors do not consider that [equality] can be pursued or [its] implementation evaluated except in relation to the combined contribution of different policies.'[44] Frank Field's study of the redistributive effects of post-war government policy is also extended beyond the 'traditional benefit welfare state' to bring four other 'welfare states' under examination: the 'tax allowance welfare state', the 'company' and 'private market' welfare states, and 'the welfare state resulting from unearned income'.[45] The importance of this device was that it revealed that the mildly progressive effects of social service provision are offset if not reversed by other forms of state activity (fiscal and economic policies), by a variety of informal processes (property inheritance, tax avoidance), and by the activities of a host of private agencies (employers, private health schemes).

These empirical assessments of the performance of the British welfare state are subject to certain limitations. The genre can be criticised on three counts, and on the basis of these criticisms it should be possible to distinguish Fabian commentary from specifically Marxist perspectives on the welfare state. The first shortcoming is particularly apparent in some Fabian research on the incidence of poverty and social deprivation. The empirical idiom of these studies and, especially, their preoccupation with the fate of individuals rather than with the political and economic structures that perpetuate social disadvantage, render them susceptible to interpretations that significantly reduce their critical impact. The persistence of social deprivation in the welfare state can be all too easily explained (away) as a consequence of personal, community or agency deficiencies. The argument is thus diverted from the more fundamental issues concerning the Labour Party's commitment to egalitarian objectives or the viability of the strategies it has selected for this purpose. This tendency was detected by Peter Sedgwick in an article written as early as 1969:

> It is evident . . . that the current reforming definition of inequality . . . has moved from the structural (involving the analysis of power and wealth) to the marginal (involving the identification of special target groups of the underprivileged). The new status of pressure groups (for the disabled, for large families, for hospital patients) . . . is a token of the shift; as is the official concern with the selective pinpointing of problem-tracts in the cities (Plowden areas, Crossman areas). However welcome and rewarding these separate concerns may prove to be, they mark a distinct retreat from the political attack upon the foundations of inequality suggested even five years ago.[46]

By default, at least, Fabian social investigation has tended to complement the selectivist drift in Labour social policy since 1966.

Our two remaining criticisms of the empirical genre are directly related to the first, and all three are rooted in the classical Fabian conception of society as 'a world of individuals with problems . . . [with] an enlightened body of civil servants and local government officials which will solve them. . . . [The] Webbs took the British status system for granted and, in part, imagined themselves as setting up a new system of educating bureaucrats.'[47] The tendency for Fabians to take the British status system for granted has exposed them to the charge that they are concerned, not with the abolition of an intrinsic-ally exploitative mode of production, but merely with securing a 'fairer' distribution of the fruits of labour in what remains a capitalist and class society. Clause 4 of the Labour Party constitution sets the objective of securing 'for the workers . . . the full fruits of their industry and the most equitable distribution thereof'. This can be interpreted as evidence that Fabians have 'taken the social structure largely for granted . . . and concentrated instead on the fate of individuals within it' (G. Hawthorne). Peter Townsend has made it clear that 'distributional justice for all' is the highest principle to which Fabian socialists can aspire.[48] Certainly, his attack was directed at *excessive* wealth and *excessive* income, at *extreme* and *unacceptable* levels of inequality, and not at the institution of private property itself, the roots of domination and exploitation in capitalist and 'mixed' economics. The limitations of an analysis that is so preoccupied with problems of maldistribution become more apparent when it is set against Marx's comment that 'vulgar socialism . . . has taken over from the bourgeois economists the consideration and treatment of distribution as independent of the mode of production and hence the presentation of socialism as turning principally on distribution.'[49] The result of emphasising relations of distribution at the expense of relations of production is that problems of class structure are analysed in terms of the relatively superficial issues of mobility, life chances and resource allocation.[50]

The distributist focus of Fabian empirical criticism and of the policies it evaluates has also been attacked from within the Fabian tradition. Richard Tawney's seminal work on *Equality* distinguished three kinds of 'measure' by which 'some kinds of inequality' can be diminished. The first consists of an 'extension of social services and progressive taxation [to] mitigate disparities of opportunity and cir-cumstance'; the second entails legislation to limit 'the ability of one group to impose its will, by economic duress, upon another, and thus soften inequalities of economic power'; and the third seeks to 'transfer the direction of economic policy from the hands of capitalists and their agents to those of an authority responsible to society'.[51] Tawney stated that 'it is an illusion to suppose that either of the first two policies can be carried forward (in any significant way) as long as the key positions of the economic system remain in private hands.' The 'strategy of equality' – the development of communal provision and taxation – is important. 'To deprecate the social services as "mere palliatives" ' is, he says, 'a piece of clap-trap'. Such a stance 'plays into the hands of the interests bent on saving the pockets of the rich at the expense of the children and the unemployed'.[52] But Tawney also insists that the strategy of equality must be seen as a complement to the other kinds of measure. The strategy of equality 'is a policy to be extended as rapidly as possible now, but which, till a radical change has been effected in the balance of economic power, will at every point be thwarted and checked'.[53] G.D.H. Cole wrote in similar vein of the limitations of the Attlee government's social programme: the social gains of 'the past five years' cannot, he argued, be held 'unless they are reinforced by the development of a mainly socialist productive system'.[54]

This brings us to our final criticism of the empirical genre. The warnings issued by Cole and Tawney acquire a distinctly prophetic quality when they are compared with some more recent Fabian assessments of the effectiveness of the Labour Party's strategy of equality. Apart from the limited range of targets to which this strategy has been directed, its tactics rest on idealist and reformist principles. They are idealist in the sense that it is assumed that significant social change can be stimulated by the provision of documentary and statistical evidence on the causes and incidence of contemporary social problems. In fact, this assumption, the principle of 'persuasion', provides the *raison d'être* for Fabian social criticism. Thus, a Fabian study of the policies of the 1964–9 Labour government was prefaced by the following statement of the authors' expectations:

> This volume is offered in the hope that it will help both to stimulate discussion and establish standards of progress towards socialism [on the grounds that] self-criticism can be a source of moral and political strength. Hope for the future depends on whether the movement can recover the purpose which it has seemed to lack since the desperate privations of unemployment and poverty in the 1930s and the immediate phase of post-war reconstruction. . . . It depends on . . . a willingness to find out the facts and face historical as well as economic and social realities. The failures have been those both of philosophy and intellectual honesty.[55]

The tactics are also reformist in the sense that the egalitarian cause is to be promoted by constitutional means, by legislative and administrative measures enacted by democratically elected governments.

These tactical doctrines would seem to be called into question by the empirical findings of some Fabian critics. Peter Townsend, for example, has concluded that he and his associates had been over-optimistic about 'the potentialities of public and political education', they had over-estimated the effects of policy legislation and under-estimated the extent to which manifesto proposals could be resisted by the Treasury and the senior civil service.[56] Towards the end of his life Tony Crosland conceded that:

> The performance . . . did not live up to the hopes which we, in the government, had entertained . . . . [the] pressure of democracy has exerted much less beneficial influence than I anticipated. . . . British society –

slow-moving, class-ridden – has proved much harder to change than was supposed. Looking back with hindsight, the early revisionist writings were too complacent in tone.[57]

And John Goldthorpe's study of patterns of social mobility turned, ultimately, to question

the strategy of seeking to attack social inequalities via legislative and administrative measures of a piecemeal kind. . . . This strategy grossly misjudges the resistance that the class structure can offer to attempts to change it; or, to speak less figuratively, the flexibility and effectiveness with which the more powerful and advantaged groupings in society can use the resources at their disposal to preserve their privileged positions.[59]

Yet none of these authors recanted his earlier commitment to reformist and idealist tactics. Crosland's bleak assessment of his Party's performance in office was followed by the proposal that we need more of the same. The 'early revisionist writings' may have been 'too complacent in tone', but they did propose 'the right reforms' and success in the future will merely require the pitting of 'a stronger will' against 'the dogged resistance to change'.[59] Townsend's response to his own analysis of past failures seemed to revolve around various proposals for ensuring that the Party mobilised its social policies in a more concerted and coordinated fashion.[60] And John Goldthorpe suggested the formulation of social policies 'which would be directed with more forcefulness towards greater equality'. With the possible exception of Goldthorpe there appears to have been no serious attempt to question the supposition that the transition to socialism can be achieved by statist or collectivist means, by 'educating bureaucrats', and by continuing to engage in the high politics of the private salon. It is only, perhaps, on the fringes of the Fabian Society, and with the revival of a certain kind of municipal populism, that this approach has been seriously challenged.[61]

## The limitations of welfare statism

This brings us to the second type of Fabian criticism – one that seems to challenge the third of our four propositions and, in particular, the supposition that the transition to socialism can be achieved through statism. It is a form of criticism that is deeply sympathetic to Cole's repudiation of social democracy and communism on the grounds that they were both 'creeds of centralisation and bureaucracy'.[62] It figured, at least indirectly, in Titmuss's vision of a 'welfare society' rather than an administrator's welfare state, and in his insistence that the future development of welfare policies must combine redistributive social justice with humanity in administration. And, since 1979, it has come to be voiced more frequently and more forcefully within the labour movement. Frank Field's *Inequality in Britain* has been condemned for its 'paternalistic collectivism';[63] Colin Crouch has argued that the welfare state 'now needs a major shift towards community level participation', and away from 'centralised professional administration', if we want socialism 'to reproduce the moral base of community life';[64] and a revival of libertarian thinking seems to be indicated by the proliferation of books and pamphlets advancing the case for 'open government', 'democratic accountability', 'decentralist' social democracy and, possibly, the work of those who advocate one or another form of 'local socialism'.[65]

The question arises as to whether this form of criticism is, in any real sense, of Fabian origin or inspiration. In one, rather limited, sense it clearly is: many modern libertarian critics have, almost invariably, secured a respectable pedigree for their position by drawing upon the work of two of the most eminent members of the Fabian Society – G.D.H. Cole and Richard Tawney. Certainly there is much that is of relevance to current debates to be found in their writings. Tawney had described collectivism as 'stage-managed fellowship', an arrangement that was designed not for men, but for tame animals.[66] The Attlee government had, he said, been very much more successful 'in dealing with the constitutional framework than with the economic and psychological foundations' of society, and its neglect of local, cooperative initiatives had resulted in a failure to create a system that was 'socialist all through and not merely at the top':[67] 'If socialism is not merely to be tolerated as a lesser evil but is to be welcomed as an emancipating and energising force, it is to men's imaginations as well as to their interests that its appeal must be addressed.'[68] And in his last book Cole issued a statement that could stand as the manifesto for all his erstwhile disciples: 'I feel sure that a socialist society that is to be true to its equalitarian principles of human brotherhood must rest on the widest possible diffusion of power and responsibility, so as to enlist the active participation of as many as possible of its citizens in the task of democratic self-government.'[69]

On the other hand, Tawney's reputation is as an 'ethical socialist' rather than as a Fabian, and Cole's early attack on Sidney Webb's collectivism would seem to have placed him well outside the Fabian mainstream and more in the tradition of Owen or Kropotkin, guild socialism or syndicalism. Webb, according to Cole, 'still conceives the mass of men as persons who ought to be decently treated, not as persons who ought freely to organise their own conditions of life; in short, his conception of a new social order is still that of an order that is ordained from without and not realised from within.'[70] For this reason Sedgwick may have been correct in describing Cole as 'a maverick thinker' who, because of his antipathy to Fabian collectivism, could only gain 'a footing in public places . . . through his personal integrity and the connections he still maintained with the official party of labour'.[71] Socialist anti-statism does, nevertheless, have some precedents in the early history of the Fabian Society and in the industrial wing of the labour movement. Even Shaw and Webb were, in the early days, anxious to dissociate themselves from those who identified socialism with collectivism.[72]

The anti-statist critique is limited in two related ways. At first sight it would seem that it is the desirability of collectivism, its compatibility with the socialist ideals of liberty and fraternity, rather than the effectiveness of collectivist strategies that is called into question. On closer examination, however, this principled objection to statism begins to pale. Some versions of the anti-collectivist argument, and even some aspects of Cole and Tawney's work, are less concerned with promoting democratic participation as an end in its own right than with emphasising, instead, its value as a means of eliciting popular electoral support for increased public expenditure and state provision. In its recent forms this argument might be regarded as a *post hoc* rearguard action against the new right and its copywriters. If, as seems likely, the electoral successes of the Conservative Party were obtained by exploiting the working-class experience of the state as an alien, oppressive, bureaucratic imposition, the popular appeal of any future Labour programme may well have to be established in the terms dictated, initially, by right-wing populist rhetoric.[73]

Second, there is a tendency for state power, the overweening power of large bureaucracy, to be conceptualised independently of economic power, the power of industrial decision-making. Both are recognised, certainly in the writings of Cole and Tawney, as problems for socialism. But the two do not seem to be connected within the framework of an overall theory of power. In this respect our fourth 'core' proposition remains unchallenged. Fabianism is, after all, a subspecies of the genus of democratic socialism: it is therefore committed, by definition, to the belief that the transition to socialism, or indeed to any of the (possibly statist) blind alleys or half-way houses along the route, can be achieved through constitutional action and by legislative and administrative means.

## Socialism and constitutional action

Gordon Lewis has suggested that the original Fabians had 'no satisfactory theory of power because they had no satisfactory theory of the state'. Not only were the Fabians unexcited by 'the adventures of ideas' but, for a variety of other reasons, 'they were content to accept the state ... as the natural vehicle for their programme'. They supposed that the 'neutral mechanism' of the state, 'once subdued to the Fabian guiding hand, would be sufficient as a means of applying the Fabian remedies'.[74]

As we have seen, this conception of the state, and the tactical principles with which it is associated, continue to serve as distinguishing and limiting features of modern Fabianism. Fabian 'optimism' on this question of the corrigibility of the state, on its susceptibility to expert intervention and control, is matched by an equally positive assessment of the extent to which the state, once it has been commandeered by socialist reformers, can mitigate and redress social injustice and inequality. The second aspect of Fabian 'optimism' has already been discussed in connection with the distributist preoccupations of Fabian empirical criticism. But at this stage it is important to recognise that these two pillars of Fabian analysis – its reformism as well as its distributism – rest, in turn, on a pluralist conception of the social, economic and political systems. From a Marxist point of view this perspective is unsatisfactory because (in the case of the analysis of inequality) it assumes the separability of the sphere of production from those of distribution and consumption and (in the case of the analysis of the state) because it divorces the economic from the political.

Fabian analysis appears to dismiss the twin possibilities that the state might serve as an instrument of class rule (even if it does not act as an arena of class struggle), and that inequalities may well persist unless and until one has transformed the economic basis upon which class relations are founded. However, it would be gross travesty to put this down merely to a misguided optimism on the part of Fabian analysts. The Fabian view is essentially 'value led'; it is the logical complement (if not the necessary corollary) of the Fabian commitment to democratic socialism. In a discussion of Crosland's arguments for equality, Raymond Plant has made the point that – from a democratic socialist point of view – equality of outcome 'may well be inconsistent with political and civil liberties'. Crosland's preference was for what he (and Rawls) called the 'democratic conception' of equality – one that is governed by the requirement that inequalities can only be justified if 'differential rewards work to the benefit of the community as a whole'.[75] This formula neatly satisfies the requirement that the pursuit of equality must command popular assent if it is to remain consistent with democratic ideals.

It is also the case that the plausibility of the analysis (and, conversely, the credibility of the critique) depend on historical and political circumstances. In the previous chapter we suggested that the ascendancy of Fabian collectivism must be understood in its political and historical context. Conditions of economic growth, the official recognition and incorporation of the labour movement, the extension of state welfare activities, and a variety of other political contingencies have all contributed to the potency of the Fabian or revisionist argument. The importance of these factors has been recognised by Fabians themselves. Crosland, for example, acknowledged that economic growth was a necessary condition for achieving the objective of equality: a rise in the general level of real incomes was itself equalising; growth makes it possible to achieve equality 'without intolerable social stress and a probable curtailment of liberty'; and, with growth, public expenditure can be increased without raising the tax burden on wage and salary earners.[76] And Andrew Gamble has argued, from a different perspective, that it was the long post-war boom that made it possible for the Labour Party to sustain some kind of commitment to universalism and civic equality, to cumulative increases in public expenditure and to the reform and expansion of the social services.[77] Conversely, it is during periods of economic recession (and at a time when both the welfare state and consensus politics are under attack) that traditional Fabian prescriptions are thrown into crisis. It was for this reason, perhaps, that in the 1930s the Webbs came to a partial recognition of 'their tactical and theoretical errors' and of the hopeless inconsistency of 'the rule of the capitalist and the landlord' with 'political democracy'.[78]

Many people are now driven to the almost irresistible conclusion that history is in the process of repeating itself. Certainly, it can be argued that the 'long boom' of the post-war years was nothing more than a period of respite in the long-term decline of the British economy. Between the mid 1960s and the mid 1970s this period of respite came to an end, and the heady optimism of the 1950s gave way to a renewed concern with the structural weaknesses of the British economy. The 'decline of Britain', with respect to its international position, had proceeded unabated throughout the period of post-war prosperity. But it was not until these trends began to be reflected in domestic inflation and unemployment rates, in the increasing severity of balance of payments crises, and by the slide in the international value of sterling that the problem of Britain's economic decline became, once again, a prominent item on the political agenda. As first the Wilson government and then the Heath, Callaghan and Thatcher administrations began to address themselves to the problem, social priorities were displaced by the perceived needs of the economy, and the social policy options that were open to government were seen as being ever more severely constrained by the imperatives of an ailing economy. The consequences for the Labour Party were clearly identified by Jim Kincaid in an article that went under the apt title of

'The decline of the welfare state':

> During the 1960s in particular, the efficient management of the mixed economy in the interests of productive growth became more and more clearly identified as *the* central objective of the Party, to which all other considerations must be subordinated. As part of this process, the 'socialism' of Party tradition and propaganda was progressively redefined to mean little more than a concern to make the welfare state more humane and more efficient.[79]

And, in a Fabian essay published a few years earlier, Peter Townsend came to a similar conclusion:

> A few years ago . . . the theme of equal rights or social equality could be said to have been the dominant domestic theme of the Party manifestos. . . . [Since then] there has been a subordination of social to economic objectives and strategies. The nation's economic difficulties have seemed so great that they have been used as an excuse for inaction in spheres which they did not seriously affect.[80]

The market, it would seem, rose like the phoenix from the ashes of the post-war settlement.

This subordination of social to economic policy has taken three forms. First, it has been assumed and argued that increases in social expenditure cannot be contemplated at a time when the economy is in crisis. Early examples of this can be found in the public and parliamentary debates that accompanied the Wilson government's 'reform' of the social security system. Ray Gunter, in a speech delivered in August 1967, dismissed what he termed 'the ingrained suspicion' in the Labour Party 'of anything that could be said to resemble the "means test" of the thirties' by questioning the supposition that 'emotional memories' are relevant 'to what is really a different world'. Gunter went on, not only to justify selective benefits, but also to enter a plea in favour of the profit motive in industry. Industrial prosperity was, he said, a precondition for the expansion of welfare provisions, and profitable industry provides more jobs. In conclusion he stated that he wished that so many of his comrades 'would stop equating profits with incest or lechery'.[81] More recently the argument has taken the form of assertions to the effect that industrial prosperity and social expenditure are mutually incompatible objectives. Bacon and Eltis, for example, have attributed the low rate of investment in the British economy to the rapid expansion of the public sector, and this is an argument which seems to have informed the expenditure policies of the last three governments.[82]

Second, there have been various attempts to tailor welfare provisions so that they *subserve* economic objectives – the objectives of economic growth and efficiency, rather than the 'traditional' objectives of social justice, compensation or social integration. The earlier and more positive examples of this are provided by the development of Labour education policy. The authors of *Unpopular Education* have traced the way in which the egalitarian goals of Labour education policy were translated, by the 1960s, into a primordial concern with education as an investment in manpower and as a stimulus to economic growth. The expansion of higher education, the formation of new ministries (Department of Economic Affairs, MinTech), the introduction of selective employment tax, the earnings-related supplement, and the enactment of the Redundancy Payments Act in 1965 – all contributed, in one way or another, to the 'shakeout' of unproductive labour, enhanced work incentives, and the development of the technical infrastructure of Labour's 'modernised' new Britain. Less positively, one could also include under this heading the various ways in which the Supplementary Benefits Commission 'clarified' its discretionary policy on the withdrawal of benefits in cases where it was suspected that the payment of social security was interfering with the incentive to work. The wage stop, the four-week rule, the work of unemployment review officers and re-establishment centres, and all the other measures designed to prevent 'voluntary' unemployment and 'industrial misconduct' can be interpreted as examples of welfare tailored to the cause of enforcing labour discipline.[83]

Third, some developments in social policy – including the Urban Programme and the growth of social expenditure under the 1970–4 Conservative government – could be regarded as attempts to find *ad hoc* solutions to the social consequences of both economic decline and economic policy. In this case social policy plays a secondary, reactive role to economic policy. It becomes a long stop in the politics of decline, performing the function of relieving the distressed and controlling the potentially dissident. Some of the best examples of this can be found in income maintenance policy. The growth of expenditure on the social services from 1970 to 1974, and the longer-term increase in the proportion of social expenditure devoted to transfer payments, have served to redistribute income for consumption from the employed to the unemployed population. Thus relief at subsistence level has been provided for the 'casualties' of a 'modernising' economy.[84] On the other hand, the long-standing government campaign against social security abuse has reaffirmed a Poor Law mentality, in which the 'deserving' are set against the 'undeserving', the 'provident' against the 'feckless', and the employed against the unemployed.[85]

It is to the credit of Fabian commentators that they have contributed to the documentation of these apparent shifts in the objectives of social policy. This, then, is our third type of Fabian criticism of the welfare state, recording what Coates and Silburn have described as 'the dismal catalogue of retreat and withdrawal from the relatively whole-hearted post-war principles of welfare distribution'.[86] Coates and Silburn go on to refer to these 'market-oriented alterations of the welfare system' an an 'apostasy'. The term is significant because it corresponds so closely to the view necessarily held by latter-day Fabians. Faced with an apparent failure of will on the part of Labour governments, their response has been to continue to act as the 'conscience' of the labour movement in the hope that at some stage in the future the Party will recover its idealism and exploit, with more determination, the constitutional route to radical social change. From the point of view of their critics, the Fabian commitment to democratic socialism and the deficiencies of their 'theory of power' have meant that they have so far been incapable of formulating the kind of intellectual and political response that is demanded by the changing character of welfare policies. This response must be based on a recognition that the current drift of social policy has, in con-tradiction to our fourth proposition, revealed the 'true' nature of the state. From this perspective the state is the mere creature of its 'bourgeois masters' acting, sometimes with a superficial benevolence, as the principal means for reproducing the conditions for capital accumulation.

## Notes

1 H. Marcuse, 'Liberation from the affluent society', in D. Cooper (ed.), *The Dialectics of Liberation* (Penguin, 1968), p. 177.
2 Ibid., pp. 191–2.
3 G. Woodcock, *Anarchism* (Penguin, 1975), pp. 458–9.
4 T. Kuhn, *The Structure of Scientific Revolutions*, International Encyclopaedia of Unified Science, vol. 2, no. 2, 1962.
5 Examples are provided by the recent writings of R. Mishra and P. Taylor-Gooby.
6 The use of the term 'pathology' in this context has been borrowed from G.S. Jones, 'The pathology of English historiography', *New Left Review* 46, 1967.
7 P. Taylor-Gooby and J. Dale, *Social Theory and Social Welfare* (Edward Arnold, 1981), p. 28.
8 Ibid., p. 21.
9 Centre for Contemporary Cultural Studies, *Unpopular Education* (Hutchinson, 1981), p. 88.
10 D. Donnison, 'Social policy since Titmuss', *Journal of Social Policy* 8(2), 1979, pp. 146–8.
11 Ibid., p. 146; see also his 'Research for policy' in M. Bulmer (ed.), *Social Policy Research* (Macmillan, 1978), pp. 54–9.
12 For a discussion of the Labour Party's commitment to the 'centralist faith', see R. Hadley and S. Hatch, *Social Welfare and the Failure of the State* (George Allen and Unwin, 1981), pp. 12–16.

13   M. Kogan, *The Politics of Education* (Penguin, 1971), p. 185. Boyd-Carpenter's description is recalled by Peter Townsend in 'Politics and social policy: an interview', *Politics and Power*, 2, 1980, p. 101.

14   R. Titmuss, 'Times remembered', in *Commitment to Welfare* (George Allen and Unwin, 1968).

15   H. Rose, 'Rereading Titmuss: the sexual division of welfare', *Journal of Social Policy*, 10(4), 1981.

16   Taylor-Gooby and Dale, *Social Theory*, p. 19.

17   P. Anderson, 'Origins of the present crisis', *New Left Review*, 23, 1964; 'Components of the national culture', in A. Cockburn and R. Blackburn (eds), *Student Power* (Penguin, 1969); T. Nairn, 'The English working class', in R. Blackburn (ed.), *Ideology and Social Science*; G.S. Jones, 'The pathology of English history', *New Left Review*, 46, 1967.

18   Nairn, 'The English working class'.

19   Anderson, 'Origins'. Cf. E.P. Thompson, 'The peculiarities of the English', in *The Poverty of Theory* (Merlin, 1978), p. 66.

20   T. Nairn, 'The nature of the Labour Party', *New Left Review*, 27, 1964; P. Taylor-Gooby and J. Dale, *Social Theory*, p. 19.

21   G.D.H. Cole and R. Postgate, *The British Common People* (Methuen, 1961), p. 423.

22   R. Tawney, *The Acquisitive Society* (Bell, 1952), p. 1.

23   Thompson, *The Poverty of Theory*, p. 405.

24   Jones, 'The pathology of English history'.

25   See H. Marcuse, *One Dimensional Man* (Routledge and Kegan Paul, 1964), chapter 1.

26   Nairn, 'The English working class'.

27   Taylor-Gooby and Dale, *Social Theory*, pp. 13–15, 17, 20–21.

28   P. Anderson, 'Socialism and pseudo empiricism', *New Left Review*, 35, 1966.

29   F. Parkin, *Marxism and Class Theory* (Tavistock, 1979).

30   Donnison, 'Socal policy', p. 152.

31   Taylor-Gooby and Dale, *Social Theory*, p. 70.

32   Cf. R. Pinker, *Social Theory and Social Policy* (Heinemann, 1971), pp. 80–92, 197.

33   R. Titmuss, 'The welfare state: images and realities', in C.I. Schottland (ed.), *The Welfare State* (Harper Torchbooks, 1967).

34   A.H. Halsey, *Origins and Destinations* (Oxford University Press, 1980), p. 1.

35   Cf. J. LeGrand, *The Strategy of Equality* (George Allen and Unwin, 1982); R. Plant, 'Democratic socialism and equality', in D. Lipsey and D. Leonard (eds), *The Socialist Agenda* (Jonathan Cape, 1981).

36   P. Townsend, 'Social planning and the treasury', in N. Bosanquet and P. Townsend (eds), *Labour and Equality* (Heinemann, 1980), p. 4.

37   LeGrand, *The Strategy*, pp. 10–12.

38   P. Townsend, 'The meaning of poverty', *British Journal of Sociology*, June 1954.

39   Some of the more recent examples of this genre include Halsey's *Origins and Destinations*; P. Townsend and N. Davidson, *Inequalities in Health* (Penguin, 1982); J. Goldthorpe, *Social Mobility and Class Structure in Modern Britain* (Oxford University Press, 1980).

40   R. Titmuss, *Income Distribution and Social Change* (George Allen and Unwin, 1962).

41   B. Abel-Smith, 'Whose welfare state?', in Schottland, *The Welfare State*.

42   A. Sinfield, 'Analyses in the social division of welfare', *Journal of Social Policy*, 7(2), 1978.

43   R. Titmuss, 'The social division of welfare' (1955), reprinted as chapter 2 of *Essays on the Welfare State* (Allen and Unwin, 1958). Cf. A. Walker, 'Social policy, social administration and the social construction of welfare', in M. Loney et al. (eds), *Social Policy and Social Welfare* (Open University Press, 1983).
44   Bosanquet and Townsend, *Labour and Equality*, p. 5.
45   F. Field, *Inequality in Britain* (Fontana, 1981).
46   P. Sedgwick, 'Varieties of socialist thought', *Political Quarterly*, 84 (Oct./Dec.), 1969, p. 399.
47   J. Rex, *Sociology and the Demystification of the Modern World* (Routledge and Kegan Paul, 1974), p. 89.
48   P. Townsend, *Poverty in the UK* (Penguin, 1979). G. Hawthorn, *Enlightenment and Despair* (Cambridge University Press, 1976), p. 248.
49   K. Marx, *Critique of the Gotha Programme* (Peking Foreign Languages Press, 1976), p. 18.
50   This point has been made in a review of Goldthorpe's *Social Mobility and Class Structure* and of Halsey's *Origins and Destinations*: see T. Johnson and A. Rattansi, 'Social mobility without class', *Economy and Society*, 10(2), 1981. For a general discussion of the theoretical issues see R. Crompton and J. Gubbay, *Economy and Class Structure* (Macmillan, 1977), pp. 5–40.
51   R. Tawney, *Equality* (George Allen and Unwin, 1964), p. 119.
52   Ibid., p. 20.
53   Ibid., p. 20.
54   G.D.H. Cole, 'The dream and the business', *Political Quarterly*, 20, 1949, p. 208.
55   P. Townsend and N. Bosanquet, *Labour and Inequality* (Fabian Society, 1972).
56   Townsend, 'An interview'.
57   C.A.R. Crosland, *Socialism Now and Other Essays* (Jonathan Cape, 1974), pp. 23, 44.
58   Goldthorpe, *Social Mobility*.
59   Crosland, *Socialism Now*.
60   Townsend, 'An interview'.
61   Cf. M. Boddy and C. Fudge (eds), *Local Socialism?* (Macmillan, 1984); D. Blunkett and G. Green, *Building from the Bottom – the Sheffield experience*, Fabian tract no. 491; J. Stewart, 'Decentralisation and local government', in *Socialism and Decentralisation* (Fabian Society, 1984).
62   Quoted in A.W. Wright, *G.D.H. Cole and Socialist Democracy* (Oxford University Press, 1979), p. 282.
63   D. Green, 'Freedom or paternalistic collectivism', *Journal of Social Policy*, 11(2), pp. 239–44.
64   C. Crouch, 'Public expenditure in socialist thought', in Lipsey and Leonard, *The Socialist Agenda*, p. 102.
65   For example, E. Luard, *Socialism Without the State* (Macmillan, 1979); G. Radice, *Community Socialism*, Fabian tract no. 464, 1969; D. Marquand, 'Inquest on a movement', *Encounter*, June 1979; P. Wilding, *Socialism and Professionalism*, Fabian tract no. 473, 1981.
66   R. Terril, *R.H. Tawney and his Times* (André Deutsch, 1973), p. 262.
67   R. Tawney, *British Socialism Today: the radical tradition* (1952)(Penguin, 1966), p. 185.
68   Speech delivered at Fabian Society dinner, May 1954.
69   Quoted in Wright, *Cole*, p. 282.
70   G.D.H. Cole, 'Recent developments in the British labour movement', *American Economic Review*, September 1918; cf. Wright, *Cole*, chapter 4.

71  Sedgwick, 'Varieties'.

72  See chapter 1.

73  Cf. S. Hall, 'The great moving right show', *Marxism Today*, 23(1), 1979; P. Leonard, 'Restructuring the welfare state', *Marxism Today*, 23(12), 1979; A. Cochrane, 'Local employment initiatives: towards a new municipal socialism?', in P. Lawless and C. Raban (eds), *The Contemporary British City* (Harper and Row, 1986); C. Raban, 'The municipalities and the future of the welfare state', in Lawless and Raban, *The Contemporary British City*.

74  G.K. Lewis, 'Slavery, imperialism and freedom', *Monthly Review Press*, 1978, pp. 251–2.

75  Plant, 'Democratic socialism and equality'.

76  D. Lipsey, 'Crosland's socialism', in Lipsey and Leonard, *The Socialist Agenda*.

77  A. Gamble, *Britain in Decline* (Macmillan, 1981).

78  Lewis, 'Slavery', pp. 242–3.

79  J. Kincaid, 'The decline of the welfare state', in N. Harris and J. Palmer (eds), *World Crisis* (Hutchinson, 1970), p. 36.

80  P. Townsend, *Social Services For All?* (Fabian Society, 1970).

81  *The Times*, 21 August 1967.

82  R. Bacon and W. Eltis, *Britain's Economic Problem: too few producers* (Macmillan, 1976).

83  Cf. N. Ginsburg, *Class, Capital and Social Policy* (Macmillan, 1979), chapter 3; Centre for Contemporary Cultural Studies, *Unpopular Education*.

84  B. Jordan, *Automatic Poverty* (Routledge and Kegan Paul, 1981).

85  For further discussion of the subordination of social to economic policy see C. Raban, 'The welfare state – from consensus to crisis?', in Lawless and Raban, *The Contemporary British City*.

86  K. Coates and R. Silburn, *Poverty: the forgotten Englishmen* (Penguin, 1970).

# Conclusion to Part I

# Criticism and Crisis

Our earlier discussion of the Fabian critique of the welfare state anticipated some of the arguments that will be developed in part II of this book. That discussion should not be interpreted as a plea of mitigation, nor as an attempt to pre-empt neo-Marxist or feminist criticism with a belated rediscovery of the radical credentials of the Fabian tradition. Its purpose has been to establish the fact that the tenor and content of Fabian analysis has shifted with the times, reflecting the current crisis in both the institutions and the ideology of the welfare state.

The terms 'crisis' and 'critique' are all too often used interchangeably. Nevertheless, they are distinct in the sense that they refer to phenomena of different orders. The former is economic and political, the latter intellectual and moral. This is not to deny that the two are connected. For example, the economic crises of the past ten or more years have served to expose the latent contradictions of the welfare state, thereby undermining the plausibility of the 'case' that has traditionally been made for it. Equally, the intellectual advances of the radical right and the radical left, and the failure of welfare-minded academics and politicians to mount a clear and appealing defence of (and case for) the social services, may have contributed to the political (or 'legitimation') crisis of the welfare state.[1] Those of us who are concerned with either the defence of the welfare state or the advance of socialism or both may, however, have been so impressed by these 'connections' as to lose sight of the powerful and independent forces exerted by the changing political and economic circumstances of recent years.

The electoral successes of the Conservatives under Mrs Thatcher and the disarray within the Labour Party can and have been interpreted as symptoms of a 'legitimation crisis'. What seems to be lacking is a body of theory and a set of political principles to inspire the voter and inform the policy-maker. The poverty of 'theory' within the labour movement, its state of intellectual bankruptcy, has been cruelly exposed by the apparently 'ideological' successes of the new right. And the ascendency of the Institute of Economic Affairs within the Conservative Party invites the conclusion that the Fabian Society must bear some special responsibility for the corresponding decline in the fortunes of Labour. The IEA was, after all, originally formed in the late 1950s to perform for the neo-liberal wing of the Conservative Party much the same function as that of the Fabian Society within the Labour Party.

This is an assessment of the current situation that is often accepted within Fabian circles. It may be conceded that, in the argument for and against welfare, the new right has secured a distinct tactical advantage and has sometimes done so by stealing the clothes woven by earlier and prematurely discredited or forgotten Fabians. Anthony Wright, for example, has pointed out that the attack on the bureau-cratic collectivism of the welfare state has invoked the concept of *The Servile State* and has drawn this image from Hilaire Belloc's book of the same name.[2] This spirit of self-mortification also produces the argument that 'the Fabian ameliorators' have found it difficult to respond to the legitimation crisis in the welfare state because their own association with welfare bureaucracy and professionalism now seems to be so much a part of the problem, and because the 'arid empiricism' of their own intellectual style has proved to be a major handicap when it comes to countering the theoretical and moral arguments of their opponents.[3]

The solution implied by this assessment involves a rejection of the collectivist and empiricist tradition of the Webbs, and a rehabilitation of the ethical socialism of Richard Tawney (interwoven, perhaps, with the various theoretical contributions of G.D.H. Cole). Tawney has a special significance for those Fabians who are anxious to find the resources for intellectual renewal within their own movement. His work seems particularly apposite in the present context. It was Tawney who had argued that 'modern society is sick through the absence of a moral ideal', and who had described the Fabian 'science of means' as a cul-de-sac which 'opened no windows on the soul'.[4] It is in Tawney's writings on the relationship between fellowship and equality that one might find the theoretical and ethical resources that are necessary to address the political tasks implied by the 'legitimation crisis' of the welfare state.[5] And Tawney's criticisms of the collectivist and centralist strains in Fabian socialism, together with the emphasis that he gave to the importance of effecting change at the level of productive relations, might also have a special appeal to those Labour activists who are intent on pioneering at local level the social *and* economic policies which might 'prefigure' the strategies of a future and more radical Labour government.[6]

There can be little doubt that the house style of the Fabian Society is changing in a way that is consistent with the mood of our time. The renewed interest in socialist theory and values should be seen not as constituting an admission of the bankruptcy of Fabian empiricism but rather as a reaffirmation of the fertility of classical Fabian thought. The empiricism of the post-war period, together with the 'technician' role that was assumed by intellectuals, was never an invariable feature of the Fabian tradition: it is more the product of *conservative* thinking wherever it is found and whatever its source. The 'superstitious reverence for accumulated facts' was, in the case of the Fabians, not the product of any inherent inability to consider issues of principle, but a feature of a particular style of thought that is characteristic of any movement which believes itself to be in the ascendant, in the vanguard if not at the acme of history. Recent political developments and current circumstances have forced the development of a more 'utopian' style – one that is more openly self-critical and speculative.[7]

It is this development which promises, and depends upon, a *rapprochement* between Fabianism and Marxism. Neither tradition is renowned for the seriousness with which it has attended to ethical and moral issues, since both sprang from the belief that socialist principles might be deduced from a scientific observation of the movements of history.[8] This sin of omission is, perhaps, marginally less pronounced in the case of Fabianism, and it is from this source that a restatement of socialist values might receive some inspiration. From a Fabian point of view, the important issues will be those concerning the moral basis for egalitarianism, and how this might be reconciled with the value of individual freedom; important, too, is the issue of fraternity and fellowship. The essential task for a democratic socialist is to provide a positive antidote to the libertarian charge (levelled from both the left and the right) that the 'strategy of equality' by collectivist means infringes the rights of individuals and destroys the very sentiments of citizenship which provide the ostensible mandate for social democracy. In their approach to this task Fabians may derive some strength from the guild socialism of G.D.H. Cole and from his conception of the proper role of the state as an instrument of community consciousness and as the expression of natural human fellowship.[9]

In chapter 3 we discussed some of the inadequacies of Fabian theory – its idealist approach to the analysis of political change and development, its distributism and pluralist understanding of power and class structure, and the limitations of its 'theory' of the state. It was suggested that these inadequacies are powerful impediments to the development of a full understanding of the shortcomings of the welfare state and the failures of Fabian efforts at social reform. The primary purpose of part II is to explore the possibility that Marxism might furnish the necessary theoretical resources without falling prey to the charges of political utopianism and intellectual totalitarianism that were reviewed in the prologue. Whether it can will depend on the extent to which its analysis of social policy issues is conceived in a genuinely 'revisionist' spirit and is thus capable of inspiring a new *realpolitik*.

At this point it is relevant to recall the distinction between the crisis and the critique of the welfare state. So far we have only discussed one aspect of the 'legitimation crisis' in the welfare state – that which is of direct concern to socialist intellectuals. Left as it is, our diagnosis of our current ills leaves much to be desired. Intellectually conceived theories and values do not in themselves win electoral contests – neither within nor between political parties. The popular support for the welfare measures introduced by the Attlee government was no more the product of Fabian evangelism than was the later apparent alienation of public support for social expenditure – the result, simply, of the individualistic values disseminated by the intellectuals of the new right.

This is to say not that ideas are unimportant, but that they must be embodied in programmes and policies that are attuned to the lived experiences of those to whom they are addressed; they must, in short, achieve 'resonance'. The need is for arguments for the welfare state, and for democratic socialism, that will appeal not only to the party tactician but also to the ordinary voter. The problem has already been recognised by those in the new generation of 'municipal socialists' who have avowedly embarked on a programme designed to 'win the hearts and minds' of the people and to lay the foundations for a new 'common sense' and, thus, for a greater popular resistance to the blandishments of 'Thatcherism'.[10]

Even in this wider sense, however, the 'crisis' of the welfare state, and of British social democracy, cannot be adequately conceptualised and dealt with as if it were only an ideological phenomenon. Its political and economic dimensions are of equal if not greater importance, and it is to be hoped that the resources of neo-Marxism might be usefully employed to asses their implications for any future reconstruction of the welfare state.

### Notes

1  For further discussion of these issues see C. Raban, 'The welfare state – from consensus to crisis?', in P. Lawless and C. Raban (eds), *The Contemporary British City* (Harper and Row, 1986).

2  R. Barker, 'The Fabian state', in B. Pimlott (ed.), *Fabian Essays in Socialist Thought* (Heinemann, 1984), pp. 32–3.

3  A. Wright, 'Tawneyism revisited: equality, welfare and socialism', in Pimlott, *Fabian Essays*, p. 97.

4  Ibid., pp. 86–7.

5   Ibid., p. 89.

6   D. Blunkett and G. Green, *Building from the Bottom – the Sheffield Experience*, Fabian tract no. 491, 1983; A. Walker, *Social Planning* (Basil Blackwell, 1984); A. Cochrane, 'Local employment initiatives: towards a new municipal socialism?' and C. Raban, 'The municipalities and the future of the welfare state', in Lawless and Raban, *The Contemporary British City*.

7   The issue of utopian thought is discussed in more detail in the prologue and chapter 1 of the present volume.

8   B. Crick, *Socialist Values and Time* (Fabian Society, 1984).

9   See the section 'The state and the transition of socialism' in chapter 1 of Barker, 'The Fabian state', pp. 33–6.

10  Cf. S. Hall, 'The great moving right show', *Marxism Today*, 23(1), 1979.

# PART II

# MARXISM AND WELFARE

## Phil Lee

Revisionism does not expect to see the contradictions of capitalism mature. . . . It wants to lessen, to attenuate, the capitalist contradictions. . . . The antagonism existing between production and exchange is to be mollified by the cessation of crises . . . [and] the contradiction between the class state and society is to be liquidated through increased state control and the progress of democracy. . . . It ends up subscribing to a programme of reaction.

Rosa Luxemburg

The decisive issue is not whether a movement seeks reforms 'within the confines of capitalism', for in reality communists as well as socialists do so. Social ameliorative reforms, such as unemployment insurance or old-age pensions, are promoted by all important labour movements out of simple necessity. Labour movements cannot afford to ignore the fact that economic insecurity, poverty and unemployment weaken proletarian solidarity and impede class mobilisation. . . . But once social democrats had chosen parliament as their battleground, once they had acknowledged the legitimacy of broader class alliances, their strategy for political mobilisation and class solidarity had to include efforts to influence government policy.

Gøsta Esping-Andersen

If the style of Fabian politics that dominated British socialist and welfare concerns in the 1950s was 'conservative', no less was true of Marxist-inspired theory and politics. Being a Marxist intellectual or member of the Communist Party in Britain in the 1950s cannot have been very comfortable. The continuous barrage of anti-communist, Cold War propaganda must have been discouraging enough but, as we shall see in greater detail in chapter 4, the theoretical stultification of much Marxist theory must have contributed towards a most bleak outlook. Retrospectively, Marxist theoretical development during this period is best described as dilatory in coming to terms with crucial post-war developments such as the boom itself, as well as the changing nature of the labour market and class structure. It was not just the intellectual myopia of post-war optimism which prompted a leading contemporary Marxist economist, Ernest Mandel, to note that Marxist theory 'now meets only with indifference or contempt'.[1] Stalinist dogma had inbred a certain slavish worship of past texts and securities which was merely aped, albeit around different events and writings, by Trotskyist breakaway movements.

For most English-language Marxist theory at this time, capitalism was simply an inherently unstable system of production containing deep and irrational contradictions. The post-war boom was little more than a final orgiastic swan-song. The whole rotten edifice would eventually and *necessarily* be swept away by working-class movements armed with a developed political awareness. Little attention was paid to the changing *forms* of capitalist social relationships, political regulation or types of political opposition to them. Questions which now dominate contemporary socialist and neo-Marxist debate – such as how the capitalist state appears to be able to act independently of ruling class interests, how gender and race issues relate to and can be linked with a politics largely based on class, and so on – were almost entirely absent. Struggles about *distributional* and *consumption* issues such as income maintenance or housing could never be divorced from the key question of how production was organised; social policy questions were little thought about and, when they were, only as subordinate to economic ones. To believe anything else – in particular, that the capitalist state was anything other than 'a machine for the oppression of one class by another'[2] – was heretical. Quite simply, Marxists did not seem to have either the will or the necessary conceptual equipment to address welfare questions. Classical Marxist writings contained very little specific guidance other than concepts, largely derived from analyses which privileged the economy.

In the late 1960s Marxist theory did experience a revival in the West. British intellectuals and students turned in increasing numbers to Marxist categories to explain events such as the Vietnam War; famine in Africa; imperialism; the arms race; the inadequacies of the post-war reforms; and the increasingly visible signs of renewed economic crisis. Large numbers of women began to question the traditional division between the genders and develop a feminist theory focusing on the power divisions between themselves and men. These feminist concerns necessarily raised questions about *distributional* struggles – those between women and men – and forced serious attention on to questions of care and welfare, in particular the unpaid care provided by women for their menfolk and dependants. Large numbers of newly politically conscious people were keen to utilise, and adapt, Marxist insights to explain developments in the form and content of 'welfare' capitalism.

Mainstream Marxist theory was at first, as we shall see in chapter 4, not very helpful in supplying adequate answers. There was an obsession with analysing the *structural* compulsions that forced capitalism's hand into conceding welfare reforms. Very little attention was paid either to the role of working-class struggle in promoting such reform, or to the possible varying *forms* that the welfare state's institutional arrangements could take. It is not until the late 1970s, under the pressure of two separate factors, that more intriguing questions begin to be asked of and about welfare by Marxists. First, many of the students attracted to Marxism in the 1960s were now often working for the capitalist state in one capacity or another – teachers, social workers, planners, health workers, etc. It is hardly surprising that they began to believe that it *had* to be possible, in the title of a timely pamphlet of 1980, to work *In and Against the State*.[3] Second, and possibly of even greater importance, there were the beginnings of the economic recession and the repeated cutbacks in welfare provision begun by Labour in 1976. Marxist theory had largely until this time seen the welfare state as doing little more than securing the logical development of capitalism and acting as a repressive mechanism of social control. Such a *theoretical* stance stood in marked contrast to the *political* actions of socialist activists, who actively organised in their thousands against the cuts. Some elements of the welfare state were clearly worth preserving and building upon. Some Marxists tentatively began to realise that welfare provision could vary in *form* and *content* under capitalism, and that some of these variations might be more facilitative of possible future socialist forms than others.

Despite these insights much Marxist scholarship on welfare is still, even today, tinged by what we describe as 'fundamentalism' – a disdain for exploring these issues too deeply for fear of losing one's commitment to 'the revolution', and the belief that only 'it' can guarantee 'real' welfare for all. Such people are still entirely sceptical of the idea of the capitalist state assuming responsibility for maintaining minimum levels of living – and can only comprehend it as part of a logic of repression. We would be the first to admit the paucity and bureaucratic inflexibility of much of the British welfare edifice; but at a time when the 'new Conservatism' of Thatcher is attempting to erode state collective responsibility, the essentially 'progressive' nature of this notion is plain for all to see. The new Conservatism has been the final element in ensuring that some Marxist commentators and activists take questions about welfare reform, content and delivery seriously. At root, welfare is about political and moral choices. The new Conservatism's attack on the welfare state – particularly that of Hayek[4] – is grounded not only in economic arguments about waste and inefficiency but in philosophical and moral ones about justice and liberty. For the new Conservatism the welfare state limits freedom and causes injustice – rhetorical appeals not unfamiliar, as we shall see, to those invoked by socialist critics. How do socialists reply to such charges? Certainly not by merely asserting an ultimate faith in the ability of planned socialist economies to guarantee human liberty – particularly given the stark and grim realities of many of the 'already' existing socialist societies. No, Marxist-influenced socialists, together with their Fabian counterparts, have to begin to re-examine the *moral* basis of their commitment to welfare and socialism.[5] If Fabianism needs to learn about the state and power from Marxism, then the latter can equally benefit from the much closer attention paid by some Fabians to the rationale behind 'the very idea of a welfare state'.[6]

The argument of this part of the book is divided into three stages. First, at the beginning of chapter 4 we outline in a simplified form the principal concepts available to Marxists for explaining the workings of welfare provision under capitalism. We have deliberately excluded any discussion of the role of class struggle, at this stage, in order to highlight how easily a Marxist perspective can fall into the trap of simply assuming that all welfare provision is functional for capitalism. In post-war Britain such arguments were particularly attractive to Marxists eager to rebut Fabian claims that capitalism not only could radically reform itself but had already done so and with entirely benign consequences. The chapter then explores further what we have described as this rather 'cynical gaze' that Marxist theory has, and still can, cast upon the welfare state; we suggest it is derived from a particular style of Marxist politics. The penultimate section of the chapter, however, rehabilitates the central concept of class struggle, revealing sharp divisions between Marxist theorists as to its precise role.

The second stage of the argument is contained in chapter 5, where we explore these divisions between Marxists in greater depth. Our contention is that much Marxist theory has tended to over-concentrate on *critique*, particularly of Fabian approaches to welfare, and as a consequence has failed to develop *political* strategies for the purpose of advancing the short- and medium-term interests of the working class, women, black people and the poor – an essential attribute of any 'socialist' political intervention in welfare. Marxist approaches, in marked contrast to the pragmatism of Fabian ones, suffer from an underdeveloped *politics* of social policy. The last stage of our argument is contained in chapter 6, where we try to indicate what a *realistic* theory and politics of social welfare, derivable from Marxism, would involve: greater awareness of politically feasible alternatives; an ability to contribute to debates about *immediate* policy alternatives; a sensitivity to just how 'real living' class (and other) struggles affect the form and content of welfare provision; and an awareness of how Marxist theory must begin to make a moral case for a 'caring' society. For as Doreen Massey et al. have reminded us, everyday discussions of welfare are 'probably the principal area in which arguments for a different caring, sharing or *socialist* society can still be heard'.[7]

## Notes

1  E. Mandel, *Marxist Economic Theory* (Merlin, 1968), p. 13.
2  V.I. Lenin, *The State*, in *Selected Works*, vol. 3 (Progress Publishers, 1971), p. 267.
3  London/Edinburgh Weekend Return Group, *In and Against the State* (Pluto Press, 1980).
4  For a useful and sympathetic guide to his arguments see E. Butler, *Hayek – his contribution to the political and economic thought of our time* (Temple Smith, 1983). For a much more sophisticated discussion see J. Gray's equally sympathetic *Hayek on Liberty*, 2nd edn  (Basil Blackwell, 1986).
5  See P. Bean, J. Ferris and D. Whynes (eds), *In Defence of Welfare* (Tavistock, 1985) for a useful collection, largely from a Fabian standpoint.
6  See R. Plant, *The Very Idea of a Welfare State*, in Bean, Ferris and Whynes, *In Defence of Welfare*, pp. 3–29.
7  D. Massey, L. Segal and H. Wainwright, 'And now for the good news', in J. Curran (ed.), *The Future of the Left* (Polity Press and New Socialist, 1984), pp. 216–17.

# 4

# A Cynical Gaze?

The social security system is concerned with reproducing a reserve army of labour, the patriarchal family and the disciplining of the labour force. Only secondarily and contingently does it function as a means of mitigating poverty or providing income maintenance. ... Similarly ... housing policy is directed towards regulating the consumption of a vital commodity for the reproduction of the labour force, and only secondarily and contingently as an attempt at providing secure and adequate accommodation for the working class.

Norman Ginsburg

The intention of this chapter is briefly to outline and then assess the Marxist approach to welfare. In the same way as part I made a distinction between 'orthodox' and more critical strands of Fabianism, this chapter will be concerned with distinguishing 'fundamentalist' Marxism from varieties more capable of adequately investigating the object under scrutiny.

## Marxist theory and welfare

A Marxist approach to the analysis of welfare in a capitalist society would largely draw upon six concepts: the state; the reproduction of labour power; the reproduction of social relations; ideology (legitimation); social control; and class struggle. These concepts have been extensively examined elsewhere.[1] Our purpose here is briefly to remind readers of the very powerful explanatory force that is achieved by their combination.

### The state

The state is seen as a direct instrument of ruling-class power, helping to secure the general conditions for the successful production and realisation of surplus value. O'Connor, in an influential text *The Fiscal Crisis of the State*, argued that the state has to perform three functions towards this end. It has to try to facilitate capitalism:

1 To obtain the conditions for *continual* successful private, capitalist production (accumulation function)

2 To obtain the conditions for the production, reproduction and harnessing of labour power (reproduction function)

3 To accomplish 1 and 2 in ways that do not provoke too much social unrest, political resistance or mass confusion, or effectively to deal with such unrest should it arise (legitimation/repression function).[2]

Welfare policies are implicated in all three of these activities, although primarily in the second and third.

### Reproduction of labour and social relations

Gough, following on from O'Connor's initial framework, has characterised the welfare state as 'the use of state power to modify the reproduction of labour power and to maintain the non-working population in capitalist societies'.[3] He goes on to argue that the welfare state's activities are directed at determining minimum levels of consumption for different groups whilst simultaneously modifying the patterns of socialisation, behaviour and abilities within the population. The welfare state is in essence 'the state organisation of social reproduction'.[4] In referring to this concept of reproduction Marxists are not just concerned with quantitative aspects, that is the necessity of guaranteeing the biological reproduction of the labour force. They are more concerned with the *qualitative* dimensions involving the type of human beings that are produced, and the sorts of relationships that accrue between people. They are keen to stress that the social relations of production have also to be reinforced and buttressed. As Cockburn has concisely put it:

> If capitalism is to survive, each succeeding generation of workers must stay in an appropriate relationship to capital: the relations of production must be reproduced. Workers must not step outside the relation of the wage, the relation of property, the relation of authority. So reproducing capitalist relations means reproducing the class, ownership, above all reproducing a frame of mind.[5]

### Ideology

Other institutions, notably of course the family, play a crucial function in this process. Many welfare interventions, as we shall see in chapter 6, precisely buttress and reinforce highly particular family relationships and familial ideologies. This concept of ideology has become increasingly important in Marxist accounts of the operation of the welfare system, not least because 'the welfare state is not just a set of services, it is also a set of *ideas* about society.'[6] It is only through exploring the determination and workings of these ideas that detailed analysis can take place of qualitative dimensions of the reproduction of the capitalist system.

*Sir Kings out more clearly.*

For Marxists the term 'ideology' conveys more than the sociological sense of interest concealment or promotion, although Marxists do use it in this way, for example to refer to professional ideologies. Following on from Gramsci's concept of hegemony there is a fascination with how the ruling class is able through transformative processes to rearticulate ideas to create forms of 'popular religion' (Gramsci) or common sense. A gloss is placed over reality, creating a taken-for-granted world that does not 'require reasoning, argument, logic, thought; it is spontaneously available, thoroughly recognisable, widely shared. It *feels* indeed, as if it has always been there, the sedimented bedrock wisdom of "the race", a form of naturalisation, the content of which has hardly changed with time.'[7] Of course such ideas are not 'natural', far from it; they are carefully constructed and worked on. Marxists are more than aware of the importance of creative agency in the dissemination and construction of ideology. Althusser, in a now classic study of the material production of ideologies, refers to the agencies that actively create and win hegemonic consent as ideological state apparatuses (ISAs) – the education system, the family, churches, the mass media and cultural institutions.[8] Such stress on wilful design can, as we shall see, all too quickly lead to conspiratorial paranoia.

Certainly it is not as if ideas are free-floating constructs sucked out of the air by Saatchi-style ruling-class copywriters! A central and intriguing element of Marxist theory's analysis of ideology is the stress on the *necessary form* that reality has to take, given commodity production. As there is no immediate *experience* of exploitation by the worker and a fair wage has apparently been paid for the work, it is as if capital had of itself the property of automatic growth and of rendering a profit to its owner; whereas, of course, this is merely a mystification stemming from the nature of the capitalist production process. This important concept of commodity fetishism is best explained through an investigation of the separation of the spheres of production and circulation. It is in the latter that our spontaneous and everyday common-sense perceptions of the system arise. It is as *consumers* that we try to buy goods as cheaply as possible, effectively blind to the conditions under which the good was produced. Welfare expenditures can all too easily 'appear' as beneficent supplements, proof of the caring nature of the system, whereas for Marxists they have much more to do with supplementing consumers' expenditure and/or guaranteeing the moral and physical well-being of the workforce – in short, legitimating continuous and apparently 'natural' exploitation.

We are in a difficult, but vitally important, territory. Marxist theories of ideology are somewhat Janus-headed. On the one hand, there is a deliberate emphasis on the necessary *form* that ideas must take under capitalism; on the other, there is an obvious appreciation of *agency* in the promotion, delivery and sealing of ideological content. The ideas themselves are far from easily distilled and often contain contradictory and complex instructions. Welfare expenditures *do* legitimate capitalism; the very idea of a 'welfare' state conjures up notions of care. Common-sense ideas about welfare, however, are also often tinged with stigma and notions of 'deservingness', receipt being regarded as proof of pathology.

Perhaps the 'agency–structure' problem is not so difficult to resolve. Golding and Middleton, for example, argued that the 'welfare scrounger phobia', so virulent in British society, is best understood as the widespread acceptance of three key ideas: '*efficiency* of the labour market and the economy; *morality* of the work ethic and self-sufficiency; and the *pathology* of individual inadequacy as the cause of poverty'. The most interesting part of their argument, however, is that such ideas may well be pervasive but their general acceptance *requires* periodic reinforcement. As they state:

> We have suggested that these ideas have lengthy pedigrees in popular consciousness. But they have been 'fixed' into the prevailing discourse in two key periods. In the 1880–1920 period . . . by the new vocabulary of the lower middle-class commercial press . . . and . . . in the second . . . period between the wars, ruling images became 'naturalised', and the now genuinely mass circulation popular press . . . provided an authoritative voice for an emasculated reformism, more concerned with social control than with the redress of injustice or inequality.[9]

Poulantzas has tried to categorise more precisely the ways that ideologies operate.[10] He suggests that we can best appreciate their general functioning in terms of three effects: (1) masking or displacing, (2) fragmentation or separation, and (3) imposition of an imaginary unity or coherence on 'reality'. He argues that Marx's 'appearances' are better understood as the *re-presentation* of certain relationships; for example, in the sphere of market relations the productive classes appear (or are represented) as mere separate economic units, and private greed appears bound by 'fair' contracts. Thus representation has the effect first, as we have seen, of shifting emphasis and awareness from production to exchange; second, of fragmenting classes into individuals; and third, of binding individuals into a passive community of consumers. It is important to recognise that this is no more than a crude inventory and that ideas under capitalism do not form a neat and harmonious whole. Moreover, many types of ideological reinforcement will have contradictory effects, not least amongst different ages and classes. Nobody though can surely fail to see the crude ideological significance of this extract from the Beveridge report:

That attitude of the housewife to gainful employment outside the home is not and should not be the same as that of the single woman. She has other duties. . . . Taken as a whole the plan for social security puts a premium on marriage in place of penalising it. . . . In the next thirty years housewives as mothers have vital work to do in ensuring the adequate continuance of the British race and of British ideals in the world.[11]

Equally well people should be able to recognise the liberal and judicial ideology at work in these two passages from the Scarman report:

It was alleged by some . . . who made representations to me that Britain is an institutionally racist society. If by that is meant it is a society which knowingly, as a matter of policy, discriminates against black people, I reject the allegation.[12]

Later in the report he is adamant that the 'direction and policies of the Metropolitan Police are not racist. . . . The criticisms lie elsewhere . . . in the ill-considered, immature and racially prejudiced actions of some officers in their dealings on the streets with young black people.'[13] We should hardly be surprised that a 'judicial gaze' can *only* understand *individual* culpability, in just the same way as it reinforces the belief that everyone has an equal chance of legal remedy in a capitalist society. In other words, it reproduces inequality by treating unequals as if they had the same resources and power. This example also serves to remind us of the previously noted dilemma concerning structure and agency. Is Scarman trapped by the apparatus (ISA) which he represents as a practitioner? Certainly he is not a free agent, but nevertheless 'he struck a more unexpected note than . . . expected . . . and awoke in the hard police lobby, not approval, but full-throated vengeance and outrage.'[14] So his ideological pronouncements may have been *constrained* within set limits, but they were *not* the mere incantations of a state puppet.

Of course, we must be alert to the fact that old ideas can take apparently new forms, when in fact they merely reinforce in a more appropriate (modern?) guise the essential elements of old repressions. Barker's most interesting notion of the 'new' racism – it is not so much that people are inferior as that they are *different* (people prefer their own types) – admirably demonstrates this.[15] This 'new' ideological form for a very old idea is exceptionally pernicious, for it is able to circumvent discussion about prejudice on ethical, political or rational grounds; it matters not what people *ought* to feel or think, for their very nature has determined their reaction. But we cannot always assume that ideologies are reconstituted in this way. Reading the *ideological* significance of past events is a risky business, for people frequently employ the term as a panacea, as if by merely invoking 'it' they have explained something. It is all too simple to judge the past as an easy stepping-stone to the present. For example, many feminists have indicted Bowlby and Winnicott's psychoanalytic theories of the late 1940s and early 1950s on maternal deprivation for being centrally concerned with lowering women's work expectations. Yet as Wilson has noted, 'their appeal was not so much in terms of returning women to the home. . . . Their work was an indictment of elitist upper-class forms of child-rearing – nannies and boarding schools – and implicitly working-class warmth and spontaneity towards children were validated.'[16] Ideas have *contradictory* effects, and they can never be neatly reduced to simple determinations.

The concept of ideology is an important one for understanding the operations of the welfare state. It would be nonsensical to try to understand the workings of Britain's income maintenance system without attention being paid to the implicit patriarchal ideologies generating female dependency. Equally, if one does not have a developed understanding of the ideologies of racism, then a most imperfect understanding of the British immigration laws will result. However, ideologies can have contradictory content and effects, and it is vital that appreciation is paid to ideologies of *resistance* and *change*. As we shall see below, some variants of Marxist theory are not very open to such considerations. Too often, and somewhat ironically, the tracing of ideological determination seeks to find structural logic. Such explanations can only locate phenomena in very general, and reductionist, ways. Equally, agency must not be handled either to produce complete contingency or, more likely in many Marxist accounts, conspiracy.

## Social control

It is because the Marxist usage of the term 'ideology' is often insensitive to questions of agency that partially explains, for us, why the concept of social control is so extensively used in their writings about welfare. It is attractive, for it appears to hold out the prospect of being able more precisely to examine the actions of particular groups in sustaining ideologies and promoting policies. However, as Cohen has persuasively shown, social control has become something of a 'Mickey Mouse' concept. For sociologists it refers to all social processes working to promote social conformity, whilst in radical writings 'it has become a negative term to cover not just the obviously coercive apparatus of the state, but also the putative hidden element in all state-sponsored social policy.'[17] A real conceptual muddle ensues. The term is admirable in locating how certain groups, particularly professional ones, are able to authoritatively define certain behaviours, persons or things. In this sense, social control can be seen – in words of Conrad and Schneider – 'as the power to have a particular set of definitions of the world realised in both spirit and practice'.[18] Their own work provides a good example of how increasing numbers of deviant behaviours (e.g. alcoholism, naughty behaviour in the classroom, child abuse, homosexuality, drug addiction and delinquency) are increasingly being regarded as the subject for legitimate, yet inappropriate, medical interventions. The medical profession and its allies, particularly the large drug companies, are criticised for actively operating as 'moral entrepreneurs' to change our understanding of deviance from a moral (badness) to a medical (sickness) one. Such work is most instructive and requires sensitivity to localised agencies, or what Foucault has called 'the microphysics of power' (see chapter 6).

Marxists are also attracted to the term 'social control', we suspect, for a very different reason, and one that re-emphasises the original sociological meaning of the term as societal regulation. Social order is clearly maintained by much more than mere legal systems, police forces and the rest; it is mediated through a wide range of social institutions from religion to family life, leisure, education, charity, social work etc. In short, a continuum of control is established with soft elements (compliance, persuasion and ideological invocation) at one end, and hard control (force and repression) at the other – the iron fist and the velvet glove. The term becomes attractive for linking these two, and opening up the possibility of 'revealing' hidden agendas or rationales lurking behind seemingly innocuous and caring social policies. This type of usage is, of course, virtually synonymous with how the term 'ideology' can be, and is, used by some Marxists. And used in this way – referring to some general requirements that the social system has for control – it really adds very little to our understanding. For as we shall see later, the more we use the concept of social control to investigate actual agencies and practices of control, the less likely we are to be persuaded by theories that wish to bring grand designs to the patterning of that control. It must be precisely such general usages of the concept that the Marxist historian Stedman-Jones had in mind when he argued that:

> It is not difficult to demonstrate that a casual usage of 'social control' metaphors leads to non-explanation and incoherence. There is no practical or ideological institution which could not 'in some way' be interpreted as an agency of social control. . . . No indication of who the agents or instigators of social control may be . . . no . . . criterion . . . whereby we may judge whether social control has broken down.[19]

Hay, in a spirited reply to Stedman-Jones, argues that the term 'social control' should be deliberately restricted to 'solely encompass the activities, actions and influence of the ruling class of Britain' by which they secure the existing basis of social relationships; it should be used 'to imply conscious action'.[20] There are two problems with this. First, it sets a very limited agenda for the scope of investigation unless we assume that state professionals merely slavishly carry out ruling-class wishes – a fault not uncommon in some treatments. Second, and not unrelated, is the problem of identifying just when such conscious action is or has been taking place. Conspiracies can very easily be invented, and intention equated with effect.

This brief outline of the major concepts (except class struggle: see the penultimate section of this chapter) employed by Marxists to account for welfare activities under capitalism, should allow us to appreciate the quite different range of concerns this body of theory brings to bear upon such questions compared with orthodox social administration. Welfare is seen as centrally implicated in the regulation of work and the control of potentially disruptive behaviour. Capitalism, by placing emphasis on profit before human need, is essentially antithetical to welfare. Human needs will only be fully realised and fulfilled after the establishment of a fully socialist, indeed communist, society. The welfare state largely serves the interests of the ruling class; and the motivation behind the provision of welfare is the legitimation of that class's rule. Welfare is not all it seems, and certainly not what the majority of people seem to assume it is. Welfare reforms have not widely redistributed income and resources from the better-off to the poor; rather any redistribution that does occur is through people's life cycle. Welfare expenditure benefits the middle classes more than the working classes, and it is downright misleading to regard welfare provision as in some way embryonic of socialism. A reformed capitalism is still capitalism. Owners of capital still extract surplus value under exploitative conditions. In short, Marxist theory has been much less concerned with immediate empirical questions, and far more preoccupied with constructing grand overarching and damning theoretical indictments. It tends to view the very possibility that capitalist societies might be able to provide adequate welfare for their citizenry with a much more jaundiced, or cynical, eye than their Fabian counterparts.

## Accommodating capitalism: the unhelpful welfare state?

Any initial appraisal of the Marxist theoretical approach to welfare has to note both its apparent unity and its marked negative analytic thrust; both are largely accounted for by the concentrations of the 'new' social policy on *critique* of capitalism and Fabianism. Offe suggests that the Marxist critique of the welfare state can be summarised in three points: '(1) ineffective and inefficient, (2) repressive and (3) conditioning a false ideological understanding of social and political reality. . . . It is a device to stabilise rather than a step in the transformation of capitalist society.'[21] Newman offers a similar appraisal under three almost identical headings: fraudulence, social control and neutralisation.[22] The last two highlight the particularity, and potential strengths, of the Marxist approach in opening up the field of social policy studies to a much richer vein of questions. The first indicates a real point of contact between the 'old' and the 'new' traditions. For as we saw in chapter 3, a major strength of the Fabian tradition has been its detailed criticisms of the actual workings of welfare systems.

The starting point of much Marxist theoretical work on the welfare state has generally been the function 'it' performs for the maintenance of capitalist stability, in marked and deliberate contrast to concentrating 'solely on its "positive" aspect, as do almost all writers in the tradition of social administration'.[23] This heavy *theoretical* emphasis on the repressive, capital-oriented aspects of state welfare is *not*, however, *always* complemented by a dismissive *political* attitude to welfare. As I have written elsewhere:

> Some friends of mine, and enemies, have accused me of having an inconsistent understanding of the welfare state. On the one hand, I have emphasised the welfare state as a repressive mechanism of social control – the schools, social work, social security agencies, housing departments, the probation service – all were seen as a means of adapting rebellious groups to capitalism. On the other hand, though, I and my ilk were perfectly prepared to defend the welfare state against the 'cuts', and always pressed for even greater extension of welfare provision.[24]

So despite their dismissive theoretical gaze, Marxists have usually been prepared politically to defend welfare services, although (as we shall see) not always in their present form. A definite and quite dramatic tension exists between Marxism as a guide to political practice and Marxism as a body of critical theory.

One reason for this is the claims by different theoretical schools and Marxist-inspired political parties to represent *the* 'real' Marxist tradition. For a conventional response to problems of theory–practice tension has been a return to first principles – to classic texts. Such a tendency is always likely to generate conservative or fundamentalist adherences. A further effect of this concentration on classic texts is an over-reliance on abstract theoretical solutions, a disdainful attitude to contemporary empirical happenings and the ascription of a low priority to issues not directly tackled by those texts. It hardly needs re-emphasising (see part I) that the issues of welfare and distribution politics are assigned a very low priority in classical Marxism. As

Mishra has observed:

> Marx's social theory is not directly concerned with the analysis of what we would describe as the institutions of welfare. For one, these institutions – in particular the social services – were scarcely developed in anything like their present form in Marx's lifetime. For another, with the notable exception of factory legislation, Marx paid little attention to the growth of state intervention in Victorian England. . . . Marx's attitude to capitalism was one of total rejection rather than reform, and much of his intellectual effort went into proving that the capitalist system was both unworkable and inhuman.[25]

This 'total rejection' of reform has clearly affected contemporary Marxism's appraisal of welfare provision, contributing to the marked theoretical emphasis on the role that welfare policies play in continuing to sustain capitalist social relations. Such arguments, we believe, are all too often pursued crudely and mechanically. For welfare policies can also be seen to involve the dispensation of monetary and personal assistance to individuals falling within certain categories of 'need', such as the aged, unemployed, sick, disabled, young and poor. As Campbell has written:

> In its wider connotation the idea of the welfare state takes in the endorsement of certain economic and social policies, such as full employment, equality of opportunity and the attainment of social solidarity through a measure of egalitarianism. . . . The welfare principle does go some way towards the objectives of socialism, more so, for instance, than the moral principles of meritorian justice or simple utilitarianism.[26]

Such an argument contains as much 'insight' as those which implicate social policy in the stabilising of capitalism, but they exist at a much lower level of abstraction. They also imply a different set of concerns to those of classical Marxism: first, an emphasis on the importance of distributional or allocative questions; and second, a sensitivity to the fact that it might be possible to utilise these questions to make political capital in order to make gradual encroachments into capitalist hegemony through immediate 'gains' by or for the working classes and underprivileged. In short, they are arguments that seem to have chosen what Rosa Luxemburg once described as not merely 'a more tranquil, calmer road to socialism but a different road – a reformist road'.[27]

Central to our argument, though, is that if Marxists take such a dismissive attitude to such issues they *cannot* possibly have anything of real importance or interest to say about *welfare*. Of course, Marxist theoretical schema are right to privilege the role of production as the basis of the economic surplus from which any allocation of consumption can be made, but consideration of such allocations should not be seen as a mere afterthought – particularly so if the object of attention is with welfare and welfare provision. Production in any political economy will pose constraints around which reproduction and consumption policies are formed, but it is also highly likely 'that growth in consumption takes on a momentum of its own fostered by the interests of those who provide it'.[28]

Classical Marxism has tended to be entirely dismissive of even loose reflection on the formulation of sets of redistributive criteria stipulating how welfare 'goods' ought to be shared out. This is Engels's rather cavalier attitude to the generation of any immediate solution to problems faced by the homeless and ill-housed:

> It does not occur to me to try to solve the so-called housing question any more than I can occupy myself with the details of the still more important food question. . . . To speculate as to how a future society would organise the distribution . . . of dwellings leads directly to utopia.[29]

It is as if social considerations, and policies, *cannot* ever theoretically venture outside the barriers set for them by the logic of capitalism's economic development. This is despite a desire on the part of those adhering to such theories to offer political sustenance to those fighting for better housing, old age pensions or whatever. This theoretical tendency has been thoroughly underscored by the debate which occurred, in the early part of this century, between the 'revolutionaries' (Lenin and Luxemburg) and the 'reformists' (Kautsky and Bernstein). This major political schism within Marxism largely turned on a theoretical disagreement concerning the role of the state. For the revolutionaries, advances sought within the bourgeois state were dangerous delusions; as Lenin stated in his speech on *The State*, 'the more democratic it is the cruder and more cynical is the rule of capitalism.'[30]

With legacies such as these from Engels and Lenin, it is hardly surprising that much Marxist theory – if it has discussed welfare at all – has been preoccupied with dismissive and often dogmatic criticism. Our argument is that Marxism has to develop a much more even-handed appraisal of the welfare state. For some it is still 'Fabian' and 'reformist' even to contemplate distributionist issues, as such reflection will do little, if anything, to alter the contours of capitalist production. This certainly seems to be the attitude of these authors:

> The state is *all* the activities employed by a ruling class to secure its collective conditions of production. Some of these like Lenin's standing armies are overtly oppressive; others, like the provision of public libraries or old age pensions, are seemingly innocuous. But what makes them all intrinsically repressive is precisely . . . *the end they serve*. From this point of view, planning agreements are just as repressive as baton charges. For . . . to maintain the conditions of production in a class society is itself to perpetuate the oppression of class rule.[31]

Such positions, we believe, betray a certain fundamentalist and unhelpful politics, and promote theoretical schema which would never allow welfare issues to be anything but secondary. This fundamentalist and often dogmatic Marxism has, in our opinion, two principal sources. First, there has been an obsession with 'correct' theory – Marxism as a scientifically accurate account of the world. The British new left has, as we discussed in chapter 3, been particularly prone to this affliction since the mid 1960s.[32] Second, this has combined with and almost unconsciously reinforced an affinity to certain theoretical–political judgements, appropriate in conditions of absolutist Russia, but often unhelpful to political struggles in advanced capitalist societies. Our next three sections will be concerned with briefly tracing the origins, the political effects and theoretical excesses of this fundamentalism.

## Origins of Marxist fundamentalism

It is a well-known fact that Marx never offered a systematic account of a future socialist or communist society, and that he considered such attempts as 'foolish, ineffective and even reactionary'.[33] This is a damaging legacy and one which finds contemporary expression in fundamentalist Marxism. For reasons obviously not pertaining in Marx's time, contemporary socialists have to pursue their goals in a world where many things have been done in the name of Marxism. Hence such a cavalier attitude to the effects of major social upheavals can no longer be seriously sustained. As we saw in part I, Marxists always differentiated between their theories and moral or utopian forms of socialism, with their ideal visions of the future; and for many Marxists it is the necessary 'correctness' of their science (theory) that will guarantee the movement to socialism and thence to communism (practice). Humans are incapable of change through mere whim, and require scientific knowledge of the limiting conditions in order to effect conscious change. Upon the accomplishment of such 'knowledge', conscious human action – the actual fusing of theory and practice – can proceed to make a rational ordering of the world possible. The vehicle for practice has usually been judged to involve the necessity for constructing a revolutionary leadership, given a generally pessimistic evaluation of the spontaneous political potential of the working classes. A further requisite is that an organisation has to act as the continuing producers of the theory and agents of the practice – a revolutionary party.

Our central charge against this body of loosely connected theoretical speculations and political assumptions that we are describing as Marxist fundamentalism is the often self-righteous confidence in the truth of the theoretical pronouncements of such parties and groups, despite real events not always matching up to them.[34] Needless to say, different groups widely disagree, yet all are equally vehement in their claims to 'the truth'. Such practice infrequently feeds back into theory, and dogmatism and atrophy all too easily result.

This book is not the place to trace extensively the origins of such atrophy, but it is essential to our argument to glance at certain key moments. The successful Russian Revolution in 1917 undoubtedly led to the fetishism of a particular fusion of theory with practice – Leninism – dominated by the idea of a clandestine revolutionary party working to establish dual power through worker and peasant soviets. The very success of this formula led to many attempts to transplant the soviet model into situations where very different traditions and problems existed. In particular, the desire to break workers from reformist illusions led in 1921 to the imposition of twenty-one conditions upon parties joining the Comintern. Claudin, a veteran Spanish Marxist, has explained the negative consequences of this:

> A large number of socialists and trade unionists who wanted to join the Comintern because they were in sympathy with the Russian Revolution and shared . . . the revolutionary objectives . . . nevertheless disagreed . . . on certain points . . . . Above all they regarded the policy of splitting the labour movement as wrong. The '21 conditions' shut the doors to all these elements . . . and, in . . . the methods adopted by the Comintern in its struggle against reformism . . . a sectarian and dogmatic spirit began . . . to clear a way for itself in the communist parties disguised under a revolutionary verbalism that concealed its remoteness from reality.[35]

This desire to clone chemically pure Bolshevik parties from working classes raised for decades on the experiences of reformist politics was to have a lasting impact on the development of world socialism. It was a decision that illustrated the worst excesses of what Lenin had previously polemised against amongst Russian Marxist circles – ultra-leftism[36] – and can only be accounted for by his misplaced optimism regarding the imminence of world revolution. Whatever the reasons, 'the divorce revealed by practice, between Lenin's ideas about the proletariat of the industrialised countries and the *actual behaviour* of this proletariat shows up . . . the *absence*, in Marxist theory, of an answer to certain political and theoretical problems concerning the road to revolution in these types of society.'[37] 'These types of society' have, of course, still to experience socialist change, and in its absence the appropriate moment for the realisation of theory has often remained either with a relatively indeterminate future (theoretical wish fulfilment), or with the progress of the allegedly already existing socialist countries. Given the stunted development of the latter, and the necessarily idealist nature of the former, it should be no surprise that many contemporary Marxists are openly discussing a crisis of Marxism.[38] The period since the Second World War cannot be said to have encouraged those who wish to see a more rational ordering of the world, and socialists have had their beliefs subject to a series of systematic body blows – from Khrushchev's 1956 admissions through to the invasion of Hungary and Czechoslovakia and recent occurrences in Poland. It is much too easy to explain these events, and the massive difficulties faced by those countries attempting to construct socialism, as simply the result of Stalinist betrayals and deviations. The recognition of such political problems and theoretical difficulties can all too easily lead to a return to the texts of the great founding fathers and mothers, with problems being seen as failures of 'correct' interpretation and practice. Such dogmatism, of course, accounts for the endless splits and splinters that characterise the practices of revolutionary groups and parties.[39] Mistakes are seen to be due hardly ever to the inadequacies of theory, almost always to wrongful application or interpretation. Indeed, even in the most infamous split within the communist movement – between Trotsky and Stalin – the protagonists were not disagreeing theoretically about the relevance of the Bolshevik model for constructing revolutionary roads; rather their differences concerned *application*. Stalin subordinated world revolution to the building of socialism in the USSR, whereas Trotsky made it dependent on the victory of socialist revolutions, in the immediate future, elsewhere in Europe. Undoubtedly Trotsky was more faithful to a central tenet of Leninism, that the Russian Revolution required revolutions in other European countries if it was to survive, but if (as we have seen) the difficulties faced in accomplishing such revolutions were under-estimated by Lenin, they were further neglected by Trotsky. By the late 1920s it was increasingly apparent that Trotsky was beginning to fall into a massive theoretical contradiction. On the one hand capitalism was seen as being in an extremely acute crisis, economically bankrupt and rent asunder by inter-imperialist rivalries; on the other he considered that, in the event of a world war, defeat of the USSR was inevitable. Contradictions such as these reveal a methodological error replete in fundamentalist variants of Marxism generally and Trotskyism in particular. This consists of perceiving the antagonisms between classes – nationally and internationally – as *absolute*, and consequently under-estimating other complex intervening determinations.

In this Trotsky was being consistent with our previously noted lacuna in Bolshevik thought – the failure to develop any real understanding of the cultural universe of the Western proletariat, and in particular its deep attachment to national and democratic values. The nation and democracy were, of course, products of capitalism but they were also conquests often won by forms of popular struggle. Perry Anderson admirably explains the gravity of this under-estimation for the development of the Trotskyist movement: 'Reaffirmation of the validity and reality of socialist revolution and proletarian democracy *against so many events which denied them* involuntarily inclined this tradition towards conservatism. The preservation of classical doctrines took priority over their development.'[40] The same might be said of other variants of Marxist fundamentalism. This conservatism has prevented many generations of Marxists working in certain traditions from adequately facing up to, let alone answering, a series of vital questions. In what precise ways are conditions for successful socialist change different than in Lenin's time? What are the reasons for the failures of those countries which have attempted socialist paths? What are the necessary preconditions for democratic socialist transition? What are the mechanics of that transition? What technical questions will have to be faced? How will egalitarian social policies be implemented? In what exact ways will life under socialism be different from that under capitalism? Too often 'the revolution' has been seen as a panacea, as a universal solution to all questions, ushering in *qualitative* changes of dramatic proportions. This has encouraged a dismissive attitude to detailed technical questions, and brusque treatment of those who have worried about the 'failures' of already existing socialist societies. 'Everything will be all right if only the "correct" political line is followed.' Let us explore in more detail the forms of contemporary arguments likely to follow from adherence to a fundamentalist Marxist politics.

## The politics of fundamentalism

There are four major fundamentalist tenets: the assumption of the impossibility of reforms; the belief in predestined class objectives; vanguardism and a frontal assault theory of revolution; and a simplistic vision of a future socialist society.[41]

### The impossibility of reforms
At 'the debate of the decade' held in London in March 1980 on the crisis and the future of the left, a leading member of the Socialist Workers' Party, Duncan Hallas, argued that 'the whole course of reform . . . depends on the possibility of the system being able to concede welfare, being able to concede reform. I don't have to make the argument that it doesn't any more.'[42] The claim that capitalism's ability to find space for reform has been eroded is a recurring theme in a certain style of Marxist argument. For example, in 1930 Trotsky noted the impossibility of further 'effective reforms within the existing

set of property relationships'.[43] He was preceded, and has been followed, by all too many revolutionaries over-eager to write capitalism's obituary. Often this has taken the form of a particularly crude economic determinism – an assertion that capitalism has reached the zenith of its natural days (matured or ripened are the usual terms) owing to the tendency for the rate of profit to fall (see the section below on the theoretical excesses of fundamentalism for further exploration). As this is not a technical book on economics, it is unnecessary to wander too far into the maze of arguments for or against this theory. In brief, it suggests that there is an inexorable compulsion under capitalism for the organic composition of capital to increase, leading to a tendency for the rate of profit to fall.[44] But it is important to note along with Hodgson that '*no one* has successfully demonstrated that there is a reliable and general mechanism for the organic composition of capital to necessarily increase under capitalism, nor is there any *clear empirical evidence* of its sustained increase over the last sixty years.'[45] Moreover Glyn and Sutcliffe,[46] amongst others, have shown that attempts to explain the present poor state of Britain's profitability as a classic illustration of this law are misguided. Evidence suggests that the fall is better explained as the result of an increase in the share of net output going to wages (before tax) at the expense of profit.

Over-zealous adherence to this law can undoubtedly lead to dubious and dogmatic political practices. For such 'laws', when inflexibly stated, altogether deny that any real long-term 'reforms' can be carried out. Indeed, 'reforms' supply further evidence of bourgeois desperation at the prospect of capitalism hurtling down its pre-ordained path to self-destruction. This is Trotsky's comment on Roosevelt's New Deal reform package of 1936: 'The New Deal represents . . . a special form of political perplexity . . . . The objective prerequisites for the proletarian revolution have not only "ripened"; they have begun to get somewhat rotten'.[47] Such an analysis may comfort and reassure the faithful but it hardly adds up to a serious assessment of a most important political development; indeed, it hinders such a possibility.

Of course, it would be naive not to appreciate the extent to which 'reforms' have shored up the legitimacy of bourgeois rule; to argue that is not, in itself, fundamentalist. Our complaint is more with the mechanistic manner in which such assessments are translated into exact 'scientific' propositions, disguising some exceptionally un-sophisticated political calculations. Another appropriate example is provided by Trotsky in a text contemporaneous with *The Transitional Programme*: 'The disintegration of capitalism has reached extreme limits, likewise the disintegration of the old ruling class. The further existence of the system is impossible.'[48] The scenario sketched out by Trotsky at the time can be summarised as follows. Capitalism was *incapable* of further expansion and was already beginning to enter decline, the basis for reformism had gone, and the communist parties were now reformist. The only alternatives were either socialism or barbarism (fascism) – either revolution and the mass participation of working people, or the growth of totalitarian regimes. Literal readings of *The Transitional Programme* have, not surprisingly, severely dogged the development of Trotskyist theory since the Second World War. For example, the pre-conference manifesto of the Fourth International in 1946 boldly proclaimed: 'There is no reason whatever to assume that we are facing a new epoch of capitalist stabilisation and development. On the contrary, the war has acted only to aggravate the disproportion between the increased productivity of the capitalist economy and the capacity of the world market to absorb it.'[49] By April 1948 the evidence for a post-war boom was undeniable, and only a newly arrived extra-terrestrial being could have failed to see it. Yet the document adopted by this year's congress was able to state without any apparent embarrassment that 'The April 1946 conference correctly analysed the changes brought about by the second imperialist war.'[50]

Our point is not that the initial analysis and subsequent reassessment were wrong-headed – though that is manifestly true, for 'the system as a whole has never grown so fast for so long as since the War – twice as fast between 1950 and 1964 as between 1913 and 1950 and nearly half as fast again as during the generation before that.'[51] Rather our point is that a certain dogmatism so pervades some variants of Marxism that an almost permanent barrier is set up between reality and analysis. Dubious and dramatically overdrawn estimations are made on the slenderest of evidence, and either wishful thinking or easy blame-mongering takes over from careful calculation.

*Predestined class objectives*
The present recession of world capitalism ironically has seen some fundamentalists less prepared to assert that 'the end is nigh'; rather they have acknowledged that the 'outcome of this crisis . . . depends on the *political* preparedness of the working class.'[52] Consequently, working-class leaderships emerge as the villains of the piece for failing to prepare their troops. As Bullock and Yaffe characteristically put it: 'We must have no illusions on this score. The greatest barrier to building a revolutionary movement in Britain today is the fact that large numbers of workers and the leadership of the working-class movement remain committed to a reformist solution to the crisis.'[53] Such an argument rests on a simple assumption: there is an inherent

socialist instinct 'running in the very blood' of the proletariat such that, if they are left to their own devices, and given the ripeness of economic circumstances, socialism will be assured. Trotsky, for example, notes that 'no matter how the methods of the social betrayers differ . . . they will never succeed in breaking the revolutionary will of the proletariat.'[54] Yet, of course, this revolutionary will only exists if the proletariat is properly led (i.e. by a revolutionary leadership steeled in Marxist science), so the masses can hardly be 'straining at the leash'. Again it is far easier to lay blame on the betrayals of reformist leaders than to face the fact that these leaders, for the most part, accurately reflect the sectionalist, nationalist, chauvinist, economistic and often racist beliefs of their members. Such arguments also enormously under-estimate the complex of factors which explain why socialist ideas have poor support in Britain. These arguments should not be taken as a recipe for despair. On the contrary, our argument is that socialists have to give far more subtle thought to how strategic interventions can be calculated to facilitate a fracturing of such ideas.

Simplistic accusations of class betrayal severely under-estimate the necessary tasks facing socialists. In particular, they fail to come to terms with the intricacies of contemporary forms of class struggle (see chapter 6) by celebrating the struggles of the male, skilled working class to the exclusion of any real concern for, or understanding of, the struggles of women, blacks and the poor. The dangers in this have been astutely noted by Sumner:

> If one froze the current scene and transformed (in the imagination) the unevenly and hierarchically developed western working class of today into a post-revolutionary proletariat, then we would have the foundation for the development of the kind of oppressive, racist, illiberal, sexist, corrupt and divided society that we see today in the socialist bloc.[55]

In the context of contemporary British politics the argument that the existence of the Labour Party diverts working-class aspirations from desirable and class-based goals simply over-estimates the sway of that Party. It fails to account *materially* for why the Party in its present form exists, and why reformist illusions are so widely found in the British working class. Instead it takes an easier intellectual posture – that the working-class movement has an implicit desire for socialism but evil men and women consistently lead it up the garden path. Panich provides a representative example: 'The function of the Labour Party . . . consists not only of representing working-class interests but of acting as one of the chief mechanisms for inculcating the organised working class with national values and symbols and in restraining and reinterpreting working-class demands.'[56] We do not wish to be misunderstood. We are more than aware of the often reactionary role of labourist politics and Labour politicians,[57] but believe these are not so much causes as symptoms of much deeper structural factors accounting for the conservatism of the British working class.

### Vanguardism and the frontal assault theory of revolution

Debates on the left, as we have suggested, have tended to become frozen into a 'reform–revolution' dichotomy. It almost seems as if this simple and oppositional set of connotations so constrains the 'grammar' of the left that no one can ever envisage anything other than a compulsive return to old ground. Most socialist thinking is governed by simple oppositions: power is there to be *either* managed *or* seized; socialism is *either* public ownership combined with bureaucratic planning by state officials, *or* an insurrectionary seizure of power by a workers' vanguard party; and so on. On the Marxist revolutionary side of this divide certain unproblematic assumptions can govern the questions of both how the break with capitalism will be made, and how socialism will actually be constructed after that initial break.

With reference to the former question, many socialists (following Lenin) argue that the bourgeois state must be entirely destroyed through frontal attacks, establishing dual power in the form of workers' councils (soviets) in order to supplant and eventually replace the old state apparatus. Such an understanding can lead to a highly dismissive attitude to any advances achieved by working people, and other forces, through democratic and social rights. For unlike in Marx's writings on actual political developments, the institutions of representative democracy, and civil and social political freedoms, are *reduced* to simple emanations of the bourgeoisie. Yet as Poulantzas noted in his last book:

> If we understand the democratic road to socialism and democratic socialism itself to involve, among other things, political (party) and ideological pluralism, recognition of the role of universal suffrage, and extension and deepening of all political freedoms . . . then talk of smashing or destroying the state apparatus can be no more than a mere verbal trick. What is involved . . . is a real permanence and continuity in the institutions of representative democracy – not as unfortunate relics to be tolerated . . . but as an essential condition of democratic socialism.[58]

For fundamentalists, though, talk of 'smashing or destroying' the state is far from verbal trickery. Lenin argued that state power *is always* the power of some class; Marx and Engels had previously described it as the dictatorship of a ruling class. Lenin explained this concept thus:

> Dictatorship is rule based directly upon force and unrestricted by any laws. The revolutionary dictatorship of the proletariat is rule won and maintained by the use of violence by the proletariat against the bourgeoisie, rule that is unrestricted by any laws. This [is a] simple truth, a truth that is as plain as a pikestaff to every class-conscious worker . . . which is beyond dispute for every Marxist.[59]

Self-evident it may be to some, but far too many important questions are brusquely swept aside if such an analysis is rigorously adhered to in advanced capitalist societies. Some of the most important of these are touched on in the following extract from a fascinating interview with Nicos Poulantzas by Henri Weber, a leading member of the French section of the Trotskyist Fourth International. Poulantzas tried, in this interview and elsewhere, to outline a possible 'third way' between the polarities of reform and revolution – an exercise that we shall be attempting to fill out in the next chapter. He suggests:

> NP:  My hypothesis may be wrong, but I think yours is totally unrealistic.
>
> HW:  Every revolutionary hypothesis seems unrealistic (to you).
>
> NP:  More or less, and everything depends precisely on that nuance.
>
> HW:  (sarcastically)
> There was nothing more unrealistic than the Bolshevik hypothesis in 1917, the Maoist hypothesis in 1949, the Castroist hypothesis in 1956!!!! To be realistic is always to be on the side of maintaining the status quo . . .
>
> NP:  Don't forget that being unrealistic has often led to disasters and bloody defeats . . . . In reality, your hypothesis is not based solely on an evaluation of the objective possibilities of a revolutionary crisis in France. It is also based, implicitly, on the possibility of the extremely rapid and powerful development of a revolutionary party of the Leninist type, to the left of the French Communist Party . . . . But I do not think that this is at all likely . . . . First, because of . . . the new reality of the state, the economy, the international context, etc. And then because of the weight of the political forces . . . . Your hypothesis implies that the Ligue Communiste Revolutionnaire (French section of the Fourth International) will grow from 7000 militants to ten or twenty times that number in a few months. That's never happened anywhere . . . (in a post Second World War context).[60]

And, even more important than the question of how the revolution will occur, Poulantzas also hints at the inherent dangers of smashing the state and replacing it with direct democracy for the actual construction of socialism:

> What I'm afraid of is that behind your 'rooting of power in work-communities' there lurks in reality the restoration of the power of the experts; in other words that you would escape the dictatorship of the

leadership of the single party only to fall captive to the discreet charm of technocratic despotism.[61]

## A simplistic vision of a future socialist society

Marx and Engels may have accused other socialists of utopianism, but without doubt Katsenellerboigen is correct to remark of their own understanding of the construction of socialism that they were the real 'romantics on this issue . . . . The classical scholars of Marxism conceived of future society as a system in which everything would be obvious. People's goals would be obvious, as would the available resources for those forming them into products needed by the population.'[62] Certainly many of their contemporary followers can be similarly accused.

A socialist society will naturally be one which attempts to eliminate and/or severely control market mechanisms for deciding what will be produced, and how the produce will be allocated. But merely to state a belief in this is not to begin to contemplate the massive difficulties involved in making socialised and just allocative decisions. One technique for avoiding paying detailed attention to such issues is to assume that communism will generate super-abundance, and so remove conflict over resource allocation; there will simply be no mutually exclusive choice, no opportunity will be forgone and, magically, no opportunity costs will accrue. Yet it was one thing for Marx to attack Malthus in the 1840s for under-estimating the unused resources of the earth; it is quite another for contemporary Marxists to believe that after the revolution citizens will be able to walk around socialised supermarkets taking whatever they need, whilst decisions about production (i.e. how the goods got there) are made without any mutually exclusive choices. As Foster-Carter has noted: 'Abundance is out; arguably it was always a meaningless notion, but henceforth scarcity will have to be accepted as more than just a bug-bear of bourgeois economics.'[63] How, then, will production and allocation decisions be made? Criticisms of the highly centralised nature of planning in the USSR and other East European countries have usually ascribed their 'failures' to a lack of 'real' democracy or 'workers' power'. The argument is that if the present planners (bosses, elite, new ruling class)[64] were removed and 'the people' took decisions, then a sense of communality and social integration would overcome the basic economic problems. The Polish economic weekly *Zycie Gospodarcze* organised a discussion on the problems of the Polish economy, and this journalist's report suggests the meeting came to a similar conclusion:

> The discussion confirms that we are faced with the enormous problem of socialising the process of economic management, giving it an authentic

social character, surmounting any technocratic difficulties which will stand in the way of management by the people. Workers' self-management will be a huge step forward in this respect. It appeared that the nationalisation of the means of production was synonymous with their socialisation and so the whole problem was firmly in hand. It is clear now the problem is definitely *not* in hand. In my view one of the basic sources of conflict was that the process of socialising the means of production was frozen. A bureaucratised, purely formal workers' self-management could not give rise to genuine control. A return to creating a role for workers in economic management creates . . . the possibility of solving the most difficult problems of the economy and so too of creating the basis for overcoming social difficulties.[65]

The really telling section of this quotation is the stress in the first sentence on 'the *enormous problem* of socialising the process of economic management'. Many can share – in rhetorical terms – the desire for a society in which there is 'effective participation of the masses in the elaboration and execution of plans',[66] in which 'the people', 'the direct producers', 'the workers', 'society' decide, but there are enormous technical difficulties of both an economic and political character to be squarely faced if such a goal is to be achieved. First, we have to recognise that neither socialism nor communism will witness 'a withering away of the state'; on the contrary, they will experience a necessary extension of the state's tasks. How, for example, will an egalitarian system of social security be established which is not centralised in some way? Second, planning for socially decided *use* does imply, however distasteful it may be to some, a *centralising logic*. If one gives production units 'real' control, i.e. real autonomy from the central plan to decide what they produce, how will effective coordination occur? Rubin was surely correct when he implied that 'if there is independence or autonomy of separate enterprises, then the transfer of products can *only* occur in the form of purchase-and-sale.'[67] Non-market (non-commodity production) methods of decentralisation are very easy to talk about, but present enormous problems for effective achievement in practice, as the experiences of Yugoslavia, Hungary, China, Cuba and others testify. Third, just what will the relationship be between the multifarious varieties of direct democracy spawned in the revolutionary process – factory based, community based, nationally based, locally based – and how do we *guarantee* there is no degeneration into the rule of a single party? We shall return to these questions in the final two chapters; our point here is that the asking of such questions cannot be dismissed as mere faint-heartedness.

Fundamentalist Marxists too often have a most irresponsible attitude towards these and other technical problems concerning transitional strategies to socialism. It is, we repeat, easy to talk of non-commodity production and decentralised workers' control, but how in practice are the two to be reconciled? Socialism will only be created in advanced capitalist societies if convincing practicable answers can be supplied. Such answers will not be generated by theory impregnated by wish fulfilment. In our opinion George and Manning, in their otherwise excellent study of welfare in the Soviet Union, exhibit just such an indulgence when trying to utilise the framework of O'Connor's *The Fiscal Crisis of the State* to explain the nature of the Soviet state and social policy. They argue:

> O'Connor's three types of state expenditure reveal the comparative limitations of social policy under capitalism. But Soviet social policies are in addition determined by a clear ideological commitment to develop a socialist way of life . . . which has no parallel in the West. . . . The crucial role of socialist ideology . . . creates an additional fourth category of state expenditure . . . one of 'social needs'.[68]

However sympathetic one might be to the general drift of their argument that 'the public ownership of the means of production and distribution and the socialist/communist nature of the dominant ideology of the Soviet Union make the fulfilment of the "social needs" function more possible than under capitalism',[69] it is a gross oversimplification to exclude the possibility of any 'social needs' being met by social policies under capitalism. It is a theoretical solution which begs too many questions, and looks entirely suspicious to those not yet convinced that planned socialised economies do meet human needs more adequately than capitalist ones.

## Theoretical excesses of fundamentalism

Marxist theoretical accounts of welfare have tended to be obsessed by the grand ambition of presenting working models of large social totalities. In these exercises 'much of the discussion' has 'tended to be indirect – a by-product of thinking about such questions as changes in the capitalist economy, the nature and role of the state in bourgeois societies'.[70] Marxist thinking on these and other issues, as we have already partly seen, can suffer both from *economic reductionism* and from *functionalist* forms of argument. It is instructive to explain in more detail what is meant by these two terms.

### Economic reductionism
We have already discussed the fact that many commentators believe that classical Marxism understood the relationship between the economic base and the superstructure in an economically reductionist manner. In other words such phenomena as political events were conceptualised as mere reflections of underlying, inexorable economic

processes. This is what is meant by a reductionist argument: one phenomenon (i.e. the political activities of the state) is reduced to another (the underlying economic logic of the system).

Economic reductionism has long plagued the development of Marxism; it led Marx himself, near the end of his life, in response to some particularly crude examples from some of his followers, to assert that he was not a Marxist! Similarly Engels wrote, in an oft-quoted passage:

> The *ultimately* determining element in history is the production and re-production of real life. More than this neither Marx nor I have ever asserted. Hence if somebody twists this into saying that the economic element is the only determining one, he transforms that proposition into a meaningless, abstract, senseless phrase. The economic situation is the basis, but the various elements of the superstructure – political forms of the class struggle . . . constitutions . . . juridical forms . . . the reflexes of all these actual struggles in the brains of the participants, political, puristic and philosophical theories, religious views . . . also exercise their influence upon the course of historical struggles and in many cases preponderate in deter-mining their *form*. There is an interaction of all these elements in which amid the endless host of accidents (. . . things and events whose intercon-nection is so remote or so impossible of proof that we can regard it as non-existent . . .) the economic movement finally asserts itself as necessary.[71]

The issue here is not whether Marx or Engels (or anyone else) was an economic determinist, but the fact that classical Marxists and their predecessors can be seen to experience considerable difficulty in ascer-taining the precise relationship between economic structures and political and ideological factors. It will be helpful to explore two clear examples of this.

The first, which we came across earlier, is the tendency amongst some Marxists to reduce the activities of the state to economic deter-minations by regarding it as a mere instrument of the dominant economic class. This instrumentalist view of the state encounters many obvious difficulties, not least of which are how to explain the variety of forms that the capitalist state can take, and why it apparently pursues certain policies seemingly opposed to the dominant class's interest. The second example compounds the first, for it involves ascertaining just what are 'class interests'. Understood in an economically reductionist manner, classes are categories of economic agents who either possess or are separated from the means of production. Yet, of course, classes also exist as *political* agents. Clearly it is a crude fundamentalist account of socialist politics that reduces class interest purely to some given economic interests of the working class. And, of course, various contributors to a Marxist theory of politics – Lenin, Gramsci and Mao – were more than aware of this.

Yet if the sphere of politics has an independence and vitality separate from economic determinations, just what is its nature and extent?

Althusser, the contemporary French Marxist, has attempted to resolve this difficulty by rejecting the conventional understanding of the relationship between the base and the superstructure. His argument is that this very imagery has to be rejected as it inevitably conjures up visions of a listless superstructure having life breathed into it by an all-powerful economic base. He argued that the economy can *never* exist in the pure form implied by this imagery. An economy simply will not work unless elements of the superstructure continuously intrude into its workings. In other words, elements of the superstructure must function as *conditions of existence* for economic processes, as in the following example: 'It is clear that the analysis of the buying and selling of labour power in which capitalist relations of production exist . . . directly presupposes . . . considerations of the formal legal relations which establish the buyer (the capitalist) as much as the seller (the wage labourer) as legal subjects.'[72] The relations of production can only be understood in relation to superstructural forms that surround them (in this example, legal relations) as so many *conditions of their own existence*.

Althusser's reconceptualisation of the mode of production suggests it is better understood as consisting of a number of distinct 'practices'. This term designates particular forms of productive activity by which the total social formation is produced and transformed. There are principally three such 'practices' – economic, political and ideological – each constituted by elements which provide each other's conditions of existence. *Economic practice* is production and reproduction of the material means of subsistence, and of the specific historical and economic production relations. This practice is constrained by the development of the productive forces and the form taken by the relations of production. However, the generation of the means of production is not the only determinant of the form the society, or the total social formation, will take. *Political practice*, producing the 'mutual relations' of social groups, their forms of organisation and the subsequent relationships of dominance and subordination, and *ideological practice*, producing subjects occupying positions within the social totality, also have to be accounted for.

These political and ideological practices (conditions of existence for the mode of production) are *not* determined by the economic practices. They exist, however, within certain limits as their basic role is to help reproduce the principal economic practices. For Althusser economic practices determine, but only 'in the last instance'. The other practices follow their own logic – or, as Althusser puts it, they are 'relatively autonomous' of the economic practices. This formulation potentially offers an escape from crude economic determinism for, according to the precise historical moment, crises can occur within and/or between the political, economic and ideological practices as specific economic contradictions are *over-determined* by others.[73] No longer need politics and ideology be conceived as super-structural supports produced by the economic base, nor politically need they be understood to change slavishly as the economic base is revolutionised. Althusser's reformulation allows for much more sensible explanations as to why certain ideologies – for example, sexist and racist ideologies in the USSR and China – continue to exist despite economic transformations. His work has drawn attention to the *totality of conditions* required for the continuous reproduction of the whole social formation, and this has galvanised Marxists into engaging with many previously neglected topics – notably women's oppression, domestic labour and the family, the importance of ideological struggle and, of course, welfare provision and the welfare state. The concept of reproduction, however, carries with it certain potential dangers when used without due care and attention – the dangers of engaging in functionalist forms of analysis. What do we mean by this?

### Functionalist forms of analysis

In short, we mean that it is all too easy to assume that 'everything' – women's oppression, racism, welfare provision – *functions* merely to buttress further the existence of capitalism. An explicitly functionalist analysis of the role of one of the social services, for example public educational provision, would proceed something like this. Compulsory state-provided education fulfils certain functions for capitalism: the implantation of discipline and the work ethic into future labour market recruits and citizens; a rationale for inequality; legitimation of capitalist values and rule; and so on. This last 'function' is, of course, infinitely elastic. It could equally well be argued that education performs quite different functions – for example, 'disenchantment with the social order' – or the same functions but much less efficiently. Certainly many adolescents develop oppositional subcultures at school which can hardly be conducive to the effective elimination of potential political opposition. Some commentators have argued that this latter experience prepares young working-class people to accept the vagaries and hardships of labour markets and low-status work, anything being preferable to more time in school.[74] Yet as Westergaard has suggested: 'Even such "cooling out" could hardly be the product of some rational calculation of this imponderable benefit for capital against the costs of talent wastage, indifferent commitment to work and grumbling discontent. The untidy social realities of the outcome are surely part "dysfunctional" for capital.'[75] Functional analysis is too neat and tidy, appearing superficially plausible but revealed as deeply suspect after more careful thought.

Critical, and Marxist-influenced, social science ironically has spent a great deal of intellectual energy criticising functionalist forms of analysis, particularly the structural functionalism of writers such as Talcott Parsons. Parsonian arguments could be summarised thus:

1   Society must be seen as a *bounded*, self-regulating *system*, tending towards homeostasis and equilibrium.
2   This organism-like, self-maintaining social system (society) must have certain basic needs or *prerequisites*, which must be *guaranteed* if *survival*/homeostasis/equilibrium is to be maintained.
3   Sociological analysis, in order to reveal the essence of the system, must focus on *the function* of parts in meeting the needs of the whole, and hence in maintaining equilibrium and homeostasis.
4   Certain types of *structural arrangements* must exist to ensure that the needs are met, and survival continues uninterrupted.

Whilst this is not the place to enter into the long history of functionalist sociology, it is important to note how a particular, highly sophisticated conservative functionalism – the *functional imperativism* of Talcott Parsons – came to dominate post-war American and British social theory. In his view, if *any* social system is to operate at all, four basic conditions have to be met or four basic problems solved. These four conditions or problems are termed functional imperatives or prerequisites: adaptation to the environment; goal attainment; pattern maintenance; and tension management and integration. The first two deal with conditions and demands from outside the system, whereas the latter two are focused more on the internal maintenance of social values. To solve these problems and so maintain existence, any society has to have four major structural features: Parsons's subsystems of the economy, the polity (politics), kinship, and community and cultural organisations. The particular form these subsystems adopt in any society is influenced by the underpinning value system. Ultimately for Parsons the cement of his functional edifice is the normative structure or, put more simply, the sets of expectations embedded in roles.

Parsonian sociology was to suffer at the hands of many critics, Marxist and non-Marxist alike. Dahrendorf, in a representative *tour de force*, argued that Parsons's system (a) reveals no real developmental history, (b) displays over-concentration on consensually shared values, (c) claims far too high a degree of integration amongst its components, and (d) concentrates only on mechanisms that preserve the status quo. Such a social system was, for Dahrendorf, a mere utopia with no essential appreciation of ubiquitous phenomena like conflict or deviance, and where mechanisms for explaining social change were conspicuous by their absence.[76] On these substantive questions Parsonian functionalism, and the varieties of radical sociology and Marxism that have cut their teeth opposing it, are poles apart. The latter insist on the inevitability of conflict, and are steeped in developmental history. But the *logical* criticisms of Parsonian functionalism seem to have a real pertinence for those theorists described above as Marxist functionalist.

The first, and major, logical criticism of functionalism is its tendency to *teleological* reasoning. Barrett explains this term in a general tirade on the inadequacies of functionalism:

> Aside from the generic difficulty of establishing the imputed 'function' of a particular social process, there is the tendency to assume that any such function, once established, can explain the very existence of that process. This is the error of 'teleology' – the view that the explanation of an object lies in a search for its *original 'purpose'*. It precludes the possibility that no purpose, or function, is relevant to our understanding, and it also precludes the possibility that the function an object now has is different from one it may have previously had.[77]

Not only, then, is teleological reasoning ahistorical; it also implies that some future consequence of an event causes that very event to occur. It should be easy to see that Marxist reasoning can also easily be dogged by the pitfalls of teleological reasoning. Indeed, the similarities between certain forms of Marxism, with their obsession with simple *reproduction*, and functionalism should be obvious by now to the reader. For the system, it is often argued, just endlessly reproduces, cloning itself in an endless orgy of similitude. It is too easy, for example, to claim that the explanation for a particular social policy, and its material and ideological effects, rests *only* with the function that it performs for the reproduction of the overall society or the dominant social force within it. This is partly because it is not altogether clear just what contribution is made by any particular social policy; or put another way, were the policy and its effects not to have been implemented and another policy pursued, or none at all, the society would presumably still have been reproduced! If this argument is conceded we must be most careful in stipulating whether a functional requirement of ensuring social reproduction actually manages to *explain* the particular practice under examination. For if we are not careful, we may have implied a possible future consequence as an explanatory cause.

The second logical criticism of functionalism is that it is prone to *tautological* or 'circular' reasoning. For example, Parsons's hypothesis of functional unity can easily be reduced to a tautology unless careful documentation is engaged in specifying how various cultural items actually promote instances of both integration and malintegration.

Any system under study must by definition be reasonably integrated; therefore, elements that are part of that system *must* promote its integration. To discover the converse would prove most difficult. There is an obvious *non sequitur* in such reasoning. Yet we have already seen how over-zealous, and not very careful, usage of the term 'reproduction' in Marxist discourse can produce exactly that result.[78]

## The state revisited

It is instructive to complete this exploration of theoretical problems presented by fundamentalism by returning to our discussion of the state, and by examining in detail how recent Marxist theories of the state suffer from some of these problems. It is now commonplace to classify such theories of the state into at least three broad categories.[79] At the beginning of this chapter we largely followed a *legitimation-crisis* theory of the state, based on the work of O'Connor; the focus of attention was on the number of crisis tendencies which are necessitated by the state's expansion of functions. Whilst we would not wish to absolve such theories of criticism (see below), we do believe they contain more insights than any other neo-Marxist analysis of the welfare state. Yet O'Connor's influential *The Fiscal Crisis of the State* is clearly rife with functionalist argument, as this passage all too clearly indicates:

> The need to develop and maintain a 'responsible' social order also has led to the creation of agencies and programmes designed to control the surplus population politically and to fend off the tendency toward legitimisation crisis. The government attempts to administer and bureaucratise . . . not only the monopoly sector labour–management conflict, but also social–political conflict emerging from competitive sector workers and the surplus population. The specific agencies for regulating the relations between *capital* and organised labour and unorganised workers are many and varied. . . . Some of these agencies were established primarily to maintain social control of the surplus population (e.g. HEW's Bureau of Family Services); others serve mainly to attempt to maintain harmony between labour and *capital* within the monopoly sector (e.g. the Bureau of Old Age and Survivors' Insurance). In both cases the state must remain independent or 'distant' from *the particular interests of capital* (which are very different from the *politically organised interests of capital* as the ruling class). The basic problem is to win mass loyalty to insure legitimacy; too intimate a relation between *capital* and the state normally is unacceptable or inadmissible to the ordinary person.[80]

It is implicit in O'Connor's position that the state is both 'relatively autonomous' of straight economic determination and of the direct political machinations of the ruling class. Yet specifying the *precise* political class interests of the bourgeoisie does present him with difficulties. His solution to this problem both in the quoted passage above and more generally is to adopt what Elster has described as an 'implicit three-tier structure of capital interests: (1) the interest of the individual capitalist out to maximise profits come what may; (2) the interest of the capitalist class, which may have to curb the individual's greed, and (3) the interest of capital, which may have to dissociate itself from class interests to ensure legitimacy.'[81] Hardly surprisingly, any state action, including social policies which imply a tacit challenge to capitalist practice and values, can be potentially viewed as functional to capital on this sliding scale of interests; for they can be explained as boosting legitimacy. It is literally impossible to conceive of anything *not* functional for capitalism, other than an immediate working-class insurrection.

The other two major Marxist approaches to the state – the class political (Miliband and Poulantzas) and the state derivationist (Müller and Neususs, and Alvater) – equally well suffer from theoretical difficulties, albeit different ones, but share a similarly pessimistic assessment of social policy. The *class-political* position is so described because the state is conceptualised as in principle abstracted from capital accumulation. In other words, the state's actions are identified with a particular political role in which its central problem is to resolve class conflict. Theoretically such an approach should avoid economic determinism, yet in practice Miliband's early instrumentalist version certainly did not.[82] He argued that the state – owing to the common cultural and economic interests between the ruling class and the elite running the state's affairs – acts as a willing instrument of that ruling class. Poulantzas, in a debate with Miliband,[83] considerably improved the class-political position, largely by establishing that the state is capitalist not because of affinities between subjects inside and outside of it, but *necessarily* owing to objective structural compulsions. Moreover, he argued, the ruling class should be perceived not as monolithic but as subject to divisions which the state helps resolve. His own theory understands the state as a distillate of the relations between the struggling classes of labour and capital. The state's actions depend therefore on the balance of class forces.

Again, as with O'Connor, economic determinism is avoided, but it is equally difficult to comprehend just how 'relatively autonomous' political processes are from those determinations. The state has to secure the capitalist nature of the society in question, and to achieve this it has to organise the contradictory interests of the ruling class into a political coherence whilst simultaneously disorganising the political actions of the working class. This is accomplished through the state providing conditions for the establishment of a successful power bloc, composed of the various fractions of the dominant class and *ultimately* acting under the control of monopoly capital. The economic may govern 'in the last instance', but this was surely never intended to mean that monopoly capital's political interests rule 'in the last instance'. Moreover, Poulantzas's argument that the state is functional for maintaining overall social cohesion within the social formation suffers from undeniable traces of functionalism, and phrases such as 'the cohesion of the ensemble of the levels of a complex unit, and as the regulating factor of its global equilibrium as a system'[84] read almost as tortuously as a Talcott Parsons text. Also, Poulantzas's bizarre habit, following Althusser, of counting most factors contributing to this cohesion – from the family to the trade union to the Church – as part of the state, makes one fear that there is a dangerous over-emphasis on the smooth reproduction of bourgeois dominance, at times bordering on the paranoid. This would certainly seem applicable to Poulantzas's views on social policy:

> It is impossible to over-emphasise the fact that the various 'social' measures taken by the welfare state with respect to the reproduction of labour-power and the field of collective consumption are at the same time geared to *police-political* management and control of labour-power. The realities are by now well known. Social welfare structures, unemployment relief networks and job-placement bureaux; the material organisation of 'social' housing space . . . ; asylums and hospitals – all these are so many political sites where legal-police control is exercised over labour-power.[85]

Our third, and final, state theory – the largely German *state-derivationist* one – is even more uncompromising than the other two in its dismissal of the possibility that the state is utilisable for 'gains' by the working class within capitalism.[86] The initial work of the state derivationists was indeed explicitly concerned with criticising the work of the crisis-legitimation school – Habermas and Offe in particular – for not specifying the absolute limits of political reformism. Müller and Neususs, in a contribution whose title encapsulates their argument – *The Welfare State Illusion*[87] – suggest that these reformist illusions have been fostered by elementary errors in theorising about the state, thus providing 'the basis of all revisionism'. The first of these is to regard the state as independent of production and its economic laws, and as existing to engage in independent political interventions to modify distributional problems. The second error was the belief that these political interventions could then be employed to alter fundamentally the cyclical and crisis-prone course of capitalist production. For Müller and Neususs the state *must* guarantee that commodities are produced within the framework of 'the capital relation'. It is this that is the prime rationale for state intervention, not those secondary activities aimed at modifying distributional problems. Thus the development of the capitalist state is due not to general requirements in modifying contradictions in the development of a complex politicised economy (as for the crisis-legitimation school), or to the necessity of politically organising the ruling class and disorganising the under-classes (as for the class-political school), but to the need to guarantee the capital relation, and capital's general interests, by interventions into the very laws of motion of capitalist development. As these alter over time, so the scope and nature of state intervention must also alter.

Although this had led to some interesting work on the periodisation of capital's 'needs',[88] there are nevertheless some real theoretical problems with this approach. First, there is an explicit functionalism, dramatically illustrated by another contributor to the school – Altvater.[89] His argument, similarly to Müller and Neususs, suggests that the state emerges because a 'special institution, outside bourgeois society' becomes necessary to guarantee certain conditions for the existence of capital in general. This institution has to fulfil certain 'prerequisites' – further shades of Parsonism – which individual capital units cannot perform, e.g. the determination and protection of the legal system. Second, there is an exceptionally severe distinction drawn between 'reform and revolution', premised upon a most naive and essentialist understanding of class interests. This can be best explored by examining Müller and Neususs's account of the British nineteenth-century Factory Acts. We should hardly be surprised that their account is explicitly concerned with resisting any interpretation of these reforms as representing the gradual advancement of 'socialist' goals within a capitalist society. For them these Acts had a number of highly functional consequences for British capital – in particular, the tutoring of working-class interests into reformist habits. Individual workers are incapable of defending their collective interests, so the state *has to* encourage the very organisation of the working class, albeit within reformist limits, to guarantee continued commodity production. Yet these very same workers – incapable of effectively resisting exploitation – are capable, if only the 'welfare illusion' could be broken, of advancing towards socialism! The 'welfare illusion', however, will only be broken when the state ceases doing what it *has to* do!

What this account, as with so much other fundamentalist literature, ignores are the actual *experiences* of the working class. Whatever the 'illusions of reformism' are, they must surely be derived from the fact that as a result of defending itself the working class does see the state as 'neutral', because that is how on occasions it actually appears to act. 'The state does act against individual capitalists, and this does benefit each individual possessor of labour power.'[90] In state-deriva-tionist theory, working-class experiences and interests are ridden over and recycled; social policies are, yet again, viewed with cynicism and suspicion: 'The development of revisionism in the workers' movement depends crucially on the experience of "social welfare" legislation enacted by the bourgeois state, . . . which makes it seem possible for capital to be gradually transformed by the means of the state apparatus.'[91]

## Status of welfare reforms

Just what is the status of social policy legislation for Marxist commentators? Judged from the majority of accounts we have examined so far, the answer seems simple: 'social policy remains essentially an instrument for preserving the status quo';[92] 'the welfare state is capitalism disguised by window dressing.'[93] In short, a reformed welfare capitalism is just a giant illusion. Certainly when Marxists are engaged in constructing formal systems there appears to be an emphasis upon reproduction and continuity. Such theoretical tendencies are reinforced in some commentaries by variants of fundamentalist politics which perceive welfare measures as always accruing long-term benefits to the ruling class. However, once Marxist commentators descend from macromodel construction and wrestle with actual empirical, historical events – such as the enactment of the NHS or the Factory Acts – there is a greater willingness to concede that welfare reforms can be delivered in a *placatory* or *anticipatory* manner. As Jones and Novak put it: 'It is, of course, the pressure and threat of class conflict, the direct and indirect challenge of labour to its continued subordination under capital, which remains the motive force of history, and it is through these struggles that social policy and state formation have taken place.'[94] There is a willingness to concede the role of *class struggle*, the importance of *strategic* responses to structural determinations, with subjective class interests and action being granted a greater significance. Indeed, when we examine both detailed accounts of historical welfare enactments and certain strategic writings, there is the glimmer of a recognition that welfare reforms may not always result in gains for capital in general.

It is, for example, worth while pondering upon these two very different assessments by Marxist scholars of the post-1945 Labour government's 'reforms':

> Welfare reforms, just as much as the nationalisation of the mines and the railways, actually facilitated the smoother running of the capitalist economy, and were in no way in conflict with the interests of power groups in private industry, so that on the whole they were tacitly if not openly welcomed, even by many in the Conservative Party, as improving the chances of industrial and social peace. . . . The welfare reforms of the 1940s

were not particularly dramatic . . . yet they were greeted as an essential part of the 'socialism' that was supposed to have been born, and continued for many years to be described as 'revolutionary'.[95]

It can be seen that the reforms of 1945 embodied a socialist *potentia*, which was not only nourished by ideal influences (the thought of Marx, of Morris, and of socialist utopians: the strategies of the British Socialist and Communist Parties) but whose *partial realisation* was fleshed by actually existent socialist values and practices within the working class community. . . . Hence this socialist *potentia* may be seen simultaneously as an *immanent actuality* and as an aspiration.[96]

The first quote – from Elizabeth Wilson – typifies a widespread position amongst Marxists, appropriate described as a capital-needs or *capital-logic* explanation of welfare reforms. The second, from Edward Thompson, is most likely to evoke sympathy when discussing detailed historical occurrences or strategy, and is best labelled the *populist* or labour-demands account. In our view, neither is entirely accurate, and their juxtaposition highlights the uneasy tension between Marxist theory and political practice – between formal abstract models and actual political events. E.O. Wright has attempted to reconcile, in a theoretical model, the complex interactions between the developing economic and political structure of capitalism and the dynamic effects of continuing class struggle.[97] Ian Gough in a seminal contribution has used a similar framework to try to account for the state's introduction of welfare reforms.[98] His theory suggests that social policies are due to the resolution of tension generated by

the degree of class conflict, and especially the strength and form of working-class struggle and the ability of the capitalist state to formulate and implement policies to secure the long-term reproduction of capitalist social relations. It is highly likely that the respective importance of each varies over different policy issues. For example, the fact that higher education is most developed in the US suggests that direct working-class pressure has not been crucial in bringing about the growth of tertiary education since the war. On the other hand, the absence of housing and comprehensive social assistance policies there, by comparison with Europe, suggests the introduction of these owes a great deal to the existence of unified labour movements.[99]

Gough modifies one of Wright's diagrams as shown in figure 4.1. This *compromise* position – social policy as a fusion of capital's needs with labour demands – is obviously a vast improvement on the other two, particularly as Gough is sensitive to the actual empirical impact of welfare provision on the capitalist economy. By trying to ascertain empirically the answers to two simple questions – who pays the taxes, and by what criteria are social benefits distributed – he is able to venture specific answers to the crucial questions of whether welfare

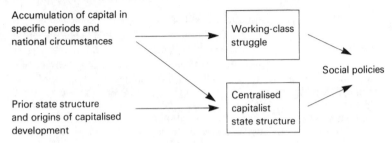

Figure 4.1 *The interaction between capitalism and class struggle*
*Source:* I. Gough, *The Political Economy of the Welfare State* (Macmillan, 1979), p. 68

policies predominantly benefit labour or capital. As he states: 'Generally speaking, the impact of welfare policies on capital accumulation will be more favourable the more they are paid for by taxes on labour rather than capital, the more they follow market criteria in distributing and awarding benefits, and the more closely are social and economic policies integrated.'[100]

The compromise position, however, should not be embraced uncritically. There is a real danger that 'class struggle' will merely be inserted into accounts in a formal manner, as a gesture. As Elizabeth Wilson has argued:

> A generalised idea of 'class struggle' remains somewhat empty. It cannot deal with the feminist critique of welfare provision . . . which raises uncomfortable problems for those who seek to stress the role of working-class demands as determinant in securing welfare reforms, as inherently progressive, since the class struggle that obtained the Factory Acts and the Beveridge Plan could certainly not be said to have operated in the interest of women who were in both cases defined as home-bound individuals dependent on a male breadwinner.[101]

Not only does this quotation force us, yet again, to recognise the difficulties faced by Marxist commentators in ascertaining the precise nature of so-called class interests – in this case, just how do considerations of gender intrude – but it also highlights the absolute necessity of paying detailed attention to empirical events. Such attention would force us to recognise the framework's apparent neglect of competition between different sections of the working class, and failure to ascertain the potentially ambiguous status of the 'new' middle classes. The skilled working class politically organised to resist the intrusions of a welfare state in the late part of the last century and the early years of this; whereas the 'old' petty bourgeoisie would have resisted higher taxation, the 'new' petty bourgeoisie are often state welfare workers themselves and, for the most part, support the extension of state services.

The potential problems with this approach are, though, even more fundamental than this. Harris, in an interesting overview of the compromise position, has argued that throughout many periods state welfare provision has benefited both labour and capital. The fact that the compromise argument appears to be able superficially to explain this fact disguises two deeper problems. First, 'to say that both labour and capital benefit from welfare services is not the same as *explaining why* those services have developed at a particular stage of capitalism,'[102] or indeed why they took *the form* (e.g. public not private) that they did. But second, and of even more significance, is the fact that the adoption of the compromise position does not necessarily resolve arguments between populist commentators (Thompson) and capital-logic commentators (Wilson). As Harris puts it:

> There is a tendency which, instead of explaining developments, looks back from the present and assumes that everything that has happened in the past to the present *had* to happen. . . . this . . . can reinforce a simple teleology by interpreting historical information in a way which suggests that the balance of needs and demands was always inevitably right for the policies that happened.[103]

Harris cites five writers who can possibly be classified as working within a compromise framework: Ginsburg, the CSE State Group, Gough, Dorothy Thompson and Saville.[104] The first two, he suggests and we agree, emphasise the needs of capital to such an extent that they occupy a position not dissimilar from the capital-logic school. Thompson, as with her namesake, is a populist, seeing the welfare state as an extension of working-class values. Saville is an eclectic, never specifying the precise mechanisms whereby the needs of capital are balanced with the demands of labour. Gough (argues Harris), despite good intentions, is also never really able to specify this relationship.

Harris accuses Gough of 'a serious confusion over the nature of the dichotomy between structure and action'.[105] By this he is referring to how the consciously organised struggles of classes (action) relate to the anonymous, largely economic forces that shape the social formation without reference to the conscious actions of classes or other agents (structure). In other words, we are back with the problem of agency and structure that we described earlier in the chapter. The implication of our argument then was that Marxist theory in relation to welfare has often concentrated too much on structural determinations, the result being a paucity of attention to agency and action. Whatever else this debate about the origins of the welfare state involves it indicates a serious attempt, within Marxist discourse, to grapple with these problems of agency. Harris's criticism of Gough in particular and the compromise position generally is that 'the questions it poses are questions about the *actions* of different classes; . . . the framework concerns *only* class conflict, action theory.'[106] In other words, anonymous structural determinations are at best underplayed, and at worst ignored. For as Harris states: 'The markets for labour, commodities and finance do impose their own constraints upon the development of the economy, the state and other aspects of society, and they would do so in an anonymous way even if trade unions, employers, traders and bankers did not play any organised political role on those markets.'[107] In short, Harris is accusing Gough of an over-concentration on 'purely political mechanisms', of being too obsessed with 'action theory' – and weak action theory at that. Whilst we would agree that political action/agency issues have been poorly theorised by Marxist discourse, we are less convinced that a return to the terra firma of anonymous economic structural determinations is the correct way forward *for scholars of welfare*. Harris seems himself to partially recognise this when he states: 'I am not suggesting that market forces are all that matters, that we should commit the error of concentrating upon structure instead of action.'[108] Yet he has nothing of real interest to say about the latter, other than the need to 'account for finer divisions of social groups – fractions of classes', hardly an original point. Moreover, he definitely privileges the resolution of anonymous economic determinations over all other determinations, as one might expect a Marxist economist to do.

Such assertive privileging is not at issue in many areas of study. However, in the field of general state expenditure, never mind welfare itself, how does such a position allow one to explain why Swedish or Danish capital requires almost half of national income to be channelled through the state sector, whilst American and Swiss capital only requires one-quarter? In regard to welfare itself, why is medical care predominantly privatised in some countries and largely socialised in others? We need a theory that is able to appreciate that what we are faced with, to quote John Clarke,

> is not the simple unfolding of some unidirectional historical logic, guided by the unerring hand of capital, but of new initiatives by capital, changing the conditions and forms of resistance from within labour, requiring new 'solutions from capital' and the state. . . . It is a permanently contradictory process of class struggle [involving] a variety of hidden and informal dimensions.[109]

Such permanently contradictory processes require a great deal of thought to be applied to action/agency issues. An adequate analysis of welfare under capitalism, of course, also has to explore the parameters established by structural economic constraints; however, there is a real danger with Harris's contribution of reinforcing a disparaging, capital-logic assessment of welfare provision. At one point he accuses the compromise school of being unable to explain international differences in welfare provision. Are we to assume that this can be done by ascertaining international differences in the structures of markets for labour, commodities and finance? Analyses which privilege such determinations are always prone to relegating 'action' questions to the theoretical margins; the only real advice for Marxists concerned with welfare is to soak themselves in Marxist economics! Of course, a Marxist analysis of welfare must trace all the interrelationships between the private accumulation of profits and the provision of welfare; but it must not exclusively concentrate on tracing the shapes to which the private capitalist economy is able to bend welfare policies and provision. Any dialectically aware critical social scientist has also to concede that social policies, broadly defined, *can* shape capitalist societies – and in significant ways.

## Conclusion

A number of issues should have become clearer in the course of this chapter. First, whilst Marxist analyses can be regarded as a useful corrective to the more over-optimistic assumptions of some Fabian commentators, there is a constant danger of excess through overly deterministic and pessimistic theorisations. This applies particularly to those analyses informed by what we have described as crude or fundamentalist politics. Second, those socialists who share our disdain for fundamentalism are faced by three choices. They can reject Marxism out of court; they can seek security in sophisticated analyses of those questions that Marxist theory has traditionally tackled; or they can attempt to develop Marxism both as an intellectual system and as a guide to political practice. Those that pursue the second course will, in our opinion, be unable to contribute *anything* to the study of welfare that is not saturated in cynicism. They may *wish* to make welfare an object of Marxist discourse, but are never able to address fully the necessary questions for fear of being accused of being the new Fabians. Our choice is the third – to try to develop certain key insights of Marxism both theoretically and politically. It is to this task that we now turn.

## Notes

1   See, for example, R. Mishra, *Society and Social Policy* (Macmillan, 1977); N. Ginsburg, *Class, Capital and Social Policy* (Macmillan, 1979); C. Jones and T. Novak, 'The state and social policy', in P. Corrigan (ed.), *Capitalism, State Formation and Marxist Theory* (Quartet, 1980).

2   J. O'Connor, *The Fiscal Crisis of the State* (St James Press, 1973).

3   I. Gough, *The Political Economy of the Welfare State* (Macmillan, 1979), pp. 44–5.

4   I. Gough, 'The crisis of the British welfare state', *International Journal of Health Services*, 13(3), 1983, p. 468.

5   C. Cockburn, *The Local State – management of cities and people* (Pluto Press, 1977), p. 56.

6   E. Wilson, *Women and the Welfare State* (Tavistock, 1977), p. 9.

7   S. Hall, 'Culture, the media and the "ideological effect"', in J. Curran, M. Gurevitch and J. Woollacott (eds), *Mass Communication and Society* (Edward Arnold and the Open University Press, 1977), p. 325.

8   L. Althusser, *Lenin and Philosophy and Other Essays* (New Left Books, 1971).

9   P. Golding and S. Middleton, *Images of Welfare: press and public attitudes to poverty* (Basil Blackwell and Martin Robertson, 1982), p. 48.

10   N. Poulantzas, *Political Power and Social Classes* (New Left Books and Secker and Warburg, 1973), pp. 195–224.

11   The Beveridge Report, Cmnd 6404, p. 52.

12   Report on Inquiry into the Brixton Disorders, 10–12 April 1981, Cmnd 8427 (HMSO, 1981), p. 11.

13   Ibid., p. 64.

14   S. Hall, 'The lesson of Lord Scarman', *Critical Social Policy*, 2(2), 1982, pp. 66–72.

15   M. Barker, *The New Racism: conservatives and ideology of the tribe* (Junction Books, 1981). See also P. Gordon and F. Klug, *New Right: New Racism* (Search-light Publications, 1986).

16   E. Wilson, *Halfway to Paradise – women in post-war Britain: 1945–1968* (Tavistock, 1980), p. 189.

17   S. Cohen, *Visions of Social Control – crime, punishment and classification* (Polity Press, 1985), p. 2.

18   P. Conrad and J. Schneider, *Deviance and Medicalisation – from badness to sickness* (Mosby, 1980), p. 8.

19   G. Stedman-Jones, 'Class expression versus social control? A critique of recent trends in the social history of leisure', *History Workshop*, no. 4, 1977, p. 164.

20   J.R. Hay, 'Employers' attitudes to social policy and the concept of social control, 1900–1920', in P. Thane (ed.), *The Origins of British Social Policy* (Croom Helm, 1979), pp. 108–9.

21   C. Offe, 'Some contradictions of the modern welfare state', *Critical Social Policy*, 2(2), 1982, p. 12.

22   O. Newman, *The Challenge of Corporatism* (Macmillan, 1981), p. 126.

23   Gough, *The Political Economy*, p. 14.

24   P. Lee, 'The welfare state: capitalist fraud or working class victory?', *Socialist Review*, 16 (Nov./Dec.), 1979.

25   Mishra, *Society and Social Policy*, p. 62.

26   T. Campbell, *The Left and Rights – a conceptual analysis of the idea of socialist rights* (Routledge and Kegan Paul, 1983), p. 194.

27   R. Luxemburg, *Social Reform or Revolution* (Young Socialist Publication, 1966), p. 34.

28   A. Cawson, *Corporatism and Welfare: social policy and state intervention in Britain* (Heinemann, 1982).

29   F. Engels, *The Housing Question* (Lawrence and Wishart, 1936), p. 98.

30  V.I. Lenin, *The State*, in *Collected Works*, vol. 29 (Lawrence and Wishart, 1971), p. 485.

31  P. Corrigan, H. Ramsey and D. Sayer, *Socialist Construction and Marxist Theory* (Macmillan, 1978), p. 10.

32  See E.P. Thompson, 'The peculiarities of the English', in R. Miliband and J. Saville (eds), *The Socialist Register, 1965* (Merlin, 1965), pp. 311–62.

33  See B. Ollman, 'Marx's Vision of Communism; a reconstruction, *Critique* no. 8, 1978.

34  For a more detailed treatment of these issues see B. Smart, *Foucault, Marxism and Critique* (Routledge and Kegan Paul, 1983).

35  F. Claudin, *The Communist Movement: from Comintern to Cominform* (Penguin, 1975), p. 108.

36  V.I. Lenin, 'Left wing' communism – an infantile disorder', in *Selected Works*, vol. 3 (Progress Publishers, 1971).

37  Claudin, *The Communist Movement*, p. 61 (our emphasis).

38  See L. Althusser, 'The crisis of Marxism', *Marxism Today*, 22(7).

39  For an interesting discussion of British Trotskyism see Big Flame's pamphlet *The Revolution Unfinished: a critique of Trotskyism* (1977). For an interesting feminist-inspired critique of certain British revolutionary groups see S. Rowbotham, L. Segal and H. Wainwright, *Beyond the Fragments: feminism and the making of socialism* (Merlin, 1979).

40  P. Anderson, *Considerations of Western Marxism* (New Left Books, 1976), pp. 100–1.

41  See G. Hodgson, 'On the political economy of socialist transition', *New Left Review*, 133 (May/June), 1982, for a similar discussion.

42  P. Hain (ed.), *The Crisis and Future of the Left* (Pluto Press, 1980), pp. 63–4.

43  L. Trotsky, *The Death Agony of Capitalism and the Tasks of the Fourth International – the transitional programme* (1938)(New Park Publications, 1970).

44  D. Coates, *Labour in Power* (Longman, 1980), pp. 170–1.

45  Hodgson, 'The political economy', 1982, p. 55 (original emphasis).

46  A. Glyn and R. Sutcliffe, *British Capitalism, Workers and the Profits Squeeze* (Penguin, 1972).

47  Trotsky, *The Death Agony*, p. 12.

48  L. Trotsky, quoted in Claudin, *The Communist Movement*.

49  'The new imperialist peace and the building of the parties of the Fourth International', resolution of the international pre-conference of the Fourth International, printed in *Workers International News*, Nov.–Dec. 1946, quoted in D. Hallas, 'Building the leadership', *International Socialism*, series 1, no. 40, 1969, p. 27.

50  *The World Situation and the Tasks of the Fourth International*, June 1948.

51  M. Kidson, *Western Capitalism Since the War* (Penguin, 1970).

52  P. Bullock and D. Yaffe, 'Inflation, the crisis and the post-war boom', *Revolutionary Communist*, no. 3/4, November 1975, p. 40.

53  Bullock and Yaffe, 'Inflation', p. 1.

54  L. Trotsky, quoted in Claudin, *The Communist Movement*, p. 79.

55  C. Sumner, 'The rule of law and civil rights in contemporary Marxist theory', *Kapitalstate*, no. 9. 1981, p. 88.

56  L. Panich, *Social Democracy and Industrial Militancy* (Cambridge University Press, 1976), p. 260.

57  See R. Miliband, *Parliamentary Socialism* (Merlin Press, 1972) for a classic critique of labourism.

58   N. Poulantzas, *State, Power and Socialism* (New Left Books, 1978), p. 261.

59   V.I. Lenin, *The Proletarian Revolution and the Renegade Kautsky*, in *Collected Works*, vol. 33, p. 236.

60   N. Poulantzas (interview by H. Weber), 'The state and the transition to socialism', *International*, 4(1), 1977, p. 10.

61   N. Poulantzas, interview, p. 8.

62   A. Katsenellenboigen, *Studies in Soviet Economic Planning* (Sharpe, 1978), p. 123.

63   A. Foster-Carter,'Neo-Marxist approaches to development and under-development', in E. de Kadt and G. Williams (eds), *Sociology and Development* (Tavistock, 1974), p. 93.

64   See B. Deacon, *Social Policy and Socialism – the struggle for socialist relations of welfare* (Pluto Press, 1983), for a discussion of the differences between these characterisations of the leading strata in such societies.

65   Quoted in G. Balzya, *Planning is Good for You: the case for popular control* (Pluto Press, 1983), p. 28.

66   C. Bettelheim, quoted in A. Nove, *The Economics of Feasible Socialism* (George Allen and Unwin, 1983), p. 29.

67   I. Rubin, quoted in Nove, *Feasible Socialism*, p. 30.

68   V. George and N. Manning, *Socialism, Social Welfare and the Soviet Union* (Routledge and Kegan Paul, 1980), p. 183.

69   George and Manning, *Socialism*, p. 183.

70   Mishra, *Society and Social Policy*, 2nd edn (1982), p. 75.

71   F. Engels, 'Letter to J. Bloch, September 1890', in K. Marx and F. Engels, *Selected Correspondence* (Progress Publishers, 1965), p. 417 (original emphasis).

72   L. Althusser and E. Balibar, *Reading Capital* (New Left Books, 1970), pp. 177–8.

73   For a useful account of Althusser's concept of over-determination see A. Callinicos, *Althusser's Marxism* (Pluto Press, 1976), chapter 2.

74   See P. Willis, *Learning to Labour – how working class kids get working class jobs* (Saxon House, 1977).

75   J. Westergaard, 'Welfare, class and distributive justice', in P. Bean and S. MacPherson (eds), *Approaches to Welfare* (Routledge and Kegan Paul, 1983), pp. 48–63.

76   R. Dahrendorf, 'Out of utopia', in his *Essays in the Theory of Society* (Routledge and Kegan Paul, 1968).

77   M. Barrett, *Women's Oppression Today* (Verso, 1980), p. 25.

78   For a highly technical but fascinating debate on Marxism and functionalism, see J. Elster, 'Marxism, functionalism and game theory', *Theory and Society*, 11, 1982, pp. 453–97. There are replies from G. Cohen, Berger and Offe and Giddens, amongst others.

79   For an interesting overview see B. Jessop, *The Capitalist State* (Martin Robertson, 1982).

80   O'Connor, *The Fiscal Crisis*, pp. 69–70.

81   Elster, 'Marxism', p. 463.

82   R. Miliband, *The State in Capitalist Society* (Weidenfeld and Nicolson, 1970).

83   See N. Poulantzas and R. Miliband, 'The problem of the capitalist state', in R. Blackburn (ed.), *Ideology and Social Science* (Fontana, 1978) for an edited version of the debate.

84   Poulantzas, *Political Power*, pp. 44–5.

85   Poulantzas, *State, Power and Socialism*, p. 186.

86  For a collection of state-derivation writings see J. Holloway and S. Picciotto (eds), *State and Capital – a Marxist debate* (Edward Arnold, 1978).

87  W. Müller and C. Neususs, 'The welfare state illusion', in Holloway and Picciotto, *State and Capital*, pp. 32–9.

88  For a most interesting contribution to this see E.O. Wright, *Class Crisis and the State* (New Left Books, 1978), chapter 3.

89  E. Altvater, 'Some problems of state interventionism', in Holloway and Picciotto, *State and Capital*, pp. 40–2.

90  J. Urry, *The Anatomy of Capitalist Societies* (Macmillan, 1981), p. 90.

91  Müller and Neususs, 'The welfare state illusion', pp. 34–5.

92  Jones and Novak, 'The state and social policy', p. 161.

93  N. Furniss and T. Tilton, *The Case for the Welfare State* (Indiana University Press, 1977), p. 67.

94  Jones and Novak, 'The state and social policy', p. 161.

95  Wilson, *Women*, p. 147.

96  E.P. Thompson, 'An open letter to Leszek Kolakowski', *Socialist Register*, 1973, p. 54.

97  Wright, *Class, Crisis*, chapter 1.

98  Gough, *The Political Economy*.

99  Ibid., pp. 64–5.

100  I. Gough, 'Thatcherism and the welfare state', *Marxism Today*, 24(7), 1980, p. 10.

101  E. Wilson, 'Marxism and the welfare state', *New Left Review*, 122, 1980, p. 87.

102  L. Harris, 'The state and the economy: some theoretical problems', in R. Miliband and J. Saville (eds), *Socialist Register, 1980* (Merlin, 1980), p. 247.

103  Harris, 'The state and the economy', p. 248.

104  N. Ginsburg, *Class*; J. Saville, 'The welfare state: a historical approach', *New Reasoner*, no. 3, 1958; D. Thompson, 'Discussion: the welfare state', *New Reasoner*, no. 4, 1958, pp. 127–8; CSE State Group, *Struggle and the State* (CSE Books, 1979).

105  Harris, 'The state and the economy', p. 255.

106  Ibid., p. 255 (our emphasis).

107  Ibid., p. 257.

108  Ibid., p. 259.

109  J. Clarke, 'Capital and culture: the post-war working class revisited', in J. Clarke, C. Critcher and R. Johnson (eds), *Working Class Culture – studies in history and theory* (Hutchinson, 1979), p. 249.

# 5
# The Politics of Social Policy

Mass unemployment is not a fatality, a necessary effect of 'anonymous and evil forces' of contemporary capitalism – it is an inherent potentiality of capitalism. But without the willing or unconscious support or strategic acceptance of right-wing politicians and economic advisers and of faint-hearted or weak-willed social democrats, and sometimes of starry-eyed trade unionists, credulously buying the liberal arguments, high unemployment could have been staved off.

Göran Therborn

This chapter sets out to clarify the political and theoretical disagreements within Marxist accounts of welfare. It argues that if these approaches are to make any long-lasting impact on the study and implementation of social policy they have to be prepared to go beyond *critique*, and to offer more than an account of the general pattern of and contextual parameters to social policy under capitalism. They have to develop a concern with and make a contribution towards *strategic* questions concerning policy development and socialist advance. In short, what is underdeveloped in Marxist discourse about welfare matters is a *politics of social policy*. In order to clarify exactly what is meant by this, three broad political perspectives derived from Marxist theory are outlined – the traditional, the prefigurative and the realist.

## Moving beyond context

Marxist scholars of welfare undoubtedly offered an alternative and theoretically imaginative response to post-war Fabian, over-optimistic assessments of both the reasons for and the achievements of welfare expansion. As we have seen, though, their own contributions were not without problems or disagreement. The largest of which was a tendency to veer towards one or the other of two mutually exclusive interpretations of the origins of welfare reforms, 'some regarding it as a functional response to the needs of capital. . . . Others see the welfare state as the unqualified fruits of working-class struggle, as concessions wrung from an unwilling state.'[1] Whilst the compromise position allowed for an apparent resolution of this conflict, it was one that left sharply differentiated political assessments, objectives and strategies unresolved. Not least of these was why, how and *what* to defend about the present welfare arrangements from public expenditure cuts. Ian Gough has suggested that the 'positive aspects of welfare policies need defending and extending, their negative aspects need exposing and attacking'.[2] This is an obvious enough solution, but one which is insufficiently attentive to the fact that some might see as negative what others regard as positive! The former's judgement will be based on the fact that these reforms merely sow illusions about the ability of the state to overcome the contradictions of capitalism and fulfil human needs. On what terms is such an assessment to be made: relief of immediate suffering, or the prospects for long-term political change? This is a particularly acute choice for workers, influenced by socialist ideas, employed by the state.

On one issue though, all Marxist commentators can agree – that of *contextualising* welfare arrangements in the wider changes occurring within the processes of capitalist production and reproduction. Piven and Cloward capture the essence of this: 'The key to an understanding of relief-giving is in the functions it serves for the larger economic and political order, for relief is a secondary and supportive institution.'[3] It follows that Marxist economists with no real interest in social policy could have a great deal to contribute to its study by offering analyses of the contextual membrane within which the distributive conflicts of social policy are played out. An excellent example of this is Glyn and Sutcliffe's text *British Capitalism, Workers and the Profits Squeeze*, written in the early 1970s, which revealed 'startling facts about the recent decline in the rate of profit on capital and the share of profits in the national income'.[4] Yet, as should be obvious to the reader by now, capital accumulation might be a necessary starting point for analyses of social policy within contemporary capitalist societies; it is not, however, a sufficient one.

No contemporary Marxist commentator on welfare doubts this, and key *theoretical* disagreements – as we saw in the previous chapter – revolve around explanations of both the origins of the state's political interventions, and the precise relationship between the state and the capital accumulation process in general and the capitalist class in particular. The capital-logic school came closest to an economically reductionist position in accounting for the expansion of state regulation as a direct effect of changing needs in the accumulation process itself; the welfare state was seen as nothing more than a political response legitimating certain overt injustices and supplying a disciplined and trained workforce. Similarly the class-political school, despite conceding the possibility of the relative autonomy of political practices from the accumulation process, maintains that even with a socialist government the state will merely protect capitalist social relations. This type of theory has tended to produce one of two types of *political* strategy for welfare – a traditional politics and a prefigurative politics.

## Traditional politics

One possible political conclusion to be drawn from much of the Marxist theoretical work on welfare, particularly when it is tinged by fundamentalism, might be that social policy is such a secondary activity – concerned only with distributive issues – that to get too embroiled in its study would be positively misleading. For such a preoccupation would detract from the really important questions concerning the international contradictions of capital accumulation, the effects on national economies of the internationalisation of banking capital, and so on. Certainly the majority of Marxist scholars appear to adopt such a position, and part of the response we saw Harris make to Gough in the last chapter reflects it: 'If economic market forces are an important structural force within which the actions and policies of different classes are constrained, a political campaign around the subject of the welfare services *will not succeed* if those structural forces maintain their constraints.'[5] Of course, Marxist theory has to privilege such structural forces, but Marxists interested in welfare have to be able to offer more than just an assessment of the *contextual constraints* to social policy. It is vital to contribute to discussions of *policy analysis* – of why particular policy options occurred and not others – if for no other reason than to be able to offer *prescriptive* advice, in the here and now, on the type of political demands that should be pursued by tenants' groups, workers in the health service, and so on. Suppose your starting point for immediate political intervention is something like the following:

> The possibility of securing a fundamental shift in the structure of class inequality in favour of the working class through administrative and policy reform or working-class political struggle is severely constrained by the essential form and functions of the state as a capitalist one, which boils down to the reproduction of the relationship between capital and labour.[6]

Then such advice very likely is going to be limited to avoiding constitutional channels, or to steeling oneself for disappointment! As Harris implies, socialist political campaigns around welfare issues become pointless, for they will *not* succeed.

Another problem with this sharp privileging of capital accumulation over political interventions is that it mirrors the conventional bourgeois separation of the study of social policy from that of economics. Zsuzsa Ferge, a Hungarian expert in social policy, urges the necessity for socialist theorists to perceive the interconnectedness of 'all aspects of social life' through the study of *societal* policy. Alan Walker uses the similar term 'structural social policy':

> first, to signify that economics cannot be separated from the politics of the society in which it operates; second, to recognise not only that economic policies and economic management cannot be disassociated from their social effects, but also that they embody social objectives; third, to provide the basis for planned social development; and fourth, when coupled with socialist values, to realise the goal of socialist welfare.[7]

For the traditionalist this last political goal is utopian, unless of course the productive infastructure has been revolutionised. The political key for achieving this end is to encourage working-class activity, often narrowly defined, to engage in revolutionary political acts to overthrow the state. Marxists interested in social welfare can write critiques of the status quo welfare arrangements, but any political activity other than this purely *intellectual* task should be devoted to separate and more important questions. These largely revolve around traditional trade union forms of struggle, and the building of a revolutionary socialist party. Of course, given the traditional manner in which economic policy is separated from social policy, traditionalist arguments that essentially 'social' struggles are doomed to failure contain some (albeit blinkered) good sense. Our point – developed below – is that socialists have to extend the scope of 'social' considerations into, and beyond, those aspects of social policy spuriously labelled 'economic'. This effectively means interventions into restructuring the labour market, reward and taxation structures, investment priorities and so on.

## Prefigurative politics

A second style of politics derivable from a theoretical critique informed by Marxist theory is best described as prefigurative. This response is equally pessimistic about the possibility of state-directed social policy developments limiting the systemic power of capital. As the authors of *In and Against the State* (*IAATS*) – the most popularised version of the prefigurative position – argue, the 'obvious lack of possibilities for reform, coupled with our eye-opening experiences of participation, have disabused us of hopes in gradualism'.[8] Nevertheless, the classical arena of reform – the state's social welfare responses – *are* regarded as important arenas for political activity. This was reinforced by the vital role that the women's movement played in the development of this new style of socialist politics.

Perhaps of even greater significance than *IAATS* was the publication
in the same year of the socialist-feminist text *Beyond the Fragments*.[9]
Dale and Foster are undoubtedly correct in their assessment that this
book 'sent ripples through the socialist movement with [its] argument
that the insights of feminism could form the basis for a new kind of
organising for socialism involving a movement of autonomous groups
around a broad political programme'.[10] Large conferences were
organised around the ideas in these two texts, largely attended by
people in 'welfare work', enthusiastically reinforcing a belief that they
were on the threshold of implementing a 'new' socialist politics of
welfare – an alternative to both Fabianism and Marxism with their
centralising, bureaucratic calculations focusing only on the structure
and distribution of public expenditure. This alternative was going to
encourage 'the fragments' from below in self-help activities so as to
promote real changes in the *social relations* between people – changes
in relations of dependency.

These adherents of a prefigurative politics retained, and indeed
added much to, the hard-edged Marxist-informed assessment of
welfare that we have described as the 'cynical gaze'. Certainly they
were suspicious of anything to do with reformist compromise; as the
*IAATS* authors put it, 'to pursue power by winning positions of
influence for the working class *within the terms of the state form of
social relations* is mistaken'.[11] 'Things are as they are', they argued,
largely due to the old errors of reformist compromise, and the
illusions that this has bred in the state's ability to deliver effective
solutions to the problems faced by the working class. Historical
analysis teaches us all this, and also draws our attention to the fact
that 'things could have been different'. Consequently, the prefigurativists are able to escape the pessimistic pronouncements generated by
their own theories by throwing themselves enthusiastically into
activist politics around welfare issues, always stressing the role of
forms of activism *marginalised* or *ignored* in the past. They reappraise
the past, appropriating lessons for future guidance in struggle.

We should not under-estimate the importance that this reappraisal
has had on the broad left in Britain. First, they certainly did point to
a largely ignored constituency in the history of socialist struggle –
women – and further recognised the importance of autonomous black
politics. Second, they privileged practical experience in struggle and
living one's politics in 'the here and now' (prefigurative politics).
Third, they stressed the need to struggle around questions of social
reproduction and social welfare, and to build on people's actual
experience – hospitals closing, bureaucratic treatment at the benefits
office and so on. The services were, after all, 'our' services but were
delivered in ways that seemed 'to limit our freedom, reduce the control

we have over our lives'.[12] In this sense, they were certainly contributing to a *socialist distributional politics*. Finally, they utilised this stress
on experience to engage in a swingeing attack on fundamentalism
generally and on the idea of a socialist seizure of power in particular:
'It is not surprising that there are not more adherents to a politics
based on the concept of the "once-upon-a-future" seizure of state
power. This way of thinking doesn't seem to bear on the problems of
everyday choice which we face as socialists *within* the state'.[13]

Yet, despite being made to feel uncomfortable by 'a politics which
pins everything on the seizure of state power',[14] and being sceptical
about the possibility of overnight change, they were equally clear that
there was no possibility of the transition to socialism 'being made
without revolution'.[15] And despite their stress on the problems faced
by socialists within the state, they offer very little in the way of real
strategic advice for state employees actually working as social
workers, health workers or whatever on day-to-day practical matters.
Rather they are highly critical of traditional forms of trade union
activity for such groups, and place much greater importance on the
vitality of a disparate range of grassroots struggles, pressure groups
and social movements. Militant activism outside workplace hours,
reminiscent of the anti-organisational libertarianism of the 1960s, is
offered with no real critical appreciation of the key problems of such
strategies: overcoming fragmentation and localism; developing city-
wide and nation-wide campaigns; and, most crucially, how to deal
with the *inevitable presence* of the state and, as they would see it, the
inevitable offer of concessions that will draw activists into its social
relations.

We are still left largely with critique, and one particularly directed
at the state's welfare provision. 'State provision leaves a bad taste in
our mouths. State institutions are often authoritarian, they put us
down, tie us up with regulations.'[16] There are some useful hints as to
what state workers can do in the here and now in a chapter entitled
'Oppositional possibilities now'. However, defending the right of
women to have separate hospital facilities; discussing how a group of
education welfare officers were able, by meeting away from their
superiors, 'to recognise that truancy is not a problem that arises in the
home or in the child, so much as a problem for the school, created by
the school';[17] and forming joint public transport groups between
workers and consumers, whilst all very laudable initiatives in
themselves, hardly amount to a 'new strategy for socialism'. Undoubtedly such activities are important, but it seems a little grandiose to
suggest that all such struggles 'challenge the capital relation and its
state form, and they do so by prefiguring socialist organisation within
the struggle itself'.[18] Certainly *In and Against the State* takes the

strategic politics of welfare much more seriously than many other Marxist-derived texts, but the analysis is based on pessimistic assumptions about what is possible, despite a certain populism (bordering on romanticism) about forms of resistance entirely untainted by statism. Indeed, a characteristic of prefigurativist politics seems to be a rather uneasy combination of romanticism and cynicism: intellectually recognising the naivety of traditional Leninist politics, but unwilling to accept that one has no choice but to engage in socialist politics *on the terrain of the state.*

Bob Deacon, in *Social Policy and Socialism – the struggle for socialist relations of welfare*, has attempted to develop many of these prefigurative ideas and apply them to both the study of and the struggle for a socialist social welfare. He is in no doubt that prefigurativism holds out the possibility of breaking politically with 'the reform–revolution dichotomy' and establishing 'a third view. . . that is neither a matter of merely democratically changing the state "from above", nor smashing the state "from inside", but transforming the state apparatus through struggle from within'.[19] Yet Deacon, even more than the *IAATS* authors, seems firmly wedded to a revolutionary politics. He is quite clear that the various visionary struggles, pressing for popular decision-making and control, have to recognise 'the necessity of overcoming capitalism if their vision is to be realised', and a 'revolutionary socialist party political organisation can be defended as the agency'[20] to effect this. This is the sharpest disagreement within the prefigurative camp. Both (despite the protestations of some) are revolutionary, but one seems to reject the idea of the revolutionary party whilst the other embraces it. Neither really contributes a great deal to our thinking about strategies or political struggles *within* the state. Indeed, Deacon's political pessimism extends so far that even his major political hope – the localised prefigurative struggle – is severely doubted. For all too easily it could become 'no more than a new form of provision capable of being co-opted into, or permitted to run alongside, the predominant state welfare form of service. (An example here might be a well women clinic that supplements but does not challenge local patriarchal medicine.)'[21]

The most refreshing aspect of Deacon's text lies in its recognition that most critical welfare texts have failed 'to indicate what socialist social policy might be' owing to their excessive concentration on criticisms of capitalism. He suggests that radical scholars can learn from the social administration tradition the merit of posing detailed empirical questions, and accordingly draws up a list of six *concrete* questions which are used to establish what an 'ideal' socialist social policy *ought* to look like:[22]

1   What priority would be afforded to social welfare provision within a socialist society, and what resources would be available to satisfy the priority?
2   What form of control over institutions of welfare might be established within a socialist society?
3   What would be the balance between the state, the market, the workplace, the community and the family in the provision of social welfare?
4   What might become of the existing relationships between users, providers and administrators of the welfare services?
5   What system of distribution and rationing of services might be developed?
6   What changes will have taken place in the nature of family life and in the sexual division of labour, and what impact would this have had on the forms of welfare policy and provision?

The answers he supplies to these questions are constructed from a fundamentalist reading of classical Marxism, combined with some recent feminist and new left writings. Two stages of goals are produced from this reading: the first establishes the criteria to be set for a social policy to be described as 'socialist', and the second establishes criteria whereby policies can be labelled 'communist'. These two sets of criteria are then applied to six 'existing' socialist societies – primarily China, Cuba, the USSR and Hungary, with 'snippets' about Mozambique and Poland. They are also used to examine the crucial question of what is 'needed to ensure the eventual realisation in Britain of socialist relations of welfare',[23] and therefore the question of the role of welfare struggles in socialist transition.

Hardly surprisingly, the standards expected of a communist social policy are most exacting, with massive ideological, political and economic changes envisaged. After socialism 'social policy would dominate economic policy and would become a matter of the realisation of human potential. . . because men and women would no longer be dominated by commodity fetishism';[24] under communism 'forms of living and housework would be communalised'[25] and 'all traces of professionalism and its converse, the experience of. . . dependence would have been eradicated.'[26] Moreover, the state will have withered away and 'the local community will predominate in the providing of services for itself'.[27] Exacting criteria indeed, and certainly we felt more convincing arguments were required to persuade us of the feasibility of some of them. For example, how could such democratic and egalitarian measures be effected without a centralised state mediating between competing local groups? The notion that sectional interest would simply vanish is hardly a convincing argument.

The criteria chosen for the half-way house of 'socialism' are surely of much greater importance in any attempt to contribute to debates about political strategy. These present 'a far more complex picture'.[28] For 'the central state will still be present'; 'the work–income connection would not yet be broken'; and 'the family would not yet have changed'.[29] For Deacon socialism must be judged by the extent to which it prepares the *preconditions* that have to be fulfilled for communism to be achieved: equalising access to education and culture; preparing for the involvement of all in democratic planning procedures; the entry of women on equal terms with men into the labour force; and so on. We are not surprised to learn that the developed 'already existing' socialist societies do not fare particularly well when these criteria are applied to their health, income maintenance and housing systems. The USSR and Eastern Europe fail to score even half marks by 'socialist' criteria, and record 'big zeros' by 'communist' ones! Indeed, the irony is – and it is a point that we develop below – some capitalist countries would score higher on the former criteria!

Moreover Third World 'socialist' countries fare rather better, despite there being 'something of a paradox'[30] about this. The way Deacon resolves this paradox reveals much about his thinking on the nature of the transition to socialism and the role of welfare struggles in this process. He argues that: 'The few apparent examples of socialist social policies that do exist in Eastern European societies. . . reflect the legitimation, labour discipline and allied needs of the ossified state bureaucratic or state capitalist regimes of those countries'.[31] By contrast, in certain Third World countries 'there is evidence that the socialist form of some welfare policies reflects the fact they were introduced in struggle either for liberation or against the problems of necessity'.[32] The paradox is answered by skilfully combining the two political themes which rest uneasily side by side within prefigurativism – romanticism and cynicism. The latter is taken so far as to condemn even the positive aspects of Eastern European social policy for merely reflecting the labour discipline and legitimation needs of the ruling elite. The former is embodied in the enormous stress placed on the importance of democratic controls from below, and the fact that it 'is the people, collectively and consciously transforming themselves and their circumstances, that are the productive force of socialism'.[33]

Now whilst such a combination does allow for some explanation of the Third World paradox, many other problems remain unresolved. The first of these is a general disdain of the complex technical problems associated with socialist transition that we discussed in chapter 4.[34] For example, Deacon concedes that deprofessionalised services in many Third World countries may reflect economic backwardness rather than conscious socialist choice. There is no real analysis of what role 'skills' will play during and after socialist transition, and, more importantly, of the limits to popular control over decisions on sensitive issues such as child-care or mental health. Second, in our opinion the problem of socialist transition is approached from the wrong way round. A check-list is established which has to be fulfilled, rather than rooting concern more firmly in actual struggles. This check-list mentality means there is little appreciation that transitional strategies for socialism, and the role that struggles around welfare play in them, may vary considerably even between similar types of society. It is as if there is one 'true' path and the role of theory is to make sure everyone sticks to it. Yet as Himmelstrand astutely notes:

> Concrete definitions of the kind of socialism adequate to a particular country must be explicated in terms of the *specific* ways in which productive forces are becoming more societal in that country . . . and in terms of the specific changes in productive relations. . . . The type of socialism adequate to that country cannot be formulated without a great deal of empirical research into the historical specificities of the forces and relations of production, the class structure and the superstructure of that country.[35]

Third, the volitional stress on 'what is always immediately politically possible' and 'democracy from below' rests uneasily with the pre-established check-list of agreed criteria. To parody, it appears that democracy is fine as long as the masses decide that which the theoreticians have already decided. Fourth, Deacon only ever partially meets his own requirement that a Marxist-inspired social policy should ask concrete 'ought' questions about welfare. Answers are sought within Marxist and feminist theory alone, and social democratic or Fabian approaches are dismissed as of little consequence. Yet a major weakness of much critical social policy, as we have seen, is the inability to satisfactorily distinguish those aspects of social policies that contribute to furthering working-class interests from those that do not. Len Doyal and Ian Gough have suggested that the only way that the positive aspects of welfare policies can be distinguished from their negative ones is by developing an adequate theory of 'human needs'.[36] Fabian-inspired theory has for many years been trying to address the problem of how human needs can be partially met in a rational manner within the confines of capitalism. Their solutions are often partial and theoretically inadequate, but the experience of that tradition cannot be dismissed as of no consequence.

Perhaps the most interesting part of Deacon's work is when he gets closest to discussing the living struggles facing socialists in Britain today – the problems faced by certain socialist local authorities in attempting to decentralise and, in a limited sense, control the exercise of professional power in their social services. The author points to a dialogue between those who suggest such changes 'can be prefigurative of socialism, and other socialists. . . who see these policies as undermining hard-won working conditions and weakening. . . trade unions'.[37] His own position is one of intense suspicion of the local authorities, betraying the prefigurativists' fear of any state initiative, even in its local guise. He also reveals a certain sympathy for those who, like the Socialist Workers' Party, argue under headlines such as 'Left Labour council bashes its workers' that: 'The councillors believe that decentralisation is a socialist proposal in itself, but how can it be if it is at the expense of the conditions of the council's workforce, and if they try to weaken union organisation in implementing it?'[38] So there is a negative response even to attempts at achieving the avowed goals of socialist welfare – at least when they are pursued in the 'here and now' by 'reformists'. He argues that this is due to the absence of a mass campaign in favour of these goals, and because the local councils lack a clear recognition 'of the need to get rid of capitalism if a socialist social policy is to be fully implemented'.[39] Both these observations beg huge questions. The first is that, in all honesty, such mass campaigns simply do not exist, despite the actions of various groups to create them. Local Labour parties have often been the *only* effective source of attempts to get mass support on such issues in recent years. The second is that the author does not really describe – and how could he, given his attraction to the theory that many of the 'socialist' countries are possibly state capitalist – *anywhere* that has effectively got rid of capitalism!

The last refuge of much Marxist theory lies, as we have seen, in the further development of more theory – *intellectualism*. This is precisely Deacon's solution to the 'decentralisation' dilemma. He writes: 'The dialogue is unconstructive. . . because of the *failure to think through* exactly what a desirable form of workers' control for social services might be'.[40] Of course clarity of thought is important, but resolution of this issue does not depend on it. It depends rather on the type of straightforward political choice that Marxist contributions to welfare debates are unused to making. Donnison, whom we cited in our introduction, accused Marxism of furnishing 'its associates with a very comfortable intellectual posture' as they never have 'to soil their hands with the compromises of reformist politics'. Despite Deacon's well-intentioned desire to avoid this accusation, his variant of prefigurative politics simply does not allow it.

We certainly would not like to be thought of as being dismissive of prefigurativist politics. Attempts to alter the *social* relations of a capitalist society by such means as, for example, workshops that privilege training for skilled jobs for women and black people, women-only forms of health provision, child centres that attempt to promote child-care as 'more than women's business' and so on, are integral to any future struggle for socialism in Britain. Our major criticism of much prefigurativism is the under-estimation by their advocates of the extent to which many of the schemes they favour rely almost entirely on local, and even national, state promotion and finance. This is an achievement not to be lightly dismissed at a time when the Conservative government is promoting, and right-wing elements in the Labour Party are accommodating themselves to, forms of welfare provided commercially, voluntarily or informally, i.e. by women's care in the home. State investment does not necessarily defuse the radical potential of far-sighted initiatives.

We would, nevertheless, wish to retain the visionary element of the prefigurativists; and we recognise that there is a danger of losing it in our argument for a more circumspect, realistic approach to socialist welfare strategy. Perhaps our argument is best expressed as a fusion of the more sanguine elements of prefigurativism with a more realistic assessment of the problems confronting the enactment of progressive structural change. Such a fusion seems to have been achieved already in the political practices of many socialist-feminist groups. Anna Coote and Bea Campbell admirably capture an apt description of the type of fusion we are looking for in the following extract: 'If we are seriously planning to transform society and liberate ourselves, we shall have to get in and swim. This doesn't mean abandoning our politics – but while we continue to organise separately and develop our own ideas and strategies, we must also carry the form and content of feminism into the mainstream.'[41]

### Realistic politics

Marxists have too often over-emphasised the compatibility of welfare reforms with the extended reproduction of capital; consequently, they have not only under-estimated the importance of such reforms for promoting the material interests of labour, but failed to recognise that some of these interests, albeit contradictory to those of capital, may *under certain circumstances* be realised *within* capitalism.[42] At root, this is the starting point of the realist's case. It is a position that has been developed most systematically in debates about welfare provision amongst Scandinavian scholars – particularly the work of Walter Korpi,[43] Ulf Himmelstrand,[44] Gøsta Esping-Andersen[45] and Göran Therborn[46] – although traces of similar political responses can be found in the Eurocommunist tradition,[47] in left variants of European social democracy and in some other recent Marxist writings. There are, of course, disagreements within this broad position, but it can be differentiated from the other two positions on four criteria.

First, realists take the politics of distribution seriously, and particularly the way that distributional conflicts are the subject of non-class-related variables (gender, consumption patterns, ethnicity, ideology etc.) as well as class-related ones. As Claus Offe has argued:

> The survival of capitalism has become increasingly contingent upon non-capitalist forms of power and conflict. Any labour movement that ignores this and avoids trying to make links with conflicts generated by consumers, clients, citizens or inhabitants of an ecosystem becomes solipsistic. . . . The crucial problem. . . is how to become more than a labour movement.[48]

Second, they display a concern for detailed *empirical* work around the changing *forms* of capitalist property and work relations – the nature, strength and manifestations of the respective classes' political power and mobilisation – and a keen interest in questions concerning the *comparative* development of the welfare state. These are precisely the types of question that need to be answered if we are going to be able to consider adequately the complex issues raised by Gough's 'either/ or' compromise position on the origins of welfare reforms. Third, such comparative studies breed a certain sensitivity to the variety of forms to which capitalism can adapt – the amazing elasticity of capitalism. For the realist some of these forms might be more *embryonic* (facilitate the eventual realisation) of socialist relations of production and welfare than others. We state the fourth criterion at the end of this section.

Esping-Andersen, in a paper whose title indicates the general drift of the realist position – 'Politics against markets'[50] – argues that the political effects of welfare state capitalism are much more contradictory and complex than fundamentalism allows. In another paper[51] he has distinguished between conservative, liberal and socialist 'ideal-type' welfare initiatives using four criteria: *stratification* (paternalism; self-reliance; universalism and solidarity); *programme organisation* (occupational/enterprise-based and status-differentiated insurance; voluntary social insurance; unified and comprehensive universal plans); *financial system* (large employer role; individual self-finance; dominant public role with progressive income tax); and *benefit structure* (occupational/status-differentiated; less eligibility criteria; benefits independent of contribution or ability to pay). He also classifies the 18 major OECD capitalist democracies according to the extent of working-class power mobilisation,[52] distinguishing five distinct patterns:

> In the first cluster (Sweden, Austria, Norway) we find countries in which the working class has maintained a high level of mobilisation and stable control

of governments in the post-war era (1946–1976). The second cluster includes countries in which working-class mobilisation has been high, but where political control of cabinets has been occasional (Denmark, New Zealand, United Kingdom, Belgium). The third cluster includes countries where working-class mobilisation has been medium to high, but where political control has been low (Australia, Finland, France, Italy and Japan). The fourth cluster (Germany, Netherlands and Switzerland) includes countries where working-class mobilisation has been medium to low, and where government participation has been partial. These countries, like the former cluster, also exhibit important religious and/or political splits within the labour movements. The fifth and final cluster includes countries where working-class mobilisation has been very low, and where it has been politically excluded (Eire, Canada and the United States).[53]

He goes on to examine, in a tentative way, the impact of this working-class power mobilisation on the development of the welfare systems of these 18 countries; in particular, their programme organisation, financial systems and the spread of means-tested social assistance and private schemes. From this investigation he concludes that some countries tend to be rather consistently 'liberal' and others consistently 'socialist' in programme organisation, and so on. From these evaluations he constructs the rough classifications given in table 5.1.

In a longer and more recent text, Esping-Andersen has clarified his earlier work on both the genesis of welfare state forms in the balance of class forces and the tripartite model of these forms.[54] The *conservative* model links selective welfare rights to occupation and status, financing welfare benefits out of an actuarially based scheme with corporatist forms of management. There is nothing egalitarian about its construction, despite sometimes extensive state involvement. It is found largely where the Church has played an important role in national social reform, and in those nations where absolutism was strongly established and difficult to erode. The commitment to full employment policies of these nations with conservative welfare forms – such as Japan, Italy, Belgium, France, Germany and, more surprisingly perhaps, Austria – varies depending on the barriers to left-wing political mobilisation and on the ability of Christian mass parties to resist liberal market principles with minimal social and economic planning. The *liberal* model provides limited welfare rights and/or means-tested benefits for individuals, financed largely out of private actuarial insurance or, for those unable to afford this, from general taxation after means testing. The commitment is to privatised, market oriented welfare with limited state expenditure on a minimum safety net social security system. Such regimes are associated with nations where the bourgeois impetus was very strong; here Esping-Andersen classifies the United States, Canada, Britain and Australia. These regimes, even when they make a formal commitment to the achieve-

Table 5:1   *A rough classification of 'Liberal/Conservative' versus 'socialist' type of stratification in the welfare state*

| | Liberal/ Conservative | Socialist | Unclear |
|---|---|---|---|
| Programme organisation, programme differentiation | Austria New Zealand Belgium Australia France Italy Japan Germany United States | Sweden (Norway) Denmark United Kingdom (Finland) | Netherlands Switzerland Ireland Canada |
| Financial system | Austria Norway United Kingdom Finland France Japan Germany Netherlands Switzerland United States | Sweden Denmark (New Zealand) (Australia) (Ireland) Canada | Italy |
| Role of means-tested social assistance | France Italy Japan Netherlands Switzerland Ireland Canada United States | Sweden Austria Norway Denmark (Belgium) Finland (Germany) | New Zealand United Kingdom Australia |
| Role of private schemes | Denmark United Kingdom Australia Japan Switzerland Canada United States | Sweden Austria Norway Germany Finland Netherlands | Belgium New Zealand France Italy Ireland |

ment of full employment, do so without the necessary political base and/or institutional framework to maintain this or other social objectives as a long-term goal.

The *social democratic* model is based on universal welfare rights attached to social citizenship, and is committed to wide-ranging egalitarian redistribution with high standards of public provision financed from general taxation. This model tends to be found in countries where there has been a relatively united and powerful working-class movement which has been able to form durable alliances with other class groupings – notably farmers in the past, and more recently the 'new' middle classes – and has been opposed by a weak or divided bourgeoisie. Esping-Andersen cites Sweden and Norway as the best illustrations of this model. There is a commitment to full employment predicated on high levels of political mobilisation by a working-class movement seeking class alliances in order 'to breed a broader, stronger, and even politically hegemonic unity and solidarity'.[55] In essence, Esping-Andersen is suggesting that the structural organisation of the social democratic welfare state can become a crucial power resource, with its programmes, services and benefits shaping the organisational capabilities of the surrounding civil society.

Göran Therborn also engages in a comparative study of the 23 sovereign states of Western Europe, North America, Australia, Japan and New Zealand (Malta was excluded, as were South Africa and Israel), in order to calculate the extent of, and prospects for, socialist advance in Western Europe. In an analysis which he admits 'will to many readers "paint" a surprisingly rosy picture',[56] Therborn attempts to ascertain the extent of socialist advance through the use of empirical criteria. His broad conclusion is that:

> The labour movement of the capitalist heartlands has experienced two periods of general growth, two momentous leaps forward, two periods of stagnation or retreat, and one split conjuncture involving defeat by fascism or less violent forms of reaction in some countries, and remarkable reformist successes in others. Today we are living in or at the end of one of the two historical periods of growth and advance.[57]

The period between 1948 and 1968 is regarded as 'two decades of organisational, electoral and ideological defensive'[58] – precisely the decades during which Croslandite Fabianism flourished in Britain. However, for Therborn 'the maturation of the welfare state in the 1960s and 1970s coincides with the second prolonged historical period of growth of the labour movement, as indicated in unionisation, labour party votes, and increasing labour strength at the workplace'.[59] Of particularly striking interest is the level of unionisation. Four distinct groups of countries emerge:

> (a) those in which the overwhelming majority of workers and employees are unionised (the five Nordic countries, Belgium and Luxembourg); (b) those in which a slight majority have enrolled in unions (Austria, Britain, Ireland, Australia and New Zealand); (c) those in which a third or so of potential union members are organised (Germany, Italy, Japan, Canada,

Netherlands and Switzerland); and (d) those in which only a fifth to a fourth of all workers and employees are unionised (France and the United States).[60]

The hetereogeneity of conditions in advanced capitalism is further revealed if we examine public expenditure levels. Here three distinct groups emerge:

> By 1982 the OECD countries fell into three clear groups (i) countries where public expenditure formed a dominant part of the national product (Sweden, Netherlands, Denmark, Belgium and France); (ii) countries where it accounted for just below a half (Canada, Austria, Germany, Ireland, Italy, Norway, UK); and countries where it comprised about a third (USA, Japan, Australia, New Zealand, Finland, Spain, Switzerland, Greece and Portugal).[61]

Of course, public expenditure falls into very different categories – arms production or purchase, public employee wages, subsidies, income transfers, public investment – producing further differences. Therborn also probes some of these — in particular, levels of welfare expenditure, sources of household income and the percentage of public sector employment as a percentage of total employment:

> Public social expenditure accounts for 10 per cent of GDP in Japan, 14 per cent in the USA, 26 per cent in (Giscardian) France, and 31 per cent in Sweden, while the share of public sector employment ranges from 37 per cent in Sweden, and 30 per cent in Britain to 6–7 in Japan. Industry employs 43 per cent of the economically active population in West Germany in 1982, but only 28 per cent in the United States. In the 15–64 age bracket, civilian employment in 1982 ranged from 79 per cent in Sweden to 46 per cent in Spain and 52 per cent in the Netherlands. In Italy, the labour market has marginalised a large proportion of under-24s, the 7:1 ratio of youth to adult employment contrasting starkly with the OECD average of 2.6:1.[62]

For our purposes the importance of this type of comparative exercise is that a number of *political* conclusions are drawn which are markedly different from those usually taken by scholars of welfare influenced by Marxist theory. First, Therborn argues from his data that it 'is simply wrong to argue that social democracy has become increasingly *embourgeoisé* and integrated into capitalism'.[63] Second, 'welfare state capitalism signifies a *partial decommodification* of social relations, which crucially complicates and restricts the range of the capital labour nexus'.[64] The potential this may have for socialist gain is spelt out by Offe: 'Areas of social life that have been decommodified by welfare state interventions can be developed, through political struggle, into relatively autonomous subsystems of life oriented to the production and distribution of use-values.'[65] Third, a large public sector, whilst not altering the fundamental dynamic of capitalism, does, owing to 'its massive influence on income determination', crucially affect 'the class relations of modern advanced capitalism. The conventional Marxist analysis of state intervention in the economy, centred on state–capital relations and on the implications of state intervention. . . is therefore inadequate. . . for the structure of public expenditure is not without significant effects from class relations.'[66] In other words, 'the arrival of welfare state capitalism. . . alters the parameters of class politics'.[67]

Such observations lead into the fourth, and final, distinguishing feature of the realistic Marxist perspective: their argument that 'the rise of welfare state capitalism is an *irreversible* development providing a fundamental basis for all future working-class struggles. The recent advances of labour therefore constitute a historical conquest which cannot be undone by democratic means: the present right-wing attacks on the welfare state are only capable of yielding marginal encroachments and impairments.'[68] Offe makes the point succinctly: 'The welfare state is. . . a highly problematic, costly and disruptive arrangement, yet its absence would be even more disruptive. Welfare state capitalist societies simply cannot be remodelled into something resembling pure market societies.'[69] The key point of realism is that some types of welfare state capitalism have severely restricted the rule of capital, and altered the *form* in which it accumulates.

## Realism and the transition to socialism

Of course, there are differences of both theoretical emphasis and political understanding within this broad realist position, particularly when it comes to the question of socialist transition. Himmelstrand is perhaps the most open in his celebration of the *maturational* nature of socialist transition strategies. He writes:

> Two alternative conclusions can be drawn on the basis of these observations. First, a socialist transformation of modern capitalist societies is neither inevitable nor particularly likely. Capitalism provokes and stimulates socialist forces of change mainly in 'peripheral' (from the Western point of view) and underdeveloped territories. Second, the seeds of socialism certainly grow in the womb of modern capitalist societies; but in the recent past few of these societies have been experiencing structural contradictions so intense and unchecked that they have been ripe for a profound socialist transformation of their social and economic orders. Sooner or later they will become ripe for socialism.[70]

Himmelstrand quite unashamedly draws the second conclusion, and is scathingly critical of those that have interpreted the development of

Swedish social democracy as further 'supporting and strengthening the prevailing capitalist system'. He argues: 'From a more genuine Marxist standpoint it would seem possible. . . . to argue that Swedish social democracy, by helping capitalism to develop and mature, in fact (if not always in a conscious and deliberate manner) has brought Swedish society closer to a socialist transformation.'[71] Socialism involves the elimination of the contradiction between capital and labour; it is *processual* in that it implies a continuous 'remodelling of the resource accumulation, decision-making and resource allocating process implied by capitalist relations of production to make them compatible with the increasingly societal character of the productive forces'.[72] For Himmelstrand the transition to socialism involves the shifting of crucial allocative decision-making to workers, and is not immediately about public ownership. Himmelstrand seems to believe that this process has already proceeded a long way in Sweden, although it is by no means complete. Others within the realist camp, including the present authors, are much more sanguine – seeing negative as well as positive aspects to such developments. Esping-Andersen is clear, for example, that much further extension of state control over the economy needs to be enacted in order to preserve the welfare achievements and hegemonic role of a radical social democracy.[73] Göran Therborn is also quite clear that 'it should never be forgotten that welfare state capitalism is still capitalism. . . . It would be a fundamental error to suggest that the fully developed welfare state has, even in appearance, removed the basic objects of working-class militancy, such as wages, working conditions, employment and social security.'[74]

In a most valuable paper Jonas Pontusson has critically summarised the arguments of what we might describe as the more 'optimistic' (in terms of socialist achievement) wing of the realist school.[75] He argues that the work of Korpi, Himmelstrand et al. and Stephens[76] can be seen as complementary – gaps in each being filled out by the others. It is Korpi's work which provides the greatest amount of material on the cumulative growth of the power of labour, yet he fails to specify in what ways social democratic policies have actually promoted labour's class interests (this is tackled by Stephens), or the extent to which capital's power may also have grown, matching if not exceeding that of labour (dealt with by Himmelstrand et al.). Korpi's argument is that the extension of political democracy has produced a much closer balance of power between the two major classes. Labour is able to assert political ascendancy, which affects the level of industrial conflict through the process of *political exchange*. As he argues: 'Labour limited itself to use its legislative power to affect the economy in the direction of increased economic growth and a more equal distribution of the results of this growth.'[77] Durable labour peace is, in this sense, dependent on constant political concessions to a strong unified labour movement capable of mobilising both electoral support and this process of political exchange. What many Marxist critics would dismiss as sheer accommodation with private capital is seen by Korpi as a subtle strategic choice, which concedes none of the overall anti-capitalist aims of the movement. Nevertheless, the increasing labour militancy of the 1970s does provide Korpi's thesis with a problem. He rejects entirely most usual Marxist explanations of this phenomenon as being to do with the world recession, increasing unemployment and the shrinking profit margins of Swedish industry. For him these strikes did not reflect the labour force's economistic wage militancy; rather they represented the *political* maturity of the labour movement beginning to make demands that capital *could not* accommodate. Whilst there seems some truth in this concerning the specific wage-earner funds demand – which we shall explain in more detail below – as a general statement it seems to underplay the importance of the largely economically determined contextual membrane which surrounds such social policy developments. Of course, it is vital to recognise the relative autonomy of political actions and decisions in the field of social policy, but this should not imply *neglect* of surrounding, and certainly pressing, economic development.

Stephens attempts to fill out the argument 'that the growth of the welfare state is a product of the growing strength of labour in civil society and that it represents a step toward socialism'[78] with an elaborate quantitative analysis of its redistributive effects. These include the provision of welfare benefits measured by the level of welfare spending, and the method of financing welfare state provision, measured by the ratio of income taxes to indirect taxes. In this sense, his work can be seen as a comparative exercise in testing some of the questions generated by Gough's compromise position. He does not analyse the distribution of control over the means of production – and it would, in all honesty, be a difficult exercise to accomplish. His data reveal that high levels of welfare expenditure combined with progressive tax structures correlate strongly with high levels of workforce unionisation and social democratic rule.[79] There are obviously many methodological problems involved with this type of research, and Therborn et al. have discussed these as well as suggesting that there may be problems with some of the conclusions drawn.[80] For example, their own historical research implies that Sweden was already a more egalitarian society than many other capitalist societies *before* the Social Democrats ever attained power!

Pontusson offers a number of other objections to the position advanced by Korpi and Stephens. First, they are both merely discussing what 'remains an exercise of power *within capitalism*, and it does not follow that income redistribution can be treated as a measure of the gradual advance of socialism'.[81] Second, 'welfare reforms which reduce dependence on the sale of labour power in one respect may reinforce it in another. The tendency towards decommodification is partial and contradictory.'[82] In making this point, however, Pontusson seems to entirely privilege analyses of the economic over that of the political and ideological, and rule out of court the prospects of any egalitarian gains during a recession – almost implying an automatic political adjustment on the part of welfare arrangements to economic processes.[83] This appears to us to be an over-harsh assessment, although his observations do point to a real danger in the more optimistic variants of the realist position. He notes that there is 'a basic problem for the theory of the cumulative growth of labour's power within capitalist society: so long as the growth mechanisms of the economy remain essentially capitalist, the advancement of labour's positions might actually generate economic processes that threaten the unity and strength of the labour movement.'[84] The third criticism Pontusson makes of Stephens is that he too easily assumes that the 'strength of labour' implies a weakness of capital. This is a problem that Himmelstrand et al. acknowledge and try to tackle.

Himmelstrand et al. define 'the systemic power of capital in terms of two partly interdependent aspects of a capitalist social formation: (i) the degree of *penetration* of the capitalist mode of production into all corners of that social formation, and (ii) the degree of *autonomy* (self-financing and self-regulation of the capitalist sector)'.[85] They then advance four arguments to demonstrate that welfare capitalism in general, and in Sweden in particular, has witnessed a simultaneous decline in capital's power in parallel with the growth of labour's strength. They suggest first that the expansion of the public sector has restricted the 'reach' of the capitalist mode of production. Second, the socialisation of the forces of production has increased capital's dependence on state financing and public regulation. They also rather vaguely imply both that economic stagnation has undermined capitalist legitimacy, and that the political aim of maintaining full employment has curtailed capital's ability to discipline labour. Pontusson argues that it is quite inadequate to regard the size of the public sector as an accurate indicator of capital's dependence, for apart from anything else the public sector itself is entirely 'dependent on the productive output of the private sector'.[86] Moreover, given how Himmelstrand statically defines class power, anything that reduced capital's autonomy would run against its long-term interests. In short,

Himmelstrand presents too pedestrian a conception of power, concentrating purely on the *volume* of resources and ignoring the capacity that one class may have to subvert the power of the other side in an actual conflict. Offe makes the same point:

> Viewed from a static point of view, the capitalist welfare state does indeed appear as an arrangement that imposes most significant constraints and limitations upon capitalist power. But viewed from the point of crisis and conflict. . . this very same arrangement may well appear to contain mechanisms which maximise the state's vulnerability to retaliatory strikes, namely to the strategic action (or simply adaptive reaction) of capital.[87]

Pontusson also claims it is highly misleading to interpret state interventionism and welfare state expansion as necessary expressions of labour's strengths, for compared with other capitalist countries 'the state has rarely infringed directly on market choices about what and how to produce. . . public ownership of industry is comparatively small in Sweden (about 5 per cent in 1976)'.[88] Rather, favourable 'economic circumstances' – successful international companies – 'facilitated social-democratic efforts to achieve full employment and welfare reforms by means of policies that conformed to market forces'.[89]

In essence, the brunt of these criticisms against this optimistic variant of realism is that they present 'an implausibly proto-socialist picture of Swedish society',[90] and one that sufficiently under-estimates the power of capital as to be comparable with the proverbial performance of Hamlet without the Prince of Denmark![91] Pontusson concludes his discussion thus:

> My discussion of the Swedish case suggests that social-democratic rule, and the development of the welfare state in particular, has contributed to the unification and strengthening of the working class and the development of a coalition between the working class and the new middle strata. But it has only very partially curtailed the systemic power of capital embedded in the structures of the economy. Rather than neutralising the crisis tendencies of capitalism, labour reformism may have accentuated these tendencies.[92]

Pontusson's criticisms are undoubtedly those of an explicitly revolutionary socialist, yet he concedes much more to what he describes as the reformist position than is usual in such contributions. For example, he admits that the mid 1970s policy proposal of the Swedish labour movement – the wage-earner funds – 'has begun to challenge private control of the investment process. . . and would involve an important element of collective ownership of capital',[93] although he regards these developments as a clear departure from traditional social democratic strategies, and not their fruition as the optimists would claim.

Just what exactly is this joint proposal of the Swedish Federation of Trade Unions and the Social Democratic Party for a system of wage-earner capital funds? In broad terms, private firms employing over 200 or 500 people – there are different versions of the proposal – would pay 20 per cent of the annual profits, in the form of shares, into wage-earner funds. Board representation rights would be given to local unions and regional labour organisations. The proposal envisages the replacement of profit orientations by criteria of resource allocation which, owing to collective labour control, would seek to optimise a balance of social benefits over costs. Undoubtedly many Marxist theorists will still regard this radical, concrete and *immediately achievable* proposal as little more than a method of shoring up a faltering capitalism. This would, in our opinion, be foolish. And the onus must surely be on them to demonstrate how any other method, particularly involving a revolutionary party, could effect the transition to greater labour control over investment without involving a trade union movement *already capable* of generating workable policies, practicable institutions and a sustaining ideology capable of delivering such goods.

## Realism, welfare and Britain

The traditional revolutionary – or 'class logic' – position on welfare tends to overlook or minimise the importance of this last point in its haste to assert the limits to any type of reform; as Norman Ginsburg has expressed it, 'while the capital–labour relation continues to exist, the form and functions of policy *cannot be altered* in their fundamentals.'[94] Little appreciation is shown of how both the form and the content of class compromise represented by welfare arrangements can vary considerably – some undoubtedly being delivered on terms more favourable to labour than others.[95]

In the case of the British welfare state, the Tory 'wet' Ian Gilmour is undoubtedly correct that the post-war consensus was largely 'founded upon making capitalism work. . . [and] was rather more of a Tory than a socialist consensus'.[96] Certainly any attempt to celebrate the arrangements of the British welfare state as 'socialist' achievement, pure and simple, would not only have to ignore 'the pre-history of the "road" to 1945 (especially the role of Liberals and one-nation Tories and the general character of the wartime coalition government) but also. . . the significance of "Butskellism" and "MacWilsonism" in the 1950s and 1960s'.[97] This absence of 'socialist' pedigree should not, however, lead us back to the bedrock of revolutionary purism.

The British post-war welfare reforms, like those in other countries, were a classical type of class compromise that *did* deliver certain important gains, albeit largely for the skilled, male and white sections of the working class. Recognition of the sheer fact of those gains, of the difficulties in preserving them from the onslaughts of Thatcherism and of modifying them along anti-racist and feminist lines, surely necessitates – once and for all – the abandonment of any simplistic partition between 'reform and revolution'. British socialism is in intellectual crisis, and the welfare state is undergoing a severe ideological and political pummelling. Times *are* hard; socialist politics has often been forced to take on defensive forms (e.g. the campaigns to preserve local government) just to defend *limited* gains. What other choice is there? As Stuart Hall has it in echoing our earlier point: 'If we cannot mobilise a full-scale popular agitation around the limited demands of maintaining and expanding "welfare state reformism", on what grounds could we conceivably conceptualise the political conjuncture as one likely to lead to an "irreversible shift of power" towards immediate working-class power?'[98]

Times are particularly hard in Britain, and we do not want our argument for a more realistic politics of welfare to be interpreted as complacency. There is little doubt that some of the arguments of the German and Scandinavian realists appear somewhat optimistic in a British, and possibly their own, context. This particularly applies to their argument concerning the 'irreversibility' of the welfare state; if capitalism cannot survive *with* the welfare state, it certainly cannot *without* it. Variants of this argument under-estimate three dangers. The first is that the present ideological and political ascendancy of the new Conservatism in Britain, whilst not as yet destroying the welfare state, is preparing the ground for its future erosion and privatisation. The second is that 'full employment (or, at least, the commitment to maintain a high level of employment) has been a principal component of the welfare state', and this 'has been abandoned in principle as well as in practice by many neo-conservative regimes'.[99] The third is that these regimes are also emasculating traditional forms of trade union power, and marginalising large sections of the workforce, particularly the young. We cannot assume, as do some of the realists, the inevitable continuation of the British welfare state.

The future of welfare in Britain depends entirely on how the labour movement, other forces that are broadly described as social democratic, and the so-called new social movements (women, blacks, anti-nuclear, ecological etc.) set about tackling the issues of jobs, production and profits *initially and necessarily* within the framework of a capitalist economy. There is no *other* immediate option – certainly not a revolutionary one. It is within such a context that the socialist realist will have to argue for forms of welfare provision that modify the 'gains' of the white, skilled and male sections of the working class. Much thought needs to be given to the form that these should take;

for example, is it realistic to pursue a policy of full employment?[100] The aims of such policies should be broadly clear: the promotion of greater degrees of job sharing; making child-care more than women's business;[101] the privileging of jobs for black people and women;[102] much more emphasis on prevention in the health and personal social services; attempts to erode professional power in appropriate areas; a 'socialist' social security scheme;[103] greater client control over resources; and so on. The 'details', to quote Engels, are much less clear, and it is vital that socialist realists attempt to work them out as soon as possible. What we *do* know is that there are no glib solutions – no panaceas.

## Conclusion

It is this commitment to detail and 'the achievable' – to what is politically feasible – combined with a much greater sensitivity to empirical detail, that has become the distinguishing feature of what we have described here as the realist position. It involves much more 'openness' than the more usual variants of Marxist theory, and a commitment to move *beyond* critique and engage in *detailed* policy analysis. Cloward and Piven capture its general theoretical drift admirably:

> The major thrust of left views has been that welfare state programmes exist because ... their economic or ... political effects are functional for capitalism. We consider that this sort of perspective may no longer serve to account for the role of social welfare .... Even if one thinks these programmes were arguably inaugurated in order to 'regulate the poor', their effects have become perverse in the sense that as social welfare benefits expanded, their longer-run consequence in the labour market *may not* have been to regulate the poor, but to *empower* them.[104]

In *political* terms the realist position recognises, first, that social democracy is, and *always has been*, the most successful expression of working-class politics in European capitalist democracies; and, far from being in its dotage – as so many on the left believe – is probably only at the adolescent stage. Second, it is vital to start where people are, not where one would like them to be. Third, welfare – broadly defined to include interventions to restructure the labour market and reward systems – is a crucial arena of struggle for any successful socialist mobilisation. Fourth, such successful mobilisations will require energy and imagination from both *above* and below. Fifth, the policy initiatives and reforms which materialise from struggles must not be fetishised, for they will help to define the future terrain and conditions of struggle.[105] Finally, the key political choice facing socialists in the metropolitan countries is no longer one of either passively waiting for the balloon to go up or *blindly* pursuing reforms. A realistic politics – aware of both the limitations and the possibilities of social democratic politics, and fine-tuning its organisational forms and political demands – is capable of facilitating significant shifts in the balance of class, race and gender power.

## Notes

1   I. Gough, *The Political Economy of the Welfare State* (Macmillan, 1979), p. 56.
2   Ibid., p. 153.
3   F.F. Piven and R.A. Cloward, *Regulating the Poor: the functions of public welfare* (Random House, 1971), p. xiii.
4   A. Glyn and R. Sutcliffe, *British Capitalism, Workers and the Profits Squeeze* (Penguin, 1972).
5   L. Harris, 'The state and the economy: some theoretical problems', in R. Miliband and J. Saville (eds), *Socialist Register, 1980* (Merlin, 1980).
6   N. Ginsburg, *Class, Capital and Social Policy* (Macmillan, 1979), p. 2.
7   A. Walker, *Social Planning – a strategy for socialist welfare* (Basil Blackwell and Martin Robertson, 1984), p. 67.
8   London/Edinburgh Weekend Return Group, *In and Against the State* (*IAATS*) (Pluto Press, 1980), p. 130.
9   S. Rowbotham, L. Segal and H. Wainwright, *Beyond the Fragments: Feminism and the Making of Socialism* (Merlin, 1979).
10  J. Dale and P. Foster, *Feminists and State Welfare* (Routledge and Kegan Paul, 1986), p. 178.
11  London/Edinburgh Group, *IAATS*, p. 138.
12  Ibid., p. 8.
13  Ibid., p. 134.
14  Ibid., pp. 129–30.
15  Ibid., p. 132.
16  Ibid., p. 9.
17  Ibid., p. 97.
18  Ibid., p. 102.
19  B. Deacon, *Social Policy and Socialism – the struggle for socialist relations of welfare* (Pluto Press, 1983), p. 248.
20  Ibid., p. 262.
21  Ibid., p. 245.
22  Ibid., p. 64.
23  Ibid., p. 244.
24  Ibid., p. 42.
25  Ibid., p. 41.
26  Ibid., p. 28.
27  Ibid., p. 37.
28  Ibid., p. 37.
29  Ibid., pp. 37–40.
30  Ibid., p. 227.
31  Ibid., pp. 234–5.
32  Ibid., p. 231.
33  Ibid., p. 53: Deacon here is quoting from P. Corrigan, H. Ramsey and D. Sayer, *Socialist Construction and Marxist Theory* (Macmillan, 1978).

34    See P. Lee, 'Review of *Social Policy and Socialism*', *Critical Social Policy*, no. 10
      (Summer) 1984, for an extended critique of the book.
35    U. Himmelstrand, G. Ahrne, L. Lundberg and L. Lundberg, *Beyond Welfare
      Capitalism – issues, actors and forces in societal change* (Heinemann, 1981), pp.
      14–15 (original emphasis).
36    L. Doyal and I. Gough, 'A theory of human needs', *Critical Social Policy*, 10
      (Summer), 1984.
37    Deacon, *Socialism*, p. 254.
38    L. Starling, 'Islington Nalgo', *Socialist Worker*, 11 September 1982 (quoted in
      Deacon, *Socialism*, p. 254).
39    Deacon, *Socialism*, p. 252.
40    Ibid., p. 255 (our emphasis).
41    A. Coote and B. Campbell, *Sweet Freedom* (Pan, 1982), p. 240.
42    J.D. Stephens, *The Transition from Capitalism to Socialism* (Macmillan, 1979).
43    W. Korpi, *The Working Class in Welfare Capitalism – work, unions and politics
      in Sweden* (Routledge and Kegan Paul, 1978) and W. Korpi, *The Democratic
      Class Struggle* (1983), Routledge and Kegan Paul, 1983).
44    Himmelstrand et al., *Beyond Welfare Capitalism*.
45    G. Esping-Andersen, 'The state as a system of stratification: conservatism,
      liberalism and socialism in the organisation of public welfare programs', paper
      presented to the public symposium on The Labour Movement and Welfare State
      in Western Europe, University of Copenhagen, March 1984.
46    G. Therborn, 'The working class and the welfare state', paper given to the 5th
      Nordic congress of research in the history of the labour movement, Murikka,
      Finland, August 1983; G. Therborn, 'The coming of Swedish social democracy',
      mimeograph, 1983; G. Therborn, 'The prospects of labour and the transforma-
      tion of advanced capitalism', *New Left Review*, no. 145, 1984.
47    See particularly P. Ingrao, 'Eurocommunism and the question of the state',
      *Eurored*, 9 (Feb.), 1979.
48    C. Offe, *Contradictions of the Welfare State* (Hutchinson, 1984), p. 285.
49    Therborn, 'The prospects of labour'.
50    G. Esping-Andersen, 'Politics against markets: de-commodification in social
      policy', paper presented at the 5th biannual Arne Ryde symposium, Department
      of Economics, Lund Univerity, September 1981.
51    Esping-Andersen, 'The state as a system'.
52    See also Korpi, *The Working Class*, and Himmelstrand et al., *Beyond Welfare
      Capitalism*.
53    Esping-Andersen, 'The state as a system', p. 23.
54    G. Esping-Andersen, *Politics against Markets – the social democratic road to
      power* (University of Harvard Press, 1985).
55    Ibid., p. 317.
56    Therborn, 'The prospects of labour'.
57    Ibid., pp. 6–7.
58    Ibid., p 8.
59    G. Therborn, 'Classes and states: welfare state developments', mimeograph, 1983,
      p. 28.
60    Therborn, 'The prospects of labour'.
61    Ibid., p. 26.
62    Ibid., p. 36.
63    Ibid., p. 12.
64    Ibid., p. 29.

65 Offe, *Contradictions*, p. 265.
66 Therborn, 'The prospects of labour', pp. 26–7.
67 Ibid., p. 31.
68 Ibid., p. 35. See also C. Offe, 'Some contradictions of the modern welfare state', *Critical Social Policy*, 2 (2), 1982; and P. Lee (ed.), 'Banishing dark divisive clouds: welfare and the Conservative government', *Critical Social Policy*, 8 (Autumn), 1983.
69 Offe, *Contradictions*, p. 288.
70 Himmelstrand et al., *Beyond Welfare Capitalism*, p. 4.
71 Ibid., p. 24.
72 Ibid., p. 12.
73 G. Esping-Andersen, *Social Class, Social Democracy and State Policy* (Copenhagen, 1980), chapter 6.
74 Therborn, 'The prospects of labour', pp. 29–30.
75 J. Pontusson, 'Behind and beyond social democracy in Sweden', *New Left Review*, 143 (Jan./Feb.), 1984, pp. 69–96.
76 Korpi, *The Working Class*; Himmelstrand et al., *Beyond Welfare Capitalism*; Stephens, *The Transition*.
77 W. Korpi and M. Shalev, 'Strikes, power and politics in Western nations', in M. Zeitlin (ed.) *Political Power and Social Theory*, vol. 1 (Greensburg, 1980), p. 321.
78 Stephens, *The Transition*, p. 89.
79 Ibid., pp. 98–112, 163–74.
80 G. Therborn, A. Kjellborg, S. Marklund and U. Öhlund, 'Sweden before and after social democracy: a first overview', *Acta Sociologica*, 21, supplement, 1978, pp. 37–58.
81 Pontusson, 'Behind and beyond', p. 80.
82 Ibid., p. 81.
83 See ibid., p. 81.
84 Ibid., p. 81.
85 Himmelstrand et al., *Beyond Welfare Capitalism*, p. 211.
86 Pontusson, 'Behind and beyond', p. 83.
87 C. Offe, 'Review of *Beyond Welfare Capitalism*', *Acta Sociologica*, 25(3), 1982, p. 316.
88 Pontusson, 'Behind and beyond', p. 84.
89 Ibid., p. 85.
90 Offe, 'Review', p. 317.
91 B. Gustafsson, 'Review of *Beyond Welfare Capitalism*', *Acta Sociologica*, 25(3), 1982, p. 306.
92 Pontusson, 'Behind and beyond', p. 95.
93 Ibid., p. 71.
94 Ginsburg, *Class*, p. 17 (our emphasis).
95 See P. Lee (ed.), *The Future of Europe's Welfare States* (Sage, 1988, forthcoming).
96 I. Gilmour, *Inside Right* (Quartet, 1978), p. 20.
97 B. Jessop, K. Bonnett, S. Bromley and T. Ling, 'Authoritarian populism, two nations and Thatcherism', *New Left Review*, 147, (Sep./Oct.), 1984, p. 39.
98 S. Hall, 'Authoritarian populism: a reply to Jessop et al.', *New Left Review*, 151 (May/June), 1985, p. 123.
99 R. Mishra, 'The left and the welfare state: a critical analysis', *Critical Social Policy*, 15 (Spring), 1986, p. 15.
100 See J. Keane and J. Owens, *After Full Employment* (Hutchinson, 1976) and M. Rustin, *For a Pluralist Socialism* (Verso, 1985), chapter 7.

101 C. New and M. David, *For the Children's Sake – making childcare more than women's business* (Penguin, 1985).

102 See K. Coates (ed.), *Joint Action for Jobs – a new internationalism* (*New Socialist*/ Spokesman, 1986).

103 P. Alcock, 'Socialist security: where should we be going and why?', *Critical Social Policy*, 13 (Summer), 1985.

104 R. Cloward and F.F. Piven, 'Moral economy and the welfare state', in D. Robbins (ed.), *Rethinking Social Inequality* (Gower, 1982), p. 221 (our emphasis). See also R. Cloward and F.F. Piven, *The New Class War* (Pantheon, 1982), particularly chapter 1.

105 See G. Ben-Tovim, J. Gabriel, I. Law and K. Stredder, *The Local Politics of Race* (Macmillan, 1986) for a sustained development of this point in relation to struggles for racial equality.

# 6

# Marxist Theory, Welfare and Political Realism

> Classes do not naturally exist, but they are made.
>
> Jean-Paul Sartre

This chapter suggests that a realistic Marxism – or what E.P. Thompson has described in another context as 'the open, explanatory and self-critical Marxist tradition'[1] – has to both sharpen and sensitise some of its theoretical concepts in order to investigate areas of welfare theory and practice previously ignored or under-examined by Marxist scholars. In particular, a *realistic* Marxism has to:

1  Advance criticisms of existing welfare practice, but in such a way as to have an awareness of 'replaceability' – of politically feasible alternatives
2  Begin to address and evaluate *immediate* policy questions, and
3  Offer *strategic* help to practitioners within, and clients of, the welfare services.

In short, it has to begin to contribute to a *realistic* politics of social welfare.

## Beyond critique: towards the politically achievable

Alec Nove recently published a most readable and interesting text entitled *The Economics of Feasible Socialism*. The author's intention was to 'explore what *could be* a workable, feasible sort of socialism, which might be achieved within the lifetime of a child already conceived'.[2] He was concerned to try to answer *practical* questions, such as how production should be organised under socialism; what balance there should be between state provision and private initiative; but most importantly, what might be *politically achievable*. He concludes one part of his analysis by suggesting that a socialist legal structure should permit the following species of social ownership:

1  State enterprises, centrally controlled and administered, hereinafter *centralised state corporations*
2  State owned (or socially owned) enterprises with full autonomy and a management responsible to the workforce, hereinafter *socialised enterprises*

3 Cooperative enterprises
4 Small-scale private enterprises, subject to clearly defined limits
5 Individuals (e.g. freelance journalists, plumbers, artists).[3]

The existence of even small-scale private enterprise might shock some purists, yet as Nove writes:

> Finally we reach *private enterprise*. Presumably even the fanatical dogmatist would accept the existence of freelance writers, painters and dressmakers. My own list would be longer. *Indeed, there should be no list*. If any activity (not actually a 'social bad' in itself) can be fruitfully and profitably undertaken by any individual, this sets up the presumption of its legitimacy. . . . Water supply is a 'natural' monopoly. If water flows from taps, private water-carriers are an absurdity. So no law is needed to forbid them. But if for some reason the water supply becomes unreliable, this can create a situation in which private water-carriers can make a living. This is indeed far-fetched. . . but. . . suppose that there appears to be an unsatisfied demand for a Peking-cuisine restaurant, Fair-Isle sweaters, a holiday booking agency, wedding-dresses, car repairs, mushrooms, sailing-dinghies, house-decorating, barley, chocolate cake, or string quartets. Large state-managed undertakings are otherwise engaged. The smaller socialised or cooperative enterprises may or may not act. . . or perhaps an individual has devised some new and economic design or method of production. Why not let him or her go ahead, and produce privately for sale?[4]

Nove tentatively suggests that a feasible socialist society would possess the following nine features:[5]

1 The predominance of state, social and cooperative property, and the absence of any large-scale private ownership of the means of production.
2 Conscious planning by an authority responsible to an elected assembly of major investments of structural significance.
3 Central management of current microeconomic affairs confined to sectors (and to type of decision) where informational, technological and organisational economies of scale, and the presence of major externalities, render this indispensable.
4 A preference for small scale, as a means of maximising participation and a sense of 'belonging'. Outside centralised or monopolised sectors, and the limited area of private enterprise, management should be responsible to the workforce.
5 Current output and distribution of goods and services should whenever possible be determined by negotiations between the parties concerned. There should be explicit recognition that this implies and requires competition, a precondition for choice.
6 Workers should be free to choose the nature of their employment and given every opportunity to change their specialisation. If they prefer it, they could opt for work in cooperatives, or on their own

account (for instance in a family farm, workshop, or service agency).

7   As an unlimited market mechanism would in due course destroy itself, and create intolerable social inequalities, the state would have vital functions in determining income policies, levying taxes (and differential rents), intervening to restrain monopoly power, and generally setting the ground-rules and limits of a competitive market. Some sectors (education, health etc.) would naturally be exempt from market-type criteria.

8   It is recognised that a degree of material inequality is a precondition for avoiding administrative direction of labour, but moral incentives would be encouraged and inequalities consciously limited. The duty to provide work would override considerations of micro-profitability.

9   The distinction between governors and governed, managers and managed, cannot realistically be eliminated, but great care must be taken to devise barriers to the abuse of power and maximum possible democratic consultation.

We offer this extended summary of Nove's book not only because we find much in it that we can agree with – although we would wish to control micromarket mechanisms more severely, and challenge power relationships more strongly than he appears to want to – but also because it seems to typify what has happened to some variants of socialist scholarship in the last few years. In a number of different areas of analysis there has developed a much more down-to-earth concern with immediate practical questions. A fine example of this is the study of crime and deviance. In the late 1960s, traditional criminology was subjected to a broadside attack from the 'radical' new criminology.[6] Whilst this was an undoubtedly refreshing and necessary experience, it left an awkward space. As Stan Cohen noted, it was 'the bridge to criminal justice *policy*' that was difficult to construct, for 'beyond filling in the picture of the system as repressive, the impact of the new theories has been slight'.[7] Very often the same people who in the late 1960s were active in demolishing the pretensions of orthodox criminology were, a decade later, complaining that it was indeed vital to construct 'an agenda which does not leave the debate to the right'.[8]

The new criminologists' first attempts at practicability revolved largely around proposals for decentralisation and beliefs in the naturally just instincts of the working-class community. As Jock Young put it:

We have to argue, therefore, strategically, for the existence of social control but also to argue that such control must be exercised within the working-class community and not by external policing agents. The control of crime on streets, like the control of rate busting on the factory floor, can only be achieved effectively by the community actually involved.[9]

Four years later, Young was to admit that such suggestions smacked more than a little of 'left idealism'[10] or what we have described as fundamentalism. More recently he and John Lea have argued that it is necessary to adopt a more realistic approach to crime which recognises 'that there is a substantial element in street crime which is merely the poor taking up the individualistic, competitive ethos of capitalism itself and that its consequences are anathema to the standpoint of socialist concerns'.[11] Ian Taylor, another contributor to *The New Criminology*, has more recently suggested that socialist criminologists must attempt to construct an alternative social strategy which will meet authentic popular needs, and thus directly challenge the 'authoritarian populist' themes within Thatcherism. He goes on to suggest that this

> reconstruction. . . must in large part arise out of practice. . . not as a result of abstract theoretical work. People are likely to deal with these questions in a vigorous and effective manner the more that they are directly affected and angered by the operation of the state (through the social security system, police or the courts), by institutionalised racism or sexism, or by unemployment.[12]

Taylor also unhesitatingly suggests that such direct and practical politics, as currently organised, necessitates involvement in the Labour Party. This advice has, of course, drawn the accusation of reformism. Nonetheless, Taylor argues for the retention of the term 'social democracy' owing to its stress on the key elements in any socialist politics – social provision and democracy. He argues that the term be 'reconstructed', though, to rescue it from the distortions of the immediate post-war period. The reconstruction is necessary owing to previous failures: first, to deal effectively with social inequality; second, to make accountable unaccountable state professionals; and third, to open up state agencies to democratic control. This 'new' social democracy would be able to try to effect such changes.

Our interest in these debates in economics and criminology is fuelled both by the stress placed by writers such as Nove, Lea, Young and Taylor on 'feasibility and replaceability' but also by certain parallels with the study of social policy. In 1981 the journal *Critical Social Policy* (*CSP*) was founded with the explicit aims both of making more widely available a critical, often neo-Marxist literature, and of contributing to policy debates.[13] Such criticisms were, of course, largely directed at the Fabian traditions, particularly of the sort outlined at length in chapter 3. At root, such Marxist critics were most concerned with rectifying the blinkered focus of Fabian *economics*, as Robin Murray has argued:

> Fabian economics has been limited in both theory and practice because it has restricted itself to the economics of circulation. It is from the sphere of circulation that it has taken its main issues of concern and definitions of socialism; inequality, market anarchy, monopoly. In demanding a 'social-isation' of ownership, it was demanding a power for the state to counter these inadequacies in the system of circulation. But Fabian economics as put into practice by successive Labour governments has consistently run into the barriers set by the requirements of private accumulation. It is the contradictory character of these requirements as they are found in the process of production that socialist economic policy must address.[14]

The stress on the limited economic focus of Fabianism led many of the new critical social policy contributors into a certain reluctance in addressing any *concrete* questions about priorities in the area of *circulation*. At the second *CSP* Conference, on socialist strategies for welfare, held in Sheffield in 1981, there was a frosty reception for contributors discussing such immediate questions around the creation of local authority employment departments; the use socialists could make of pension funds; and possible social policy proposals for the next Labour Party manifesto, whether on housing, social security or whatever. Such people were dismissed as being *mere* Fabians, with little or nothing of importance to contribute. The critique of Fabianism, in other words, bred within many people involved with *CSP* a real reluctance to actually engage in specifying any concrete proposals about immediate issues for fear of being accused of the dreaded plague – new (dare we suggest 'born-again') Fabianism.

The study of social policy simply is *not* the study of political economy! It has quite different concerns – concerns that were properly reflected at later conferences of *CSP*, when the whole three days were taken up with discussions which had earlier been almost taboo. Our position is a simple one. First, socialists concerned with social policy have to engage in controversies about *immediate* questions within the sphere of circulation, and this has to be more than mere verbal intervention pointing out the myopia of a certain kind of Fabianism. Second, many of the critiques of Fabianism offered by the new critical social policy have, as with the new criminology's critique of orthodox forms, been overdrawn.

Murray, whilst aware of the theoretical limitations of Fabianism, nevertheless calls for a shift in the agenda of the labour movement, involving immediate demands on the state around questions of cir-culation and consumption:

1 Industrial restructuring through planned intervention.
2 The development of publicly controlled technology and systems

design, geared to the skills and concerns of labour, and to social needs.

3    A redefinition of planning, as popular planning for labour in and against the market.

4    The transformation of public services and state corporations, in terms of their internal organisation and their relations with their manual workforce and with the users of their services.

5    A concern with the quality of consumption rather than its mere quantitative aggregate. The Fordist mode of production has been particularly inappropriate in food, culture, health, and education – all key parts of a new mode of consumption, replacing that based on mass-produced consumer durables.

6    The attack on inequalities within production (particularly the division between conception and execution) which feed back into income inequalities, and inequalities between men and women and between black people and whites.

7    The integration and direct planning of the public economy, and its expansion to ensure a job for all those who are currently unemployed.[15]

Our concern is that these types of conventionally regarded 'economic' demands become integral to the concerns of socialists pressing for 'socialist' forms of *welfare*. Rather than use political economic analysis to always locate, and usually criticise, the kind of developments being encouraged by Murray and others, use it to struggle as hard as possible to achieve *accomplishable* goals.

### Dismissing the Fabian tradition?

One does not become tarred with the same political brush as more conservative variants of Fabianism by addressing immediate questions in a practicable manner, and fighting for those goals on the terrain of the state. Far from it; one dons the mantle of Fabianism by fetishising the technical means of achieving practical solutions, and losing sight of the long-term *ends*. Fabianism may often involve pragmatism, but *practicability* is the hallmark of any effective political intervention. During the 1950s, Croslandite or revisionist Fabian socialism lost sight of *ends* to such an extent that a socialism of equality became, to use Wright's words, 'variously replaced, at least rhetorically, with a socialism of growth, efficiency, technology, stability, economic management and government'.[16] Crosland's politics, despite a commitment to the goal of egalitarianism, were predicated on the belief that capitalism was a tamed beast and the task was to improve an already improving society. It is largely memories of this variant of Fabianism, mixed with uneasy feelings about the uncritical attitude of the Webbs to welfare professionalism and state bureaucracy, and gelled with knowledge about the problems associated with Tawney's and Titmuss's idealism, that have for many people become *the* Fabian tradition. Again, as Wright has it, 'for most purposes "Fabianism" now obscures more than it reveals, a loaded shorthand when a discriminating longhand is required.'[17]

Certainly it does not seem unfair to accuse some of the more vitriolic critics of Fabianism of a somewhat limited understanding of the object under scrutiny. How many people who use the word 'Fabianism', almost as a term of abuse, have read the works of G.D.H. Cole, Tawney or Titmuss? If they were to do so they would, we believe, be somewhat surprised. This is G.D.H. Cole writing in 1954: 'But the welfare state is, all the same, not socialism. . . it is at most only socialistic – if even that.'[18] In *New Fabian Essays* even Crossman argues that what has been created is little more than a 'capitalist adaptation', and therefore not a specifically socialist enterprise.[19] Tawney was always aware of the limitations of minimally redistributionist strategies; they should be 'extended as rapidly as possible now, but. . . till a radical change has been effected in the balance of economic power, will at every point be thwarted and checked'.[20] And, of course, neo-Marxist critics of the welfare state should always try to remember what Hilary Rose once reminded them: their own relatively late recognition of a gender dimension succeeded that of certain Fabians, whose 'preoccupation with the social relations of redistribution, perhaps we could speak not too strainedly of the social relations of reproduction or consumption' was accompanied by 'an unusual sensitivity to the position of women'.[21]

Despite the fluidity – Pimlott describes it as a 'stimulating diversity' – of the Fabian tradition,[22] too many critics from its left insist on referring to it as a homogeneous entity. For example, Peter Beresford and Suzy Croft note a shift to the right in the Fabian *consensus* when discussing the recent spate of writings from social administrators critical of the state's centralised and bureaucratic form of service delivery.[23] But just what is being referred to by the term 'consensus'? It certainly cannot be the predominant Croslandite form of Fabian politics of the post-war period, Wilsonian technocratic collectivism or the Webbsian statist tradition; for Beresford and Croft's target is 'welfare pluralism', which seeks a *decreased* role for the state and an enhanced one for the informal, market and voluntary sectors in the production and delivery of welfare services. The major text arguing for this position is Hadley and Hatch's *Social Welfare and the Failure of the State*.[24] This book has found itself in the almost unique position of being welcomed by *all* the major political parties, and superficially at least one can even discern similarities between certain welfare pluralist ideas and the suggestions of some Marxist prefigurativists – such as Beresford and Croft – for radical deprofessionalisation and decentralisation. The differences revolve around Beresford and Croft's perceptive examination of the welfare pluralists' motives for, and desire of, real change. First, they suggest that many of the practical schemes devised by the welfare pluralists – for example, patch-based social service reforms[25] – far from eroding, or challenging professional power, enhance it: 'Yet whatever local variations there may be, patch can generally be said... to be based on... anachronistic and gender-loaded notions of "community"; the reprivatising of responsibility for care; the unpaid labour of women; and the continued hegemony of the social work profession.'[26] Second, whilst some welfare pluralists – notably Hadley, Bosanquet and Gladstone[27] – reject the further expansion of the commercial sector for social services, even they 'seem to over-estimate the capacity of the state to regulate the slice of the welfare market the commercial sector takes and the quality of its provision, once the state sector and state controls are reduced in accordance with welfare pluralist philosophy'.[28] In short, some welfare pluralists do not realise the *long-term* consequences of their own prescriptions, whilst others not only recognise but openly embrace them. Third, and as a consequence of this, Beresford and Croft are convinced that welfare pluralism is a concept behind which Fabian ideas have adjusted themselves rightwards: 'For the welfare pluralists the spectre of free-market dominance is a disturbing reality, which not only meant that their traditional state-oriented position was no longer tenable, but also that it was necessary to stake out a new defensive position against market ideas which would ensure their future.'[29]

Whilst we have some sympathy with many of Beresford and Croft's points, particularly the last, the quality of their argument is undermined by their insistence on referring to Fabianism as a uniform doctrine. Near the end of their article they do concede that 'some Fabians have moved to the left' but this is not elaborated upon, and developments under Labour councils such as Islington and Sheffield are treated with the same contempt as 'experiments' by Conservative councils. There is no recognition at all of the growing *rapprochement* between certain Marxist and Fabian positions. Surely the ideas expressed in David Blunkett and Geoff Green's Fabian Society pamphlet *Building from the Bottom – the Sheffield experience*[30] are markedly distinct from those of welfare pluralist writers who have now firmly placed themselves outside the Labour Party? The former can hardly be accused of acting as stalwart defenders of market forces when their major argument is that whilst 'we cannot ignore the central economic forces of our market economy. . . there are alternative forms of organisation which challenge its political and ideological supremacy'.[31] Blunkett and Green address precisely the sort of questions raised by prefigurativist Marxists about the need to change fundamentally the social *relations* of welfare, and display a keen awareness of what is *politically possible*.

Beresford and Croft's ire is drawn by the fact that it is always 'the council' determining what the scope and nature of these political possibilities will be. They are sceptical, and quite rightly, of participatory schemes for clients or tenants which are more often than not 'a window-dressing display more to deny people any real say than to allow it'.[32] They, along with many other neo-Marxist critics, automatically question any scheme that comes 'from above' and is not generated 'from below'. This is not surprising, as Beresford and Croft perceive a huge divide between local working people and the 'corps of outside middle class, professional social workers whose colonialist control. . . with its guarantee of middle-class status and reward. . . is sometimes difficult not to equate with that of a nineteenth-century cleric'.[33] Most socialists, including some social workers, will have some rhetorical sympathy for such views – indeed, Blunkett and Green's pamphlet comments on how some of Sheffield's councillors would like to see social workers live in the community they serve – but what *practical* policies flow from such a polarised class analysis? It implies, first, a process of localised social service recruitment – a proposal that is beginning to be experimented with in some local authorities – and, second, a long-term strategy of dismantling the social service bureaucracy/hierarchy and deprofessionalising the services. Again, many socialists would have sympathy for such *goals*. However, we come back to the fact that neo-Marxist writings on social policy have been very poor in their analysis of *how* to achieve them, have been good on 'why' questions but weak on 'how' ones.

For us the most refreshing aspect of recent theoretical developments amongst British socialists, and particularly the alternative new left policies being developed by some Labour authorities, is the firm emphasis they place on answering such 'how' questions.[34] Their advocates are more than aware of their limitations – that they are not creating little oases of socialism. John Benington, until 1985 the head of Sheffield Council's employment department, offers a typical observation:

> If you look at the recent experience of the labour movement. . . certain kinds of ideas. . . periodically grip its imagination. . . . The Lucas experiment gripped the imagination of both sections of the trade union movement and parts of the 'intellectual left', and became a kind of metaphor or parable for an alternative way forward. . . . Now the left Labour councils are maybe

offering that kind of hope.... Of course they sometimes generate fantasies ... and all kinds of false expectations surround what is possible. But maybe... we will nevertheless be able to develop certain forms of practice and initiative which provide, if not models, at least metaphors for a way of tackling things; a source of hope and experience to analyse critically.[35]

It is short-sighted and politically nihilistic to dismiss such 'experiments' as a mere Fabianism. Many of their architects – including Murray above – explicitly recognise debts to Marxist analysis; even orthodox, self-proclaimed Fabians such as Heald acknowledge the importance of Marxist analyses of the state in helping fill a lacuna in their own work.[36] In our opinion, it is necessary to redraft the political map to recognise that there are at least three 'Fabianisms' on offer in the 1980s: the 'old' corporatist tradition of Wilsonian technocratic centralism; welfare pluralism; and the 'new left' alternatives. The last group has much more in common with those we have described as 'realistic' Marxists than it does with the other variants of Fabianism.

**Towards a critical policy analysis**

Without doubt, neo-Marxist investigations of welfare have provoked a much more rigorous concern with the *long-term* aspects of *why* certain policy developments occur. By contrast, the strengths of Fabian approaches lie in attention to detail concerning more empirically demonstrable and *immediate* questions about *what* actually occurs at the *legislative moment* (which pressure groups were involved; the role of particular individuals; the precise nature of government, or local authority, departmental trade-offs; etc.) and *how* the resultant social policy actually works out in practice (the precise effects of particular legislative acts; the possible consequences of alternative policy options; etc.).

*Questions of the middle range*
Risking over-simplification, it is possible to diagrammatise (see figure 6.1) the three key areas that have to be addressed if any successful social policy analysis is to occur. Whilst it would be a nonsense to suggest that Marxists do not engage in studies of detailed acts of legislation or the day-to-day operations of agencies – indeed, one of the distinguishing features of the new critical social policy has been the attention paid to the operations of agencies such as building societies and pension funds, largely ignored by conventional social policy[37] – it is, nevertheless, undoubtedly true that their major energies have been spent on the more distant terrain of the *contextual membrane*. The types of questions that have dominated most Marxist investigations

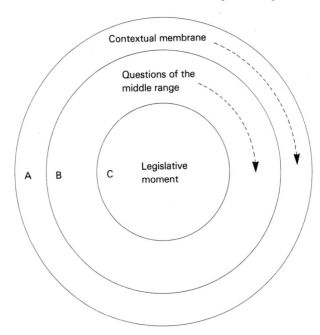

Figure 6.1    *Questions for successful social policy analysis: the middle range*

are those concerning the state of the economy; the relative strengths of different fractions and forms of capital (rentier, industrial, finance); the general balance of class forces and the state of particular political conjunctures; and so on. Equally, it would be a gross caricature of Fabian studies to imply that their primary emphasis on legislative enactment leaves them bereft of any wider concerns. A more sensible argument would be that both sets of theorists tend to utilise concepts *primarily designed* to investigate either *structure* (in the case of Marxist theory) or *agency* (in the case of Fabian theory) to explore the crucial arena of the middle range where structures mould, but do not entirely predetermine, actions and outcomes.

The key question – and it is one we have come across before – is just how do we investigate this complex set of correspondences between the practice of agents and the operation of structural processes? Recent Marxist contributors have recast this question as being one about contrasting popular needs with those derived from capitalist compulsion.[38] Such formulations are a partial help, but what is necessary is to clarify the nature of Marxist contributions to the study of social policy. The concepts of Marxist political economy are best suited to structural type A questions (see figure 6.1) and can become unwieldy if drafted in to address issues for which they were not intended, i.e. about immediate empirical actions. We saw in chapter 4 how the term 'social control' – a concept by no means exclusively used by Marxists – has often been called upon to avoid the obvious rigidities that result from employing structural concepts in pursuance of answers to action-oriented questions. It is worth while pursuing an example at this point.

How can we account for the occurrence of those peculiar social policy developments of the late 1960s – the Urban Programme and related community initiatives such as the Community Development Projects (CDPs) and the Comprehensive Community Projects? Most commentators are in agreement as to the contextual factors that provoked these demonstration projects – the 'rediscovery' of poverty, prompting a serious questioning of the performance of welfare services, combined with the government's fear of inner city riots at a time of growing racist agitation.[39] Such superficial agreements, however, gloss over what are, for our purposes, very revealing methodological and political disagreements in approach. Bridges,[40] a Marxist, in our opinion correctly privileges structural determinations but does so in a manner that emasculates sensitive considerations of agency. He argues:

> Each of these projects was designed to absorb, contain and divert the emerging protest of the urban poor, both black and white. The Community Relations Commission and Race Relations Board were destined to become a dumping ground for any black person who complained to anyone about anything and were used as such by housing officials, social welfare agencies, the police and politicians. The function of the Urban Aid Programme was to buy out community-based organisations by giving them relatively small sums of money for 'safe' activities such as adventure playgrounds and legal advice centres. The Community Development Projects had the same function on a larger and more concentrated scale.[41]

He further inquires as to 'whether the Comprehensive Community Projects... do not amount to internal labour reservations'.[42] McKay and Cox[43] adopt a much more conventional, dare we say Fabian-style, policy analysis approach, privileging immediate empirical developments and taking exception to precisely the type of account offered by those such as Bridges who regard the main objective of the projects as 'being to manipulate and placate potentially rebellious urban masses with token gestures'.[44] They argue 'it is clearly necessary' to avoid such grandiose arguments and 'refer to the *immediate* events surrounding... inception'.[45] They conclude: 'The Urban Programme developed as a result of the popularity of particular ideas on poverty and urban deprivation which at the time apparently offered to bureaucrats and politicians a highly acceptable and "low cost" solution to an imperfectly understood social problem.'[46] No one could really disagree with the latter half of this extract, but the whole hardly adds up to an adequate explanation. How did these 'amorphous academic ideas' actually become popularised so as to be able to influence the bureaucratically dominated policy system?

Neither of these accounts is satisfactory. McKay and Cox have, in effect, found their traditional and pluralist social policy analysis wanting. Explanations couched in terms of interest group representation, political party or bureaucratic influences simply do not offer viable accounts. Consequently, they have resorted to a source of policy change *outside* their traditional frame of reference. The concept of ideology is invoked in the shape of 'fashionable ideas'. McKay and Cox, in other words, recognise the necessity to employ structural concepts in addressing type B questions (the middle range: see figure 6.1) and employ the notion of ideological determination. They use the concept, however, in an entirely *empiricist* manner as if it were being used to address type C questions (the legislative moment). No attempt is made to produce a developed account of the ideological system referred to, or to trace the reason why particular groups found such ideas useful. The events are, in short, simply *redescribed*.

Bridges' account is inadequate for the reverse reason. He employs structural explanations all right but does so exclusively, bringing structural concerns to bear on questions of agency. His use of the term 'social control' suffers from precisely the limitations we described in chapter 4. Of course there were social control concerns present in these programmes – as in all social policies – but, as Loney suggests, their aims 'were rather more modest' than Bridges implies, and were rooted more 'in traditional social work attitudes toward what were seen as individual, family and community pathologies. Social control was to be directed at delinquents not agitators.'[47] Bridges uses the term too indiscriminately, to imply both effect and conscious design. His preference for analyses addressing type A questions (figure 6.1) means he brings this concern for structural certainty into his investigation of issues of the middle range (type B questions) – bringing a structural finality to actions which are much more ephemeral and contradictory than his heavy-handed approach allows for. Type C questions – concerning actual empirical happenings – merely form a *selective* backdrop to his account; that which fits is mentioned, that which does not is discarded. For example, there is no mention of the fact that the CDPs produced a highly critical literature and were without doubt the breeding ground for a new generation of radical community activists.[48] Many of those at present engaged in the new left, local government 'experiments' learned important skills working for the CDPs. Bridges' account is a classic example of a genre of 'radical' literature that provides *no* useful analysis whatsoever about what practitioners can do *in practice*; community workers simply become 'soft cops'.

Neither account adequately comes to terms with crucial questions lying in the middle range – in particular, the growth of professional influence over, and in some cases monopolisation of, decision-making. How autonomous can we assume central government policy-making is from the influence of professional bodies? The type of initiative planned by government may bear little resemblance to the finished product once it has been influenced by various intermediaries – in particular, professional administrations and service deliverers. Certainly, one cannot understand these 'experimental' programmes without recognising the major importance of the social work and community work lobbies. Social work ideas offered a practical remedy to social problems which did not depend on large-scale expenditure or fundamental social change.[49] Social work professionalisation was the major agency carrying and popularising the ideas that McKay and Cox credit with creating these programmes. Social and community workers were also in the vanguard of Bridges' social control efforts. When considering middle-range questions it is facile not to admit that whilst structural considerations allow us to recognise why government chose a policy option which did not propose radical social change, the resultant policy initiatives did not always mean that conflict was institutionalised.

*Exploring the middle range*

The key question is: do adjustments have to be made to Marxist theory, and concessions made to the insights of other theoretical systems, to enable it to contribute more effectively to these middle-range debates? Some readers will suggest that even to pose the question in this manner is to do a disservice to Marxism's essential unity. Our response to such reactions is simple. Such people may have a philosophical point, but they leave Marxist theory with a very limited range of questions that it can ask about social policy. You may wish for such a restrictive agenda, but why bother to study social policy if you cannot adequately explore questions of policy analysis? In our opinion, Marxist theory has to be modified to handle questions for which it was not principally designed. Alan Cawson has written that 'Marxism does not provide the key, but it does help define the lock'.[50] That is not quite correct. On some questions, as we have seen, *only* Marxist theories can effectively open the door (type A questions); in order to address other questions some modifications and supplementations will have to be made (the middle-range questions). How can Marxist theory successfully operate in this arena? Answers to this complex question are likely to generate an enormous amount of controversy. Our explanation will necessarily be both selective, and entered into somewhat tentatively.

## Sensitising concepts

### Determination in the last instance?

Much of our argument so far has implied that conventional Marxist theory has a tendency to treat capitalist social formations as if they were simply constituted by their relations of production. We further suggested in chapter 4 that much of the blame for this state of affairs lay with the traditional manner of conceptualising the economic base as an active force breathing life into an otherwise listless superstructure, whereas Althusser's formulation of relatively autonomous ideological and political *practices* produced less reductionist conclusions. How are we to apply this concept of relative autonomy to real world events? The last decade has witnessed some bitter arguments about this question. Althusser suggested that it was possible to separate those ideological and political practices that *had* to operate as *conditions of existence* for capitalist economic practices from those that were not necessary for this purpose. The latter were consequently able to follow their own 'autonomous' logic. For some, in particular E.P. Thompson, this concept of relative autonomy was never anything more than a warning against the possible danger of reductionism, offering no real guidelines for detailed empirical or historical analysis.[51] For Hindess, Hirst and others, the concept and its qualification of 'determination in the last instance by the economic' is little more than 'a logically flawed, half-baked defence of reductionism' (Cutler et al.[52]). Their argument is that it simply is not possible for something to be simultaneously determinate and autonomous.

Important political implications result from this observation, as can be appreciated by examining Cutler et al.'s understanding of class. For classical Marxist theory, classes are viewed both as part of the determinate relations of production (that is as carriers of economic structure – wage labourer, land owner etc.) and as social subjects more widely engaged in politics (members of a political party, trade union or community group) and struggles over ideas (sexism, racism etc.). The crucial question for Marxist theory is: can classes in their economically defined form become real living, active, political forces? Or put in theoretical terms: can classes conceptualised in economic terms become represented (literally *re*-presented) as homogeneous living political and ideological forces? For Cutler et al. the answer is simple: 'Classes do not immediately and directly represent themselves. When we examine political and ideological struggles, we find state apparatuses, political parties and organisations, demonstrations and riotous mobs... but we cannot find *classes* lined up against each other.'[53] Subsequently, the 'choice for Marxism is clear. *Either* we effectively reduce political and ideological phenomena to class interests determined elsewhere (basically the economy)... *or* we face up to the real autonomy of political and ideological phenomena.'[54] Their rejection of the relative autonomy formulation stems from an objection to Althusser's usage of the concept of representation. Althusser differentiates between *what* is represented and its *represented form*, implying that there is something determinate about, and specific to, the *means* of representation. Cutler et al. argue that if the means of representation (i.e. political institutions) are specific, determinate and therefore *independent* it can make no sense to conceive of them as tending to be or actually being constrained by something outside themselves (i.e. economic relations); nor is it logical to speak of them representing anything in particular. Bew et al., amongst others, have defended the logic of the relative autonomy concept using the following analogy:

> Consider an independent means, the camera, by which visual images can be represented in photographs. The camera exists perfectly independently of these images. They do not conjure it into existence. Its conditions of production are social, economic and technological. There can be a plurality of types of camera, each with a specific way of being effective. Yet a genuine constraint is present. To function *qua* camera, it is constrained to produce photographic representations of visual images. If it does not, then it ceases to be a working camera. For all its independence of origin and independent effectivity it can only represent a strictly specifiable set of entities. There is no necessary incompatibility between the effectiveness of a practice and a constraint upon it to represent a set of entities. Nor, more generally, is there a necessary incompatibility between autonomy and its limitation. Cutler et al. fail to demonstrate that 'representation' is an incoherent notion. It is not the concept of relative autonomy which is half-baked, but their objections to it.[55]

This problem of specifying the degree and precise functioning of the concept of 'relative autonomy' is undoubtedly one of the most important confronting contemporary Marxist scholars, particularly those concerned with social welfare. Students of social policy face a stark choice, as welfare matters are so obviously a function of determinate economic forces, the state's and other agencies' political interventions, as well as ideological factors. Do they attempt to employ the concept of relative autonomy and, if so, how? Or do they go along with Cutler et al.'s notion of a necessary non-correspondence between practices, i.e. the absolute autonomy of all practices? To facilitate the making of such a choice it is instructive to explore an area of study where the concept has been operationalised, and which is of great importance to social policy – the family form and the precise nature of women's subordination.

### Accounting for women's oppression

Until fairly recently, many Marxists did not separate specific concepts used to account for women's oppression (e.g. the sexual division of labour) from those concepts (e.g. relations of production) used to explain capital's general development.[56] For example, Olivia Adamson et al., writing in 1976, argued that women's oppression was both created by the capitalist relations of production and functional for capitalism; consequently 'the struggle against capital *is* the struggle against domestic work and the struggle against domestic work is the struggle against capital'.[57] Other feminists influenced by Marxist theory have explicitly rejected such functionalist and reductionist arguments, and have spent much of the past decade engaged in a wide-ranging debate about the extent to which women's oppression is constructed *independently* of the economic processes of capitalist production. Some of the early contributions to this debate emphasised the ways in which the family system helps to create and reproduce the necessary conditions for capitalist production, highlighting particularly how domestic labour (housework and caring for dependants) plays a vital economic role in capitalist reproduction. Later contributors to this domestic labour debate introduced additional concepts such as patriarchal ideology and the sexual division of labour to help explain why *female* wage labour offered these advantages for capital.[58]

Even with supplementation, such analyses were not capable of convincingly demonstrating why it should be in the interests of capital in general to pay women wages that required the payment of a larger wage to their husbands, or why the privatised system of reproduction should necessitate *women* performing domestic duties. Politically, these analyses still collapsed the struggle for women's liberation into the generalised class struggle, failing to appreciate the extent to which the interests of women workers in the nineteenth century had been subsumed under and eventually defeated by those of the organised *male* working class. Some Marxist feminists turned to the concept of patriarchal power in order to explain such events. The key question became: what is the exact relationship between class power and gender power? Are there two separate systems, one governing production and the other reproduction, or one single related system? Single-system analyses appear, as we have seen, to slide into functionalist and reductionist arguments. Dual systems, such as the capitalist–patriarchy approach of Heidi Hartmann, *openly restrict* the applicability of Marxist concepts, arguing that their sex-blindness needs to be compensated by new concepts derived from that of patriarchy.[59] Such restrictions make sense to us, although such analyses do admit difficulties in satisfactorily linking the two types of power hierarchy. Michelle Barrett is not so willing to narrow the applicability of Marxist theory, and in *Women's Oppression Today* she attempts to utilise the concept of relative autonomy to satisfactorily explain the relationship between capitalist production and male power.[60]

The key to women's oppression, for Barrett, is a complex she terms 'the family-household system'[61] which is made up of a particular social structure (the household) and, crucially, a given ideology (familial). Although the two are connected, they are not parallel. The former is made up of a number of people, usually biologically related, dependent on both the wages of a few adult members (primarily the husband/father) and the unpaid domestic labour of females (primarily the wife/mother).[62] The latter, the ideology of familialism, enabled the bourgeoisie 'to secure a hegemonic definition of family life: as naturally based on close kinship, as properly organised through a male breadwinner with financially dependent wife and children, and as a haven of privacy beyond the public realm of commerce and industry'.[63] Barrett's principal argument is that this family-household system is not inherent to capitalism but has emerged through a complex series of processes that have incorporated an ideology of 'natural' female domesticity into the relations of production. To some extent these ideological notions predated capitalism but were reinforced by the acceptance of the male industrial working class. Brenner and Ramas paraphrase Barrett's argument:

> Once the family-household system was in place, a sex-segregated labour market was almost inevitable. ... Working-class men fought for the family-household system because it was in their short-term interests. However, in the long run, Barrett argues, this represented a real defeat for the class as a whole because it split the interests of working men and women. Working-class men could have organised to raise women's wages, a strategy that would have unified and thereby strengthened the working class. Instead, they fought for a family wage and unions for men.[64]

As the capitalist class derives long-term *political* benefits from these fundamentally conservative arrangements, it has continued to buttress them through protective legislation in the nineteenth century and welfare provisions in the twentieth, despite *economic* costs. Barrett's analysis therefore stresses both how the state expands 'welfare provisions to enforce women's dependence within the household' and how this provision plays 'an important part in structuring the different opportunities open to men and women, the ideology of women's dependence upon a male breadwinner, and in constructing women's "dual relationship" to the class structure'.[65]

Such a view is a dominant one amongst Marxist feminists,[66] yet it does not necessarily flow from adopting the concept of relative autonomy; nor has it gone unchallenged.

Brenner and Ramas suggest this view over-emphasises state policies which reinforce women's dependence and ignores the contradictory trend whereby the welfare state developed services to care for dependent adults and, to a lesser extent, children *outside* the family. They go on to argue that since the Second World War welfare developments have not emphasised 'a firmer location of responsibility for dependants within the family, but a halting, grudgingly-given movement toward the narrowing of familial responsibility'.[67] Certainly Barrett's account of working-class acceptance of the family-household system, and the promotion by an enlightened bourgeoisie of welfare arrangements based upon it, smacks of conspiracy. Undoubtedly, men's needs and male assessments of priorities have dominated working-class struggle – promoting high males wages as a major priority and relegating concerns about quality child-care. Jane Humphries criticises most Marxist-feminist accounts for their one-sided emphasis on capital's needs. According to her the working classes have defended and strengthened the family form as it 'reflects a struggle... for popular ways of meeting the needs of non-labouring comrades within a capitalist environment'.[68] The family-household system represents a partial victory for the working class as it offers protection from the worst ravages of capitalism's trade cycle.

Methodologically, Barrett seems to have theorised ideology as relatively autonomous of economic processes, but *not* of political control of the male-dominated bourgeois state. Indeed, it seems a little odd that an account stressing such a degree of freedom for ideological determinations, with all their uneven complexity, should so privilege such *coherent* state interventions. Other writers, following Donzelot (many of whom have sympathy for the total autonomy position of writers such as Cutler et al.), stress the disparate nature of the political and ideological interventions into family life.[69] This is Hodges and Hussain's explanation of Donzelot's method: 'The essential feature of the modern family is that it is a subject of intervention from a number of different directions and all of these... have specific effects upon it.... The family is less of an institution or organism than a *point of intersection of different social practices*: medical, judicial, educational, psychiatric, etc.'[70] We will have cause to return to Donzelot's methodology below, but for our present purposes it is important to note how these analyses, also concentrating on ideological determinations, reject the assumption that the family-household system *must* reproduce the established social order.

Barrett's attempt at operationalising the concept of 'relative autonomy' appears partially successful. She has certainly pointed out the foolishness of economic reductionism, and in a most graphic manner has demonstrated the effects of gender divisions on class solidarity. Her employment of the concept of ideology, however, suffers from an embarrassment of riches; a blend of relatively autonomous, capitalist and patriarchal ideologies are called on to explain the social compulsions for the formation of a particular type of family form as well as generalised mass investment in the values of family life. There is both a particular and a general problem with this. The particular problem is that in her limited discussion of the mechanisms through which people acquire gender ideologies she stresses the *passive* internalisation mechanisms of stereotyping, compensation, collusion and recuperation, and there is no real explanation of why particularly working-class women should have adopted an ideology that does not meet their real material needs. The more general problem is a failure to specify the very question we wanted answered – the precise nature of the relationship between the different levels of determination.

Barrett has retrospectively conceded some ground to these criticisms in a very interesting reassessment of her own and other socialist-feminist work on the family. This auto-critique – co-authored with Mary McIntosh – focuses largely on their original inadequate theorisation of how the family-household system and familial ideologies are differently structured for, and experienced by, black women. They admit to ethnocentric assessments, and urge white feminists to develop a fuller understanding of the different *forms* that a critique of the family might have to take in different contexts. More specifically, they argue that usage of the concepts of *ideology* and *reproduction* (see chapter 4) should be reappraised. The former should be more sensitive to how the ideological construction of white femininity has often been at the expense of highly offensive distortions of black femininity and sexuality; and the latter should incorporate into analyses the general reproductive abuse of women from the Third World and ethnic minorities, e.g. campaigns of mass sterilisation and the use of morning-after contraceptives. However, the key theoretical issue here – and it is one that British socialists and feminists are only just waking up to – is how racial oppression relates to forms of class power. In the case we have been examining the issues become even more complicated as the question of race has to be added to the already clouded relationship between gender and class. Barrett and McIntosh wonder whether it is possible to 'argue that racism, like women's oppression, has independent origins but is now irretrievably embedded in capitalist social relations'.[71]

Perhaps it is not possible to lay down precise rules for the employment of the relative autonomy concept. It certainly appears self-evident to us that the scope of strict economic determination will weaken the nearer one gets to type C policy analysis questions (see figure 6.1). Yet to opt for *complete* autonomy, even on these questions, is merely to confront the problem faced by much empirical sociology and orthodox social policy – masses of data with no organising principle to govern their explanation. Perhaps there are simply varying shades of autonomy, and no general principle to be learned; separate policy analysis issues may require separate specifications.

*Rediscovering civil society*
John Urry's recent work has altogether rejected the concept of relative autonomy, suggesting that capitalist society is better investigated through the concept of civil society mediating between the economy and the state.[72] Civil society in effect replaces the notion of ideological practices or levels, for Urry claims that ideologies cannot be conceptualised as a coherent instance or structure on a par with the economy or the state. The latter two can be regarded as having a structural unity; the economy is structured around capitalist relations of production entailing a definite set of immanent laws of capitalist development, whilst the state's unity is derived from the Weberian notion of a 'monopoly of physical coercion'. Civil society has no such unity; rather it is made up of three spheres – circulation, reproduction and struggle – lying between the state and the economy. Thus civil society embraces widely divergent practices, from family relations to commodity markets, from trade union organisations to religious bodies.[73]

Urry's is undoubtedly a helpful book, not least because (like Barrett) he demonstrates the futility of regarding capitalist societies as unitary totalities, and goes on to demonstrate how civil society must be seen as a locus of struggles for which there is *no* structurally determined outcome. The state's interventions, too, are conceptualised in a helpful manner as 'resulting from the interdependent relations between the economy and civil society: the former sets its demands, the latter provides the context within which it struggles to resolve them'.[74] So it is never simply a matter of regarding the state as an automatic pilot for smooth capitalist rule:

> Nor is it correct to consider that the state is always able to implement the 'correct' policy from the viewpoint of capital accumulation: indeed the state may often implement the 'wrong' policy, or the 'right' policy but at the wrong time. The state must not be viewed as automatically reacting to the demands of capital accumulation. Indeed, for substantial periods there may be no power bloc established at all; merely a number of politically dominant

classes, fractions, and social forces with no particular organisation, unity or policy.[75]

Such a view seems compatible with Gabriel and Ben-Tovim's discussion of racism.[76] In a most interesting article – reviewing the Marxist literature on the subject and socialist strategies to resist racism – they suggest that racism is best conceptualised as an almost indiscriminate range of practices that cannot be unitarily regarded as 'pure' effects of either dominant economic class relations and/or the political will of the ruling class. They imply that socialist political activity may often have to be structured around achieving important ideological 'gains', e.g. combating and overcoming racism and sexism, within a capitalist framework (see the section 'Living, breathing class struggle' below, and the conclusion to part II, for development of this point).

It is these two crucial Marxist concepts – the state and class struggle – that we are forced to return to yet again. In which ways do they need modifying or *sensitising* for effective employment in policy analysis questions? In a sense the resolution of the major theoretical difficulties we have come across in this text could be seen as resting on clarifications within these two areas. Is it possible to differentiate between state functions and rationales for state actions and retain a unitary Marxist theory of the state? Or do we have to jettison Marxist concepts if we adopt a more fragmented view of the state? Similarly, when explaining these different state interventions as partially the result of the *actions* of different groups (class fractions, professional associations, trade unions etc.) how does one proceed, and how far can one go before one abandons the structural propensities of Marxist theory altogether?

### The state and policy formation

As we saw in chapter 4, O'Connor's work, with its clear conceptual distinctions between different categories of state expenditure, constituted an important breakthrough for Marxists concerned with state policy. Around the time of its publication Marxist writers began to make other crucial distinctions – for example, between the local and the central state – and pay much greater attention to the complex nature of the demands placed on the state. As the authors of *Unpopular Education* put it: 'If schooling is to contribute to reproducing hierarchies of control, it faces acutely contradictory demands: to develop in some the desire to manage the labour of others, in others a limited technical mastery and, for the great majority of young people, to ease the transition towards essentially subordinate positions in the hierarchies of labour.'[77] O'Connor's work was much more fruitful in generating awareness about such complexities than in understanding the precise reasoning behind state interventions. Which state actions were dependent on the outcome of pressure and struggle, and which occur regardless of them? This was precisely the question Offe tried to answer with his distinction between *allocative* and *productive* policies.[78]

Allocative state intervention involves the state in what Harrington has described as a *responsive* mode, differentiating between competing demands about available goods and services.[79] The state becomes an arena for power struggles. Productive state intervention is said to occur when 'something more and different from this is required to assist capitalist accumulation';[80] the state has to produce goods and services required by the accumulation process owing to market failures to supply some aspect of constant or variable capital. This type of intervention, described as the *independent* mode by Harrington, is unable to rely on political pressures as some of the principal groups exerting such pressure will have been party to producing the original market failures. The state has to resist, for example, the demands of certain of the principal actors in the development process, notably property speculators and builders, if it is to effectively combat inner city congestion and pollution.

There are a number of immediately obvious problems with Offe's distinction. First, he is only really concerned with the state's economic policies; social policies might require more subtle distinctions. Second, the productive policy classification leaves many questions under-explored, not least those appertaining to the alleged independence of the state from political pressure. Offe argues that the rationale for state interventions is 'the stabilisation of the accumulation process' representing 'the well-being of capitalism as a whole'.[81] This is a highly notional kind of independence. No answer is supplied to the question of *how* the state has come to represent these long-term interests. Surely an approach more sensitive to how class forces influence the state would have to add a historical dimension. Such an addition might lead one to similar conclusions as those made by Harrington: 'What seem to be "independent" (internal) state initiatives may in fact merely represent a reaction to earlier (external) social forces. ... The state's independence would refer to nothing more than its unresponsiveness to a current set of social interests due to its continued responsiveness to the previous influence of another set.'[82] Whilst this is undoubtedly a correct observation, we cannot agree with the theoretical or political motivations behind it. For, somewhat ironically, Harrington's argument seems to further preclude any *political* possibility of state agencies (local or national) being able to act against capital's long-term interests. He states:

[If] it is accepted that past pressure may become internalised within the structure of the state – e.g. in the organisation of its machinery, in the policy-making techniques it adopts, in the ideology of policy-makers – then it follows that the failure of various current external social interests to influence policy is not an indication of state independence from external influence. It merely indicates that other social interests or other demands than those presently being aimed at the state are influencing the formation of policy.[83]

In other words, the state's scope for independent action lies *only* with the autonomy of certain professional groups within the state – an autonomy which Harrington argues will for the most part resist and bamboozle popular political pressures through the use of technical jargon and other distancing techniques.[84] Theoretically, Harrington implacably opposes what he describes as dualist models such as Offe's, i.e. theories which imply that *different* empirical objects might be best explained by *different* theoretical systems. He suggests that the 'problem with this approach is very simple: that by splitting up the empirical objects... it draws attention away from any connections between them'.[85] This argument does not, however, lead him to want to use Marxist theory in a unitary or holistic manner, as such approaches place serious restrictions on the 'things to be explained'. We would certainly concur with this rejection of unitary Marxist theory in social policy studies for, as we have seen, such theory has marginalised questions of social policy analysis. Harrington's solution, following Pickvance,[86] is to adopt a multi-theoretical approach but one stressing different levels of abstraction rather than different empirical objects. This appears to us little more than a unitary method in not so subtle disguise!

## The fragmented state?

Alan Cawson and Peter Saunders are two theorists who have consciously attempted to develop the type of dualistic theory rejected by Harrington.[87] Cawson, in the most extended presentation of the thesis, argues that both functionalist Marxist and monetarist variants of political economy reduce politics to economics, and that it is necessary to develop a new political economy. For as

a larger and larger share of national output came to be produced by fewer and fewer giant firms, it became evident that they could exert not just economic power in the market but also sectional political pressures for discriminatory economic policies. Thus was born the dual state and the dual economy. Overlaid upon and increasingly dominating the competitive market sector of the economy, in which a large number of small firms remained subordinate to the market, was a corporate sector which grew both as a cause and a consequence of state intervention. At the same time the democratic political market was beginning to be eclipsed by the power of interest groups, especially those of the economic producers, both capital and labour.[88]

We are fortunate that Cawson offers a diagrammatic presentation of this historical development (see figure 6.2). In the same way as the corporate and competitive sectors are differentiated, so too can we 'distinguish between a corporate sector of interest representation and a competitive or pluralist one'.[89] Neither the economy nor the political system are becoming uniformly corporatist; rather a dual economic and political structure is emerging.

Cawson's and Saunders's work seems hell-bent on trying to achieve quite precise explanations of any given state intervention. They explicitly reject the relative autonomy formulation for this purpose owing to its tendency to explain 'everything and nothing. As a description, it is undoubtedly valid, but as a causal explanation it is fatuous and empty.'[90] In their search for greater precision they effect a series of conceptual distinctions, 'breaking down the concept of "the" state into its levels, functions and modes of intervention, so as to permit an exploration of state policy from the starting point that the state's relationship to different kinds of interest may vary depending upon what we are looking at'.[91] The *functions*, following O'Connor, are described as production, consumption and legitimation. The *levels* of state operation are the self-evident ones of central, regional and local. The *modes of intervention* are more complicated. The first is the *market mode*, with its characteristic feature being the limitation of state activities to those which are required for private markets to operate. The second is the *bureaucratic mode*, reliant upon 'an extensive state which constitutes all links between state, economy and society into a public sphere, and comprises a set of authoritative command relationships which define the rights and duties of individuals';[92] and thirdly, the *corporatist mode* in which 'the state is neither directive nor

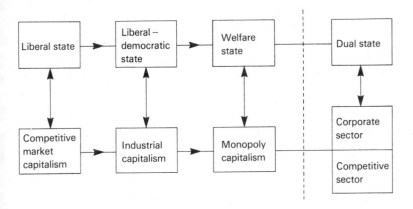

Figure 6.2   *A dual economic and political structure*
*Source:* A. Cawson, *Corporatism and Welfare* (Heinemann, 1982), p. 11

coupled to an autonomous private sphere'.[93] Cawson again provides a diagrammatic guide:

|   |   | Market mode | Bureaucratic mode | Corporatist mode |
|---|---|---|---|---|
| 1 | Role of the state | facilitative | directive | interventionist |
| 2 | Basis of legitimate decisions | law-governed | rule-governed | bargain-governed |
| 3 | Distribution of power | diffuse/ pluralistic | centralised/ concentrated | polycentric/ hierarchical |
| 4 | Form of legislation | regulatory | detailed | enabling |
| 5 | Form of planning | non-planning | imperative | indicative |
| 6 | Associated ideology | competitive individualist | state socialist | social democratic/ reformist |
| 7 | Ideological basis | private property | egalitarianism | security/efficiency/ abundance |

Figure 6.3    *Modes of intervention*
Source: Cawson, *Corporatism and Welfare*, p. 67

The dual state theorists present the reader with an incredibly neat 'ideal-type' formulation. Its neatness stems, however, from not as yet having to dirty its hands with real-world applications. Will the concepts hold up and be capable of producing precise accounts of exactly how different types of real-world political struggle affect state policy decisions? Certainly, they seem to start off in the right manner, expressing unhappiness with Gough's compromise formula because 'people do not merely identify their political interests by reference to... a common class position but also by common *functional* locations'. In other words, 'horizontal class relationships grounded in a hierarchy of dominance are cut across by sectional and functional dimensions which lead to socio-political alignment around vertical positions'.[94] Without doubt conflicts do develop around what Dunleavy has termed *consumption sectors*[95] so that 'when people mobilise... over questions of consumption, they do so not as members of a class, but as consumers of a particular commodity or service; as commuters, civil servants, parents, book-borrowers and so on'.[96] If anything, though, these are further *conceptual* refinements to a model which, as we shall see, is far from satisfactory.

First, the model makes far too many dubious assumptions: for example, that everything at the local level is 'pluralist' or 'competitive'. No real questioning occurs as to whether local services (e.g. council housing, education and personal social services) could be organised on a bureaucratic basis, and it is very unclear how we are to categorise the locally organised police and fire services. Second, a major problem with O'Connor's state expenditure classification was always how to render his conceptual distinctions into suitable forms for empirical study; as he often pointed out, most spending falls into all three categories. Cawson and Saunders compound these difficulties, and their well-intentioned search for specific detail all too easily ends up as an imposition of inappropriate and rigid categories. Third, their careful taxonomic exercise can be seen to be inflexible if it is asked to perform comparative duties; not only does the model not properly identify the key concerns of British local government (a rather haphazard development of some public utility types of social investment combined with important social consumption provision), but also its ethnocentrism prevents it from properly appreciating alternative developments (e.g. in France, where education is centrally controlled and social housing is both centrally and locally organised).

Fourth, for all their concern with detail, the model is only limitedly applied and then with scant attention to historical developments. Huge generalities are offered, for example that 'the NHS can be seen to comprise corporatist and bureaucratic elements... [and] the post-war history of the NHS can be persuasively analysed as an unfolding interplay between professional and managerial elements in the context of the unionisation of health service workers'.[97] There is nothing of any substance about 'the details' of class, professional or functional struggles within the service other than this rather brief observation: 'The structure of producer interests has changed markedly, with a succession of challenges to the dominant position of doctors and consultants mounted by administrators and other occupational groups such as nurses and ancillary workers'.[98] Of course, health policy is largely determined by the control of doctors over access to patients and the principle of 'clinical freedom', but can it seriously be argued that 'policy is now *much more* subject to the influence of other provider groups amongst which managers have come to play a more significant... role'?[99] Perhaps it can, but we need much more information, and an answer to *why* this has occurred. If not, there is a danger such arguments will seriously misconceptualise the nature of professional power and influence, treating professions as solely nationally-based interest groups within the corporatist sector. Powerful professional groups, such as the medical profession, are able to originate policy change through *ideological* dominance and localised practices. The fifth problem, then, is the failure adequately to conceptualise the nature of professional power. Local policy inputs are seen as relatively free and open to popular/pluralist demands; but this picture excludes from view the way professional groups internally organise nationally and then are able to effect local shifts in policy, influencing one local authority after another. Two recent examples of this process are the influence of the social work profession on the adoption and form of intermediate treatment and community care.

The sixth, and final, problem is the rather dismembered view of class struggle on offer. As noted earlier, Cawson distinguishes between a corporate sphere of interest representation (politics) where political groups come together through common class position or functional location (interest deriving from objective social categories) and a competitive sphere where interest is derived from subjective choice. This is an interesting idea – the separation of objective from subjective interests – but one whose application produces some perverse conclusions. The Campaign for Nuclear Disarmament is classified as a non-class group (which does not tell us very much) and trade union struggles, which were once regarded as part of the competitive sphere, are now thought better categorised within the corporate sector, owing to the fact that they have an established and legitimate role within the relations of production. This formulation hardly allows for any exploration of struggles between trade union leaderships and their rank and files. A most anaemic view of the give and take of real political struggle results from this obsession with slotting everything into different boxes. The corporate sphere becomes dominated by organisations *directly* representing class interests – monolithic capital confronting a uniform labour! As Allan Cochrane has noted, this is an absurd view, reducing class struggle to confrontation at the NEDC.[100] Cawson seems to recognise as much:

> Politics in the corporate sphere... does not exhaust all issues and other functionalist interest groups (which may have a class character but which do not *directly* represent class interest) will be important in the analysis of many aspects of social policy... in health, education and the personal social services... The competitive and corporate spheres overlap.[101]

This is a most tortuous passage and one that virtually concedes many of the central problems in their whole exercise. Similar arguments apply to their virtual denial of any role for class struggle in the sphere of consumption. The vital question is: just *how* do consumption sectional struggles mesh with those that clearly do have a more direct class component? Of course, as we have seen, some Marxists see class struggles anywhere and everywhere, but one does not improve upon such views by replacing them with a model so unwieldy and lifeless as to bear comparison with the worst excesses of the capital-logic school!

Perhaps we are being over-harsh in our judgement on the dual-state theorists, for they have at least attempted to come to grips with many of the problems faced by Marxist theory in trying to specify the relative autonomy of ideological and political instances from economic ones. Certainly, they are correct to point to separate arenas of class struggle and the way that consumption sectional struggles can cut across traditional class divisions, e.g. in housing sectors (home ownership versus tenant). Our objections to their work are largely the same as those we directed at some variants of fundamentalism – the iron-case rigidity of their theoretical system. Living, breathing political forces become simply unrecognisable; the peculiar concrete linkages between tenants, organised workers, radical professionals and the poor which make up the Labour Party, for example, simply disappear into a multitude of disparate boxes! Trade unions become quintessential corporate bodies with little attention to localised plant, combine or workshop organisation or conflict. Are we asking too much? Is Marxist theory capable of simultaneously being acutely sensitive to actual political struggles whilst concentrating on the more structural aspects of social policy determination?

## Living, breathing class struggle

By now it should be apparent that there are widespread disagreements amongst Marxists on how best to explain concrete political struggles. This is no mere question of interpretation and involves large differences of opinion about the very class location of certain occupations, many of which contribute to the delivery of welfare. How, for example, would Marxist theory assess the class location of a teacher? How would his or her potential as an ally in working-class struggle be evaluated?

Eurocommunist traditions have always emphasised catholic criteria for membership of the working class, stressing broad anti-bourgeois political positions easily encompassing the teaching profession. Many recent Marxist writings have also pointed to the routine deskilling and proletarianisation of white-collar work.[102] Marx himself certainly credited teachers with working-class status: 'A schoolmaster is a productive labourer when, in addition to belabouring the heads of his scholars, he works like a horse to enrich the school proprietor. That the latter has laid out his capital in a teaching factory, instead of a sausage factory, does not alter the relation.'[103] Marx's discussion identifies membership of the working class with productive labour, and there has been a great deal of recent controversy about what is involved in such labour. Many teachers, of course, now work for the state; would this have altered Marx's opinion? Certainly many contemporary Marxists do not regard teachers as productive workers, although some do suggest that teachers' indirect contribution to the creation of surplus value (i.e. their contribution to the reproduction of variable capital) allows them to be classified as such.[104] Most nevertheless seem determined to assign all white-collar workers – the majority of whom they regard as being engaged in supervisory and non-productive work – into some sort of 'new' or reconstituted middle class.

Carchedi, for example, argues that there is a new middle class which consists of those who carry out the global functions of capital (control and surveillance) whilst simultaneously carrying out the functions of the collective labourer.[105] Poulantzas similarly uses political and ideological criteria, in addition to an economic one, to separate off the proletariat from what he describes as the new petty bourgeoisie.[106] Workers, for Poulantzas, are defined economically by direct involvement in productive labour (i.e. material commodity production) – a position which reduces the working class to a near minority in most European countries, and to pygmy proportions in the USA! Those engaged in supervisory work are *politically* defined as part of the new petty bourgeoisie, and in addition the alleged expert knowledge of non-manual workers (i.e. their role in mental labour) *ideologically* separates them off into this new stratum. Poulantzas's discussion of ideology is most revealing in relation to our enquiry into the teaching profession. He argues that: 'Agents of the state personnel who go over to the side of the popular masses often live their revolt in terms of the dominant ideology... and... do not challenge the reproduction of the social division of labour within the state apparatus... nor... do they normally challenge the political division between rulers and the ruled.'[107]

It would appear that teachers, and all other middle-class state personnel, are caught between the two major classes, *incapable* of effectively challenging dominant ideologies or political forms. This same position is adopted in the only serious attempt by British Marxists to explain the class location of teachers: 'Trapped between the developing power of monopoly capitalism and the advances of the working class, professionalism can be understood as a petty bourgeois strategy for advancing and preserving a relatively privileged position.'[108] Wright also emphasises the essentially ambivalent status of middle-class existence.[109] For him teachers have to be placed between the petty bourgeoisie and the working class (in terms of productive relations) and between the bourgeoisie and the working class (at the ideological level) in a *contradictory class location*. Approximately 50 per cent of the population can be placed in such positions, as shown in figure 6.4. As these 'contradictory locations' have contradictory class interests 'they are objectively torn between class forces within the class struggle and can potentially be organised into more than one class capacity. Class struggle itself therefore determines... the complexities of the class structure' and the class formation.[110] Olin Wright's work potentially allows for a much more fluid understanding of class struggle as a process involving temporary alliances and trade-offs. With reference to teachers, for example, he concedes 'how they potentially subvert bourgeois ideology'.[111] However, he never really employs his schema to account for any

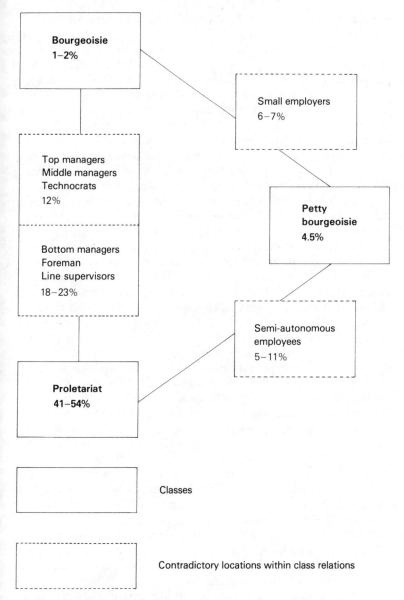

Figure 6.4   *Class locations*
*Source:* E. O. Wright, *Class, Crisis and the State* (New Left Books, 1978), p. 86

actual contemporary outcome. As with so much of this work on class location, it is at a very high level of abstraction, sharing with the dual-state theory a real difficulty with focusing on specific empirical situations. The whole exercise is more like a grand theoretical game, and it seems that very different conclusions could be drawn just by changing the conceptual rules. Other Marxist theorists could use the same terms but come to very different political conclusions. For example, Ozga and Lawn in their study of the teaching profession argue that: 'Productive and unproductive workers are more *united* by their *common* exploitation and their fundamentally antagonistic relations with their employers than divided by the technical application of the criteria of surplus value production'.[112] We are forced to conclude that the Marxist theorisation of the class status of the middle classes, and the role of professionalism, is most underdeveloped. 'Deprofessionalisation' is valued as an important political goal, but little has been thought through concerning either a viable strategic programme or what practicably to replace professionalism with.

The analysis of professions is an excellent example of how radical welfare theory almost exclusively concentrates on *critique* (e.g. their lack of accountability; failures of responsibility and self-evaluation; disabling effects; etc.). Paul Wilding's work is a representative example of this, despite rejecting the usual assumption that professional autonomy and power varies inversely with the level of state intervention. If anything this unconventional approach, emphasising 'how bureaucracies can free professionals from many of the constraints and inhibitions of single-handed private practice',[113] further reinforces the image of the all-powerful profession. By always highlighting the pervasiveness of professional power – capacity for policy determination, definition of client needs, control over resources, authority over clients, and control of the work situation – Wilding fails to enquire sufficiently into how different bureaucratic contexts may develop radically divergent conditions for the execution of power by professional groups. Another related weakness is his concentration on the generalised medical profession as his major example, failing to penetrate sufficiently into the medical division of labour and the power differentials between consultants, junior doctors, general practitioners, radiographers, opticians etc. as well as the differences between this profession and other welfare professionals. All too often the power of the people at the top end of a profession – chief education officers, headmasters, directors of social services etc. – is equated with the power of the lay members of the profession. Such work is not very helpful in specifying the precise nature of professional control or in helping us account for activities such as sympathetic industrial action undertaken by social workers in support of housing workers over deteriorating services to clients.

Again, Urry's work seems to offer a potentially more useful approach. In *The Anatomy of Capitalist Societies* he suggests there are three spheres of civil society – circulation, reproduction and struggle – and there are no 'pure' classes defined economically. Rather:

> Classes only exist in struggle within civil society; they do not exist first... as economic classes which may/may not realise their economic interests at the political/ideological level.... The form... they take is given first by the current patterns of capital accumulation and between the functions of capital and labour; second, by the form of gender, age, racial, regional and national interpellation within civil society; and third, by the forms of political organisation and state apparatuses.[114]

Following Laclau,[115] Urry suggests class struggle should be understood as taking place within three separate arenas. The first is 'class struggle', where struggles centrally implicate classes structured by the appropriation and production of surplus value; this is the traditional understanding of class struggle. The second is 'classes in struggle', where struggles involve categories of subject who occupy a common position in relationship to the means of production but not one entailing direct antagonism with another class; these are groups, to use Wright's term, in contradictory class locations. Finally, 'popular-democratic struggle' involving the organisation of 'the people' on non-class forms of interpellation, i.e. gender, generation, region, race, nation etc. The implications of this tripartite division appear most useful for any investigator trying to ascertain the precise effects of class struggle on social policy outcomes. First, it allows us to get away from the fundamentalist insistence on the essential nature of a particular class – pent up, frustrated and waiting to be released. Second, the particular structure of civil society provides a diversity of boxes for class and non-class forms of political mobilisation. Third, these other forms of struggle will often interact with, and minimise or heighten, the salience of class struggle; indeed, attempting to establish the salience of class is very probably the major form that class struggle takes in contemporary capitalist societies.

In a recent paper on the effects of deindustrialisation, Urry has applied his model and suggested that the particular organisation of local labour markets are of great significance in structuring patterns of industrial location.[116] Consequently, local politics has been affected by a continuing decomposition of national class divisions, and a heightening of the importance of non-class-based politics. Struggles are often defensive in nature and concerned with recapitalising the local economy and preserving a semblance of local democracy (defend the GLC; save Merseyside; Sheffield's 'Services worth saving' etc.). Moreover, there is a shift in political forms away from exclusive preoccupation with the politics of production to a more widely conceived politics of *consumption*. The struggles of women, the young unemployed and ethnic minorities are increasingly looked to as the principal force for progressive social change. Certainly, we should not under-estimate the importance of what Dunleavy has described as 'consumption sector struggles'.[117] Vic Duke and Stephen Egdell have demonstrated, in a most interesting study on the effects of public expenditure cuts, how predominantly private consumption processes (e.g. public education and health provision) generate fragmentations within middle-class groups, and public consumption processes (council housing and public transport) generate divisions amongst the working class.[118] Their study also indicates that recent party political alignments have been influenced more by consumption location profiles than by occupationally defined social class.[119] They are, nevertheless, reluctant to under-estimate the marked and continuous importance of social class, and disagree with the dual-state theorists that 'the boundaries of consumption sectors bear a necessary non-correspondence to class boundaries'.[120]

Clearly, much further work still needs to be done on clarifying the precise ways in which generalised political struggles determine social policy outcomes. In addition, it is important to try to clarify how struggles over ideas can translate into material gains for particular groups. Many radicals are now acutely aware of the need to struggle on *ideological* questions.[121] A good example of this is the many feminist-inspired critiques of the Labour Party's alternative economic strategy for blindly aiming to create jobs which merely reflected hierarchical and sexist divisions. No attention was being brought to bear on how job-sharing schemes could be encouraged and how the family wage system might be undermined.[122] Such an example underlines yet again the immense difficulty faced by the broadly defined left in ascertaining what constitutes a gain for the working classes. Another, and even more perplexing, example involves an assessment of the post-war expansion of the personal social services and the precise role of social workers. Mike Prior and Dave Purdy have argued that 'this development has served to highlight the need for the community to take responsibility for coping with "individual" problems such as mental or physical handicap or juvenile delinquency. . . . From this standpoint the modern social worker is a carrier of collectivist values which are alien to the standards of capitalism.'[123] The more usual account of this process amongst socialists is that social workers reinforce conservative attitudes towards family life and effectively school deviant people into socially acceptable ways of behaviour.

A final, equally perplexing, example is highlighted by the debates around the use of racism awareness training (RAT) by 'socialist' councils concerned about racism in the delivery of their services. In very powerful critiques both Ahmed Gurnah and Sivanandan have criticised RAT for its individualism and ethics. This quote from the latter captures their tone:

> Racism is not, as RAT believes, a white problem, but a problem of an exploitative white power structure; power is not something white people are born into, but that which they derive from their position in a complex race/sex/class hierarchy; oppression does not equal exploitation; ideas do not equal ideology; the personal is not the political, but the political is personal (changing society and changing oneself is a continuum of the same commitment – else, neither gets changed), and personal liberation is not political liberation.[124]

Such strong negative responses from some black intellectuals and activists have been experienced as a particularly bitter blow by many committed socialists – both white and black – who were convinced that RAT was a 'progressive' political initiative. Certainly, Gurnah's conclusions seem somewhat more conciliatory than Sivanandan's: 'this is not meant to imply that all anti-racist education and anti-racist consciousness raising is ineffectual and harmful. Quite the contrary: both are extremely important, but need to be done in the context of concrete action... in policies and conditions.'[125] We appear back again with the dilemma of structure and personal action. Our point is that 'critical', Marxist-influenced social policy studies are somewhat in their infancy with regard to the necessary political calculations that are required to evaluate not only what is a working-class 'gain', but also what are gains for other oppressed groups. The real world is a complicated place in which separate struggles merge and gell. Life is not all a Manichaean struggle between good (labour) and evil (capital); rather it is a place where very difficult 'political' choices have to be made. For example, during the abolition of South Yorkshire Metropolitan Council the unions in Sheffield managed to get Sheffield City Council to 'ring-fence' certain jobs, which meant they could only be offered first to ex-South Yorkshire employees. Such a decision, of course, cut across the other agreements to employ more women and more people from ethnic minority groups; the majority of South Yorkshire's professional employees were white and male. Many activists in Sheffield were extremely angry and accused the unions and the Council of racism and sexism. Were they right to do so? Surely at a time of attacks on, and erosion of the unions' power, it is vital for their continued credibility that they are able to demonstrate some ability to protect jobs. How socialists judge when best to make gains on a variety of fronts simultaneously and when best to hold back and emphasise other issues is something that needs much thought in the coming years.

**A new view of power?**

The increasing awareness amongst Marxist theorists of the need to specify the independence of the struggles of women, black people and others from the wider class struggle has led many to abandon Marxism altogether. For thinkers such as Hindess and Hirst, as we saw earlier, it was impossible accurately to assess the degree of relative autonomy of ideological and political practices from economic ones, and from such observations it was but a small step to an intellectual position that celebrated the complete autonomy of all processes! These thinkers found the work of the French philosopher Michel Foucault very useful in their search for what they describe as a 'non-essentialist' view of power. Wickham provides this example to explain what they mean:

> An analysis produced through a framework built around the essence economy must consider its object, say the demolition of a group of houses to make way for an office building, only in terms of... the maintenance of a capitalist economy (the potential profits of development and finance companies etc.). And it must do so at the expense of considerations of this object and its *specific conditions of existence in their own right,* free from any essence (government policies on development and housing, housing laws, council procedures, deliberations of planning bodies etc.). A policy of resisting the demolition of the houses based on such an essentialist analysis will be limited to strategies and tactics concerned with critiques and attempts to change companies' concentration on profitability... at the expense of strategies and tactics concerned with the specific conditions of existence.[126]

This seems to us not to solve the problem of relative autonomy, merely to repose it; that is, just what is the relation in such works between analyses of the economy and the other, albeit specific, conditions of existence? However, we take the general point that much greater attention has to be given to certain questions underplayed in some Marxist analyses.

Certainly, the questions posed by Foucault's genealogical analysis of history are important ones for the development of a critical social policy. His methodology rejects emphasising grand events and linear processes and seeks to establish and preserve the singularity of previously discredited and neglected episodes and phenomena, e.g. sexuality, madness, punishment and reason.[127] The focus is on complexity, contingency and the ultimate fragility of all historical forms. In addition, he highlights the historicity of phenomena and qualities previously considered ahistorical – sentiment, feelings and the physiology of the body. Foucault is particularly interested in this latter issue, the interrelationship between the body and history, relishing the demonstration of how even our physiology cannot escape the play of historical forces. Essentially, Foucault's work is concerned with showing how:

> Things weren't as necessary as all that; it wasn't as a matter of course that mad people came to be regarded as mentally ill; it wasn't self-evident that the only thing to be done with a criminal was to lock him up; it wasn't self-evident that the causes of illness were to be sought through the individual examination of bodies.[128]

In exploring such fascinating questions, Foucault concentrates attention less on the marxisante questions of 'Who has power?' or 'What aims do the ruling power holders have?', and more on questions about the continuous and uninterrupted pervasiveness of power for those on the receiving end: the interminable ongoing subjugation which controls our bodies, governs our gestures and dictates our very behaviours; the processes through which subjects are constituted as effects of power. For Foucault, these areas of power diffusion – the microphysics of power – were not invented by the bourgeoisie, but have been adopted and deployed by them from the moment they realised their political and economic utility. In effect, Foucault's conception of power is suggesting that it is most effective and tolerable when its operations go undetected, whereas Marxism concentrates too much on the overt or 'judico-discursive' conception of power, i.e. power as emanating from the formal rules of states. For Foucault: 'Power isn't localised in the state apparatus, and... nothing in society will be changed if the mechanisms of power that function outside, below and alongside the state... on a much more minute and everyday level, are not also changed'.[129] The attraction of Foucault's work for students of social policy should be obvious from this extract.[130] In particular, three aspects of his work should intrigue radical scholars of social policy. The first is Foucault's obsession with discipline – methods of observation, recording, calculation, regulation and training to which the body had to be subjected in order to eliminate individuality and produce regulation and normalisation, e.g. the rise of the Poor Law, schooling and prison systems. The second is the non-correspondence between various social, political and economic practices. As Gordon has expressed it: 'Our world does not follow a programme, but we live in a world of programmes, that is to say in a world traversed by the effects of discourses'.[131] Finally, there is the appreciation of the difficulty of effecting radical social change – the sheer stubbornness of certain practices despite changes of political rule or economic logic.

We can see all three of these themes in Jacques Donzelot's work. Donzelot is particularly concerned with investigating what he describes as 'the social', that 'enigmatic and worrying figure no one wants to take stock of for fear of losing one's way or one's Lenin'.[132]

In effect, 'the social' signifies a specific level or arena which is coterminous with the emergence of a series of technologies of power. As Barry Smart has put it:

> The emergence of 'the social' and the associated measures and mechanisms directed towards such dimensions of population as fertility, age, health, economic activity, welfare and education, not only represents a major development or shift in the form of the exercise of power, but in addition it has produced significant changes in... social relationships, and has since the mid-century effected a particular form of... solidarity.[133]

Donzelot's best-known work in English is *The Policing of Families*. This work attempts to demonstrate that the essential feature of the modern family is that it is the subject of interventions from a variety of different social practices – medical, judicial, educational, psychiatric etc. – all of which have specific effects. Donzelot's account is very detailed and complex – and space precludes an extended outline here – but what fascinates him is how the state is able to exercise control *through* families, with the active cooperation of members. As Hirst states in a most useful summary:

> Families are tied into networks of supervision through the school... juvenile courts... public housing and social security. Failures in relation to or *claims upon* these institutions bring the family under what Donzelot calls 'the tutelary complex' [which attempts] ... to manage the effects of 'failures'... and adjust families to social norms. Increasingly the deficiency of or claim by *one* member of the family, for example a truant child, becomes the ground for supervision of the family as a whole.[134]

The patriarchal father figure also loses his authority to this 'tutelary complex'. Central to the expansion of welfare and legal control over the family has been the expansion of psychoanalysis – or more specifically what Donzelot describes as the 'psy complex'.[135] Psychoanalysis has supplanted religious, medical and other techniques in the management of personal and relational difficulties; and this form of control allows for flexible standards of normality and competence (the concept of adjustment). Donzelot and his followers suggest that their complex account offers a much more fruitful explanation of why people invest so much in family life than the Marxist one of ideological conditioning.

We should, not, however, allow ourselves to be dazzled by Foucault's and Donzelot's work. Certainly, it promises many interesting avenues of research, particularly in the area of how ideologies are constituted and reproduced. Their work, indeed, seems to offer a more sophisticated approach to social control than that contained in much Marxist literature; yet in actuality it suffers from excessive conspiratorial overtones. Miscellaneous and disparate agencies are able to seek and secure their interests virtually at will. And whilst at first it appears their work has 'filled in' the missing space in Marxist discourse – the problem of agency – a moment's thought reveals that 'agency is in fact the central refusal of Donzelot's text'.[136] Their work explicitly rejects the imagery of strict causation but does not fight shy of continually implicating the effects of processes for which they cannot specify a cause! Much of Foucault's discussion of power reminds one a little of a science fiction film in which bodies are being implanted with alien elements and nobody, not even the recipient, knows.

The precise specification of agency does, nevertheless, remain a problem for Marxist analyses of social policy. We have attempted in this chapter to argue for a theoretical approach which is pragmatic and eclectic, utilising Marxist theory where appropriate and modifying and borrowing from other systems if a better explanatory purchase can be gained. We have also suggested that much more attention has to be paid to empirical happenings, if even this pragmatic Marxism is to have anything of utility to say about *immediate* policy analyses and strategies. Our argument is not that we should abandon Marxism's insight into structural determination, merely that we should complement it with greater precision.

## Conclusion

In the introduction to this chapter we intimated that a realistic Marxist theory concerned with welfare had to grapple with three sets of issues. It had to be able, first, to generate politically feasible alternatives; second, to attempt to address and evaluate immediate questions of policy; and third, to offer strategic help to practitioners within, and clients of, the welfare services. Little explicit attention has been paid to this last question, but our extended discussion of the first two has continuously borne it in mind. Marxist-informed theory about welfare issues has come a long way since the end of the post-war boom. No longer are practitioners harangued by radical theorists only too willing to point out how their actions merely shore up capitalism. In 1975, Paul Corrigan wrote that throughout 'the Western world, states are characterised by one of the two major symbols of control in capitalist society: the tank or the community worker'[137] – and this in an analysis that partially recognised the possibility of *radical* community work! Far more analyses in the 1980s begin from the type of position outlined by Kevin McDonnell in a very interesting piece on working in housing aid:

> I started from the position that housing aid is a valid area for socialists attempting to act in accord with their politics while simultaneously having a job that will pay them. For me the first priority... is in some way to help increase the power and self-confidence of the working class and other

oppressed groups. While sometimes... you may think you are moving in this direction, at the same time there is always a constant battle to avoid... ways of doing things characteristic of capitalist society.... There are definitely limitations involved... but the eventual outcomes are not determined from the beginning... There will be failures... successes may only be partial and temporary. But at least as socialists we can attempt to make the best of the opportunities that do exist and... extend them in every way possible.[138]

Much of this chapter has been an extended commentary on just how we might best be able to *evaluate* these successes and failures, on the types of realistic political calculations that are required. In coming to terms with these calculations, Marxist-influenced theoreticians have revealed quite large differences between themselves. We have deliberately drawn out these differences and sided with a version of Marxist theory that is so fragmented and eclectic that other Marxists might barely recognise it as the theory to which they adhere. We would concur with their arguments, for the whole purpose of this text has been to demonstrate the possibilities for a *rapprochement* between a critical or left Fabianism and a pragmatic Marxism, and a rejection of conservative Fabianism and fundamentalist Marxism.

## Notes

1   E.P. Thomson, *The Poverty of Theory and Other Essays* (Merlin, 1978), p. 361.
2   A. Nove, *The Economics of Feasible Socialism* (George Allen and Unwin, 1983), p. ix.
3   Ibid., p. 100.
4   Ibid., p. 206.
5   Ibid., pp. 227–8.
6   I. Taylor, P. Walton and J. Young, *The New Criminology – for a Social Theory of Deviance* (Routledge and Kegan Paul, 1973).
7   S. Cohen, 'Guilt, justice and tolerance: some old concepts for a new criminology', in D. Downes and P. Rock (eds), *Deviant Interpretations – problems in criminological theory* (Martin Robertson, 1979).
8   Ibid., p. 20.
9   J. Young, 'Working class criminology', in I. Taylor, P. Walton and J. Young (eds), *Critical Criminology* (Routledge and Kegan Paul, 1975), p. 81.
10  J. Young, 'Left idealism, reformism and beyond: from the new criminology to Marxism', in National Deviancy Conference/Conference of Socialist Economists, *Capitalism and the Rule of Law* (Hutchinson, 1970), pp. 12–13.
11  J. Lea and J. Young, *What is to be Done About Law and Order?* (Penguin, 1984), p. 117.
12  I. Taylor, *Law and Order – arguments for socialism* (Macmillan, 1981), p. 123.
13  *Critical Social Policy* is published three times a year and is available from Longman Group Ltd, Subscription (Journals) Dept, Fourth Avenue, Harlow, Essex, CM19 5AA.
14  R. Murray, 'New directions in municipal socialism', in B. Pimlott (ed.), *Fabian Essays in Socialist Thought* (Heinemann, 1984), p. 218.

15  Ibid., pp. 218–19.

16  A. Wright, 'Tawneyism revisited: equality, welfare and socialism', in Pimlott, *Fabian Essays*, p. 75.

17  Ibid., p. 81.

18  G.D.H. Cole, 'Socialism and the welfare state', *Dissent*, Autumn, 1954, p. 319.

19  Quoted in Wright, 'Tawneyism', p. 91.

20  R.H. Tawney, *Equality* (George Allen and Unwin, 1964), p. 43.

21  H. Rose, 'Re-reading Titmuss: the sexual division of labour', *Journal of Social Policy*, 10 (4), 1981, p. 481. It is worth while noting that it has been feminist writers who have been much more concerned with issues of immediate practical concern (and the question of replaceability), particularly in the very interesting debate about community care.

22  Pimlott, *Fabian Essays*, p. vii.

23  P. Beresford and S. Croft, 'Welfare pluralism: the new face of Fabianism', *Critical Social Policy*, 9 (Spring), 1984, p. 19.

24  R. Hadley and S. Hatch, *Social Welfare and the Failure of the State – centralised social services and participatory alternatives* (George Allen and Unwin, 1981).

25  See R. Hadley and M. McGrath (eds), *Going Local: neighbourhood social services*, NCVO occasional paper no. 1 (Beresford Square Press, 1980).

26  Beresford and Croft, 'Welfare pluralism', p. 33.

27  See N. Bosanquet, 'Services for mentally handicapped people in Britain 1968–82: a case study in the mixed economy of welfare', paper given at the Social Administration Association conference, 1983. See also N. Bosanquet, 'Choose or we lose', *The Guardian*, 27 July 1983, p. 11; and F. Gladstone, 'Wet blanket', *Voluntary Action*, Autumn, 1981, p. 30.

28  Beresford and Croft, 'Welfare pluralism', p. 25.

29  Ibid., p. 33.

30  D. Blunkett and G. Green, *Building from the Bottom – the Sheffield experience*, Fabian tract no. 491, 1983.

31  Ibid., p. 16.

32  P. Beresford and S. Croft, 'Community control of social services departments: discussion document', 1980, p. 17 (available from Battersea Community Action, 27 Winders Road, Battersea, London SW11).

33  Ibid., p. 5.

34  See M. Boddy and C. Fudge (eds), *Local Socialism – Labour councils and new left alternatives* (Macmillan, 1984) for a survey of these developments.

35  'A parable of how things might be done differently – interview with John Benington', *Critical Social Policy*, 9, 1984, p. 76.

36  D. Heald, *Public Expenditure – its defence and reform* (Martin Robertson, 1983).

37  See M. Boddy, *The Building Societies* (Macmillan, 1980); N. Ginsburg, *Class, Capital and Social Policy* (Macmillan, 1979); R. Minns, *Pension Funds and British Capitalism – the ownership and control of shareholding* (Heinemann, 1980); P. Barnes, *Building Societies: the myth of mutuality* (Pluto Press, 1984); R. Minns, *Take over the City – the case for public ownership of financial institutions* (Pluto Press, 1982); E. Schragge, *Pension Policy in Britain – a socialist analysis*, (Routledge and Kegan Paul, 1984).

38  See I. Gough, *The Political Economy of the Welfare State* (Macmillan, 1979). See also end of chapter 4.

39  For useful overviews, see M. Loney, *Community against Government – the British Community Development Project 1968–78* (Heinemann, 1983); J. Edwards and R. Batley, *The Politics of Positive Discrimination – an evaluation of the Urban*

*Programme 1967–77*, (Tavistock, 1978); J. Higgins, N. Deakin, J. Edwards and M. Wicks (eds), *Government and Urban Poverty: inside the policy making process* (Basil Blackwell, 1983).

40　L. Bridges, 'The ministry of internal security: British urban social policy 1968–74', *Race and Class*, 16 (4), 1975, pp. 375–86.

41　Ibid., p. 376.

42　Ibid., p. 385.

43　D. MPcKay and A. Cox, 'Confusion and reality in public policy: the case of the British Urban Programme', *Political Studies*, 26 (4), 1977, pp. 491–506.

44　Ibid., p. 500.

45　Ibid., p. 499.

46　Ibid., p. 565.

47　Loney, *Community*, p. 38.

48　See ibid., for full bibliography of this literature.

49　Ibid., pp. 18–25.

50　A. Cawson, *Corporatism and Welfare: social policy and state intervention in Britain* (Heinemann, 1982), p. 3.

51　Thompson, *The Poverty of Theory*.

52　A. Cutler, B. Hindess, P. Hirst and A. Hussain, 'Marxist theory and socialist politics', *Marxism Today*, November 1978. See also A. Cutler, *Marx's Capital and Capitalism Today*, vols 1 and 2 (Routledge and Kegan Paul, 1977 and 1979).

53　Cutler, *Marx's Capital* (1977), p. 232 (original emphasis).

54　B. Hindess, quoted by P. Corrigan and D. Sayer, 'Hindess and Hirst: a critical review', *Socialist Register, 1978* (Merlin, 1978), p. 179 (original emphasis).

55　P. Bew, P. Gibbon and H. Patterson, *The State in Northern Ireland* (Manchester University Press, 1978), pp. 214–15. This text is a most interesting attempt to employ the concept of relative autonomy.

56　See the major contributions to what has been described as 'the domestic labour debate'. For an instructive overview see M. Barrett, *Women's Oppression Today – problems in Marxist-feminist analysis* (Verso, 1980).

57　O. Adamson, C. Brown, J. Harrison and J. Price, 'Women's oppression under capitalism', *Revolutionary Communist*, 5, 1976, p. 12.

58　V. Beechey, 'Women and production: a critical analysis of some sociological theories of women's work', in A. Kuhn and A. Wolpe (eds), *Feminism and Materialism* (Routledge and Kegan Paul, 1978).

59　H. Hartmann, 'The unhappy marriage of Marxism and feminism: towards a more progressive union', *Capital and Class*, Summer 1978.

60　Barrett, *Women's Oppression*.

61　A term originally used by M. MacIntosh; see 'The welfare state and the needs of the dependent family', in S. Burman (ed.), *Fit Work for Women* (Croom Helm, 1979).

62　Brenner and Ramas have suggested that this formulation merely reproduces the type of 'dualism' of which Barrett accuses Hartmann. See J. Brenner and M. Ramas, 'Rethinking women's oppression', *New Left Review*, 144 (March–April), 1984, pp. 33–71.

63　Barrett, *Women's Oppression*, p. 204.

64　Brenner and Ramas, 'Rethinking', p. 36.

65　Barrett, *Women's Oppression*, pp. 230, 233.

66　See MacIntosh, 'The welfare state'; E. Wilson, *Women and the Welfare State* (Tavistock, 1977); Hartmann, 'The unhappy marriage'.

67  Brenner and Ramas, 'Rethinking', pp. 64–5.
68  J. Humphries, 'Class struggle and the persistence of the working class family', *Cambridge Journal of Economics*, 1 (1), p. 250.
69  J. Donzelot, *The Policing of Families* (Hutchinson, 1980).
70  J. Hodges and A. Hussain, 'La police des familles', *Ideology and Consciousness*, Spring, 1979, p. 90, (our emphasis).
71  M. Barrett and M. MacIntosh, 'Ethnocentrism and socialist-feminist theory', *Feminist Review*, 20 (Summer), 1985, p. 41.
72  J. Urry, *The Anatomy of Capitalist Societies – the economy, civil society and the state* (MacMillan, 1981).
73  Ibid., p. 31.
74  Ibid., p. 122–3.
75  Ibid., p. 105.
76  J. Gabriel and G. Ben-Tovim, 'Marxism and the concept of racism', *Economy and Society*, 7 (2), 1978, pp. 118–54.
77  Centre for Contemporary Cultural Studies, *Unpopular Education – schooling and social democracy in England since 1944* (Hutchinson, 1981).
78  C. Offe, 'The theory of the capitalist state and the problem of policy formation', in L. Lindberg (ed.), *Stress and Contradiction in Modern Capitalism* (Lexington Books, 1975).
79  T. Harrington, 'Explaining state policy making: a critique of some recent dualist models', *International Journal of Urban and Regional Research*, 7 (2), 1983, pp. 202–17.
80  Offe, 'The theory', p. 129.
81  C. Offe, 'The abolition of market control and the problem of legitimacy', *Kapitalstate*, no. 1, p. 111.
82  Harrington, 'Explaining', pp. 207–8.
83  Ibid., p. 208.
84  See P. Malpass, 'Professionalism and the role of architects in local authority housing', *Royal Institute of British Architects Journal*, June, 1975, p. 628.
85  Harrington, 'Explaining', p. 215.
86  C. Pickvance, 'Review', *Critical Social Policy*, 2 (2), pp. 94–8.
87  Cawson, *Corporatism and Welfare*; P. Saunders, *Urban Politics* (Hutchinson, 1978); A. Cawson and P. Saunders, 'Corporatism, competitive politics and class struggle', in R. King (ed.), *Capital and Politics* (Routledge and Kegan Paul, 1983).
88  Cawson, *Corporatism and Welfare*, pp. 10–11.
89  Ibid., p. 42.
90  Cawson and Saunders, 'Corporatism', p. 9.
91  Cawson, *Corporatism and Welfare*, p. 48.
92  Ibid., p. 66.
93  Ibid., p. 66.
94  Ibid., p. 64.
95  R. Dunleavy, 'The urban basis of political alignment: 'social class', domestic property ownership, or state intervention in consumption processes', *British Journal of Political Science*, 9, 1978.
96  Cawson and Saunders, 'Corporatism', p. 24.
97  Cawson, *Corporatism and Welfare*, p. 91.
98  Ibid., p. 91.
99  Ibid., p. 92.
100  A. Cochrane, 'Some criticisms of the dual state thesis', unpublished paper presented to the MA sociology (community studies) course, Sheffield City Poly-

technic, May 1984. Much of this section is reliant on ideas stimulated by this paper.

101   Cawson, *Corporatism and Welfare*, p. 64.
102   See E. Mandel, 'Introduction' to *Marx's Capital*, vol. 1 (Penguin, 1974).
103   K. Marx, *Capital*, vol. 1 (Foreign Language Publishing, 1961), p. 508.
104   See A. Hunt, 'Theory and politics in the identification of the working class', in A. Hunt (ed.), *Class and Class Structure* (Lawrence and Wishart, 1977).
105   G. Carchedi, *On the Economic Identification of Social Classes*, (Routledge and Kegan Paul, 1977).
106   N. Poulantzas, *Classes in Contemporary Capitalism*, part 3 (Verso, 1978).
107   N. Poulantzas, *State Power and Socialism* (New Left Books, 1978). p. 154.
108   D. Finn, N. Grant and R. Johnson, 'Social democracy, education and the crisis', cultural studies no. 10, University of Birmingham, CCCS, p. 170.
109   E.O. Wright, *Class Crisis and the State* (New Left Books, 1978), chapter 2.
110   Ibid., p. 108.
111   E.O. Wright, 'Intellectuals and the class structure of capitalist society', in P. Walker (ed.), *Between Labour and Capital* (South End Press, 1978), p. 208.
112   J. Ozga and M. Lawn, *Teachers, Professionalism and Class – a study of organised teachers* (Falmer Press, 1981) (our emphasis).
113   P. Wilding, *Professional Power and Social Welfare* (Routledge and Kegan Paul, 1981), p. 67.
114   Urry, *The Anatomy*, p. 66.
115   E. Laclau, *Politics and Ideology in Marxist Theory* (New Left Books, 1978).
116   J. Urry, 'De-industrialisation, classes and politics', in King, *Capital and Politics*, pp. 28–48.
117   Dunleavy, 'The urban basis'.
118   V. Duke and S. Egdell 'Public expenditure cuts in Britain and consumption sectional cleavages', unpublished manuscript, 1983.
119   See also S. Egdell and V. Duke, 'Reactions to the public expenditure cuts: occupational class and party realignment', *Sociology*, 16, 1982, pp. 431–9.
120   Cawson and Saunders, 'Corporatism', p. 20.
121   See S. Goss, 'Women's initiatives in local government', in Boddy and Fudge, *Local Socialism*, pp. 109–32.
122   See A. Coote, 'The AES: a new starting point', *New Socialist*, 2 (Nov./Dec.), 1981; J. Gardiner and S. Smith, 'Feminism and the AES', *Marxism Today*, October 1981. See also various contributors to 'Socialist feminism and economic strategy', *Socialist Economic Review* (eds D. Currie and M. Sawyer), 1982, pp. 29–108.
123   M. Prior and D. Purdy, *Out of the Ghetto – a path to socialist rewards*, (Spokesman, 1978).
124   A. Sivanandan, 'RAT and the degradation of black struggle', *Race and Class*, 26 (4), 1985, p. 27.
125   A. Gurnah, 'The politics of racism awareness training', *Critical Social Policy*, 11 (winter), 1984, pp. 17, 19.
126   G. Wickham, 'Power and power analysis: beyond Foucault', *Economy and Society*, 12 (4), 1983, pp. 468–9. (our emphasis).
127   M. Foucault, *The Order of Things: an archaeology of the human sciences* (Vintage, 1973); *The History of Sexuality, Vol. 1: An Introduction* (Allen Lane, 1979); *Discipline and Punish: the birth of the prison* (Allen Lane, 1977).
128   M. Foucault, 'Questions of method: an interview with Michel Foucault', *Ideology and Consciousness*, 8, 1981, p. 6.

129  M. Foucault, *Power/Knowledge: selected interviews and other writings 1972–1977* (ed. C. Gordon) (Harvester Press, 1980), p. 60.

130  See M. Hewitt, 'Bio politics and social policy: Foucault's account of welfare', *Theory, Culture and Society*, 2 (1), 1983, pp. 67–85; P. Squires, 'The emergence of the social state', unpublished paper, Dept of Social Administration, University of Bristol.

131  C. Gordon, 'Afterword', in Foucault, *Power/Knowledge*, p. 245.

132  J. Donzelot, 'The poverty of political culture', *Ideology and Consciousness*, 5, 1978, p. 85.

133  B. Smart, *Foucault, Marxism and Critique*, (Routledge and Kegan Paul, 1983), pp. 120–1.

134  P. Hirst, 'The genesis of the social', *Politics and Power*, 3, 1981, p. 74 (original emphasis).

135  Donzelot, 'The poverty'.

136  M. Barrett and M. MacIntosh, *The Anti-Social Family* (Verso, 1982), p. 102.

137  P. Corrigan, 'Community work and political struggle: what are the possibilities of working on the contradiction?', in P. Leonard (ed.), *The Sociology of Community Action*, sociological review monograph 21, University of Keele, 1975.

138  K. McDonnell, 'Working in housing aid', *Critical Social Policy*, 2 (1), 1982, pp. 76–7.

# Conclusion to Part II

# Necessary Revisions: A Third Way?

> People are unhappy with existing services, but they are not prepared
> to see their complete destruction. This is probably the principal area
> in which arguments for a different, caring, sharing or *socialist*
> society can still be heard.
>
> Doreen Massey, Lynne Segal and Hilary Wainwright

The arguments at the end of part II for a more realistic Marxist
approach to welfare were largely *theoretical*, revolving around the
desire for greater sensitivity in accounting for capital's needs; the state
and its actions; power; class and its relation to other sources of social
inequality, notably gender and race; and, last but not least, the
possible forms any future socialist society might take. Of course,
theoretical clarification alone is never sufficient; only socialist political
*practice* will ensure the achievement of a welfare socialist society.
Certain important issues have nevertheless been placed on the agenda – theoretical issues that do require urgent clarification if such a
goal is ever to be properly defined, never mind achieved.

We should not under-estimate the severity of the crises that have
been affecting both British socialists – of all hues – and the British
welfare state during the 1980s. 'Just why am I a socialist?' and 'What,
if anything, has the presently constituted welfare state got to do with
socialism?' are questions that have persistently demanded searching
answers over the last decade. Both British socialism and the British
welfare state have been under sustained attack – externally from the
renaissance and pervasiveness of right-wing ideas and practices, and
internally from their own supporters' re-evaluation of their achievements and potential. For many old securities have been lost and new
ones have not been found – or sought.

## The crisis of socialism

John Westergaard wrote in the mid 1960s that 'competition with the
Conservative Party is almost always likely to work in the latter's
favour if the terms of reference are those of "legitimacy" of authority,

"respectability" and "efficiency".'[1] The same might now be argued of the question of individual freedom, as David Selbourne has perceptively put it:

> The fact that the right's proclamations of the virtues of self-reliance are obnoxious to socialists, at a time when public provision for job creation, for welfare or for reflation have political and ethical priority in the socialist scale of values, is no more than obvious. But merely to reiterate, in conventional socialist fashion, that the right has shamelessly nailed the colours of freedom to its political mast, notwithstanding or because of the economic crisis of capital, no longer meets the case, or the political challenges socialism faces. Instead, socialists must fight first on the ground chosen by the right, and with its weapons.[2]

Of course, the banal incantations of fashionable right-wing ideologues (e.g. Milton Friedman's 'freedom to choose') are little more than cynical vehicles to shift the terrain of public discussion away from capitalism's all-too-obvious recurrent structural crises on to arguments about seemingly obtuse ideas such as personal liberty or family virtue. But do not the correcting of wrongs perpetuated on individuals, and the creation of a morally 'just' order, lie at the very heart of the socialist project? So many variants of Marxism concede ethical ground to the right before they start with their argument that more meaningful personal freedom will only be generated after the conquest of power and the transformation of the means of production. 'What do you expect if some people are alienated? You are, after all, living under capitalism.'

If capitalism is so patently unjust and immoral why, as we argued in chapter 4, was it not overthrown years ago? It really is no longer good enough to rest contented in the belief that it is the capitalist mass media, or some other ruling class strategy, which induces docility into a working class that otherwise would be full of revolutionary ardour. The simple fact is that many right-wing arguments evoke genuine desires in ordinary people to, as Mill put it, 'frame the plan of our life to suit our own character'.[3] Socialist arguments all too often are *only* concerned with collective forms of liberty. Exhortations that genuine freedom is an illusion unless all *equally* have access to control over productive property has, as yet, no such immediate or practical appeal. Marxist-influenced socialists have under-estimated the extent to which the British people's collective understanding almost uncritically equates the right to property with individual liberty; socially owned public property has an altogether inferior moral purchase. Raphael Samuel has written feelingly about 'the waning of collectivity' in British political culture, desirous as he is of its return: 'In the 1940s . . . the principle of collectivity was dominant . . . in every department of national life. An ideology of "fair shares" – Labour's master concept – linked post-war reconstruction to the stratagems of wartime survival, opposing communal effort to selfish interest and private gain.'[4] Such a state of affairs certainly no longer exists, and perhaps it only occurred temporarily in wartime conditions, to be experienced particularly vividly by a Jewish, working-class lad brought up in a family with commitments to the Communist Party? Just how do we advance communal values – communality not community[5] – whilst making people realise that socialism is also about retaining respect for personhood and individual autonomy? The answer is not to become all nostalgic for something which was probably only a temporary phenomenon romanticised in a childhood memory. Perhaps Samuel's point is a simpler one – that we are no longer clear what 'socialism' itself really stands for.

Is it simply about enabling people at the bottom of the heap (and does this enablement imply achievement of equality of opportunity, or equality of outcome?); eradicating the market (to what extent?); or identifying a commitment to the communal and the collective at the expense of individualism?[6] 'Arguments for socialism cover a wide variety of moral and intellectual positions – self-denying struggle against the evils of competition, the solidarity of the exploited, uneasy middle-class altruism, or more public spending on the welfare system.'[7] And socialists are often so much clearer about what socialism is *not* than about what it is; it certainly is *not* embodied in British Rail or the National Coal Board, or the presently constituted National Health Service. This book is making a plea that in such a perplexing political climate there is something to be gained from amalgamating some of the strengths of a 'realistic' Marxism with those of a 'critical' Fabianism. In respect of the classical arguments that socialists engage in, we are proposing first and foremost 'a third way' between the Scylla and Charybdis of reform and revolution. Our argument is for creative constitutional actions by socialists until such time as constitutionalism is abandoned by the right in their attempt to overturn the achievements of an elected left-wing government. Those who suggest that this 'third way' is merely a barely disguised reformism would do well to reflect on André Gorz's observation that 'the choice of this road, incorrectly called "the peaceful road to socialism", is not the consequence of an *a priori* refusal of violent revolution or armed insurrection. It is a consequence of the latter's actual impossibility in the European context.'[8]

Second, we are arguing that Marxist theory has to base its arguments more clearly on *moral* premises; it has to enter into moral debate about 'Why socialism?' and 'Why should people's welfare be collectively provided for?' In this it has something to learn from the

Fabian tradition. Liberal arguments about liberty are a powerful edifice, and are too often expropriated by the right. Rawls has suggested that Hume, Smith, Mill and Bentham are 'social theorists and economists of the first rank. The moral doctrine they worked out was framed . . . to fit into a comprehensive scheme'; and 'those who criticised them often did so' – in their own times *as now* – 'on a much narrower front, whilst failing to construct a workable and systematic moral conception to oppose it.'[9] The arguments of the right now dominate the agenda on questions about social and moral progress; and Marxist-influenced socialists *have* to appreciate that it is partly on ethical grounds that any effective antidote will be constructed.

Third, this moral argument has to be blended into a much more realistic 'politics of the possible'. People are not inherently socialist: far from it, they have to be cajoled and argued with. By far the most satisfactory form of argument is to build their confidence through the gradual achievement of things that they can recognise as gains and improvements in their own lives. How one politically calculates the nature of these gains is not easy, and is undoubtedly another source of socialism's present crisis. How should feminist and anti-racist demands be amalgamated with class-based ones? Intense arguments rage on these questions, as we have seen.

Our position is open to one major accusation – that by trying to achieve what, at first, will necessarily only be piecemeal 'gains' (albeit for a reconstituted British working class), whatever is achieved will only be at the expense of oppressed groups in other parts of the world (in particular, the peasants and workers of the Third World). Of course, in an abstract sense there is some real truth in this, but it is not something that has been ignored by groups who hold a 'third-way' type of politics. For example, the Labour Coordinating Committee's book *The Alternative Economic Strategy* contains extensive discussion on how trade could be more effectively planned to benefit Third World countries.[10] Of course, as Coates has argued, there are some cruel paradoxes to be faced up to here.[11] For example, if a left Labour government achieved improved living standards for the working class, this would possibly prompt multinational capital to move to areas where labour costs were cheaper – hence removing some of the material base fuelling the Labour Party's strategy for economic recovery. But are we to assume from Coates's argument, or that of any other fundamentalist, that 'revolutionary' socialists are in some ways unconcerned about the living standards of British workers? Are we to assume that revolutionaries continuously argue in their propaganda *against* British job protection: 'Well, you know, you are quite lucky here compared with Brazilian peasants!' Of course not. If you engage in the day-to-day business of practical socialist politics *in any developed country* you are open to the accusation of encouraging the exploitation of the Third World. This is as true for revolutionaries as it is for reformists or revisionists. A Third Worldist political perspective privileging the needs of people from that part of the globe can be, and is, adopted by many, but it generates a very different set of political demands to those of British revolutionary groups.

### The crisis of welfare

The crisis of the British welfare system mirrors in many respects that of British socialism. For so long substantial parts of the former were held up as shining examples of the achievements of the latter, and now they too are under sustained intellectual and political attack from the right. For the Marxist-influenced left much that is wrong with British socialism – its parochialism, statism, chauvinism and inflexibility – is also to be found in the workings of the welfare apparatus. Some of these criticisms are not alien to the right's attack on welfare; nor, incidentally, do the right's arguments always display a lack of concern for the worst-off members of society. Their position on welfare – briefly summarised – is as follows. First, unrestrained market activity would help the poor through a 'trickle-down' process whereby the entrepreneurial energy of today translates into the mass consumption of tomorrow. Second, the notion of a welfare 'right' is a politically dangerous one, and its extension should be resisted, for it means that demands on the resources of the state become infinite. Third, this elastic concept of welfare needs and rights is fuelled by the welfare professionals and other deliverers of services; the beneficiaries are not the clients but the welfare bureaucracies and their employees. Fourth, and following directly on, welfare services are therefore inefficient in their own terms; they do not redistribute resources from rich to poor. Fifth, they are in any case misconceived, as it is not feasible to utilise criteria of social justice to alter market operations; any attempt to do so will induce coercion, and only fuel further injustice. Sixth, economic growth encouraged by lowering taxation and so enhancing incentives is much more likely to benefit the worst-off than more welfare and planning.

This admittedly breathless summary of the right's arguments should still indicate why the left's response might be somewhat equivocal.[12] On the one hand, certain parts of it were just what the left had always been saying: heavily bureaucratic structures and practices, overall paternalism and professional self-interest. The broadly defined left was certainly quick to pick up on how Thatcherism was able skilfully to exploit the majority of the working class's negative experience of welfare provision and delivery. Stuart Hall, in a very influential thesis, suggested that certain 'authoritarian populist' themes were adroitly employed by Thatcher to equate post-war social democratic 'gains' with a bureaucratised and failing socialist experiment.[13] Paul Corrigan went so far as to argue that 'the bureaucratic state form' of the welfare services has 'turned significant sections of the population away from the welfare state as a progressive set of institutions'.[14] Ramesh Mishra in a recent article has evaluated these claims, and even-handedly suggests that there was no evidence that Thatcherites in 1979 openly 'campaigned on a platform opposed to the welfare state', and that the notion that the welfare state had lost popular support suffers from over-generalisation, i.e. 'the tendency to tar the whole of the welfare state with the same brush'.[15] This is precisely the same dilemma, from another angle, that we came across at the end of chapter 4: just how do we separate out those aspects of the welfare state we wish to defend and build upon from those we wish to reject? This is not simply an *intellectual* exercise, but one into which the day-to-day realities of politics rudely and continuously intrude.

In a very useful paper Bob Deacon has recently built on his earlier work (which was largely intellectual in content – see chapter 5 for discussion) by separating out six alternative *political* strategies for welfare: the free market; welfare pluralism; welfare corporatism; alternative social planning; local socialist welfare; and social revolution.[16] In effect, potentially five different 'socialist' welfare strategies. We might expect each of these to offer very different answers to our dilemma. Welfare corporatism – as championed by Mishra[17] – is chastised, perhaps a little over-harshly, for merely offering more of the same, 'a contract between capital and an *unreconstructed* working class'. Welfare pluralism – as we again saw in chapter 6 — can mean 'all things to all people', and is rejected by Deacon in its right-wing form for 'providing further legitimacy to the damaging privatising policies of the Tories', although he concedes that in more left-wing versions 'it prioritises . . . the needs of those whom the welfare state has marginalised.' His fear that even these left-wing versions will incorporate elements of market delivery make him ultimately unsure of this strategy. His favoured position is the 'revolutionary' one, with its characterisation of socialist social policy as policy and provision that 'embodies [within it] a new set of social relations . . . of "reciprocal collaboration".'[18] However, some concessions are made to 'alternative' socialist planning (represented by Walker's work[19]) and the local socialist[20] variant of this, owing to their ability to 'begin the task of accommodating . . . [to] the interests, needs and demands of women'[21] (and, we presumably might add, blacks and other oppressed minorities). Ultimately, despite the value of their visions of how human need could be planned for democratically under socialism,

both approaches are rejected by Deacon for their reformism – ultimately resting upon the election of 'left' Labour governments and
councils. Perhaps a useful way of characterising the 'third way' represented in this text – the fusion of a critical Fabianism and a
realistic Marxism – is the combination of the alternative social
planning and local socialist welfare strategies with some of the 'progressive' elements of welfare pluralism and corporatism, as shown in
the accompanying figure.

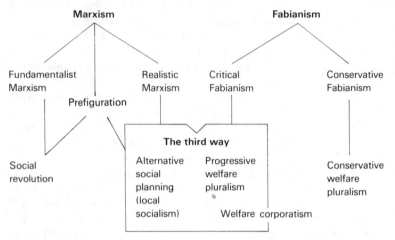

*The third way: critical Fabianism and realistic Marxism.*

The flowering of these various consciously developed political
strategies in one sense represents the growing maturity of socialist
thinking about welfare. Those Marxist-influenced socialists who think
seriously about welfare questions – and there still are not all that
many – have in some cases begun to modify the excesses of their
'cynical gaze'. The slowly modifying position of the Labour Party on
council house sales[22] graphically illustrates what most socialists began
to realise in the late 1970s: 'that if the welfare state does not have the
function of increasing freedom, rectifying injustices, and responding
to the moral claims based upon needs, it hardly seems worth
defending'.[23] Slowly it has dawned on 'the generation of 1968' that
many welfare state arrangements, whilst not always entirely defensible
and certainly *not* to be celebrated, *do* have some worth beyond merely
servicing the machinations of a capitalist economy, and are infinitely
preferable to the egoistic ravages of the market. Older socialists such
as Ralph Miliband – highly sceptical of the arguments of this text,
which he would describe as 'new revisionist' – probably have always
known this:

That the 'relations of production', and for that matter the relations of life, are less oppressive for most workers than they were a hundred or even fifty years ago is in very large measure due to class struggle and pressure from below exercised upon employers and the state, and to the direct and indirect impact which the working class has had, via its representative agencies, upon the political system of these countries. This has not involved the storming of Winter Palaces, and it has certainly not produced the revolutionary transformation of capitalist societies. But it has been much more significant in its reach and results than is conveyed by such labels as 'economistic', 'corporate' and the like. The advances which have been made have not ended exploitation and oppression, least of all of women and racial or ethnic minorities. That point needs to be made, but it should not obscure the benefits which many of these advances have brought, or the degree to which they have served to raise expectations and to foster demands and advances.[24]

Many socialists engaged in welfare politics in the mid 1980s have taken stock of Miliband's timely assessment; they have begun to take the challenge of the right and the need to morally justify welfare provision much more seriously. Arthur Scargill, that *bête noire* of the right, has recently argued that in a socialist society 'there would of course be the right of every individual to own their own home and own their own garden'.[25] We are sure he does not mean by this that socialism should stop at the garden gate; his remark certainly does not necessarily imply it! The interesting point is that the necessary critiques of statism and professionalism – from the left, right and centre – have prompted the left to think much more seriously about the appropriate usage of voluntary effort for welfare;[26] ways in which informal and community caring might possibly be modified so it largely did not end up as women's work;[27] what proper balance might be struck between decision-making by trained experts and wider forms of community control; how far socialist initiatives can promote self-help schemes for women, black people and others without removing their radical core; and so on.

There is a much greater sensitivity to what we earlier described as 'the politics of the possible', and the necessity of struggling on ideological issues. From the crisis a certain maturity has bloomed. There are, of course, still many fundamentalist Marxists – they are not, as we are sure some will argue, a figment of our imaginations – who still believe along with Trotsky that 'the conception of individual freedom is essentially *petit bourgeois*'.[28] Many more are now persuaded by arguments such as those of Len Doyal and Ian Gough that it is vital for any socialist welfare project to evaluate how far social systems enable *individual* needs to be met, and that it is possible to specify 'what is and is not generalisable about the human condition', i.e. the need for autonomy and learning, health and survival, and so on; for if it were not, 'how could *any* rational decisions about production, consumption or resource allocation be made under socialism?'[29] There is a danger, of course, that such specification of a dynamic conception of how to optimise basic need satisfaction can lead to a dogmatic imposition of expertise. That, though, is precisely the danger of the socialist project; socialism is fuelled by a desire to make the world a more equal, 'better' place. Marxists should face these issues squarely – face up to the realities of human rights – rather than hide behind a moral relativism that can all too easily deny them.

There is also now an acute awareness among those on the left in Britain about how difficult it is to make socialist-inspired calculations that advance the welfare interests of a reconstituted working class. The growth of discussion on this topic amongst socialists is, in our opinion, an entirely healthy thing. Many people are now aware that ritual sloganising and a simple politics of revolution will not suffice. Even those revolutionary socialists that take welfare seriously – and there are, as Bob Deacon has lamented, pitifully few of them – have begun to appreciate how in 'concrete instances socialists and feminists in their union may conflict with socialists and feminists as consumers'.[30] They have begun to appreciate, albeit in a small way, the delicacies of the political calculations that have to be made in socialist welfare politics. This may even have to include, as Deacon has noted, the following recognition:

> A political strategy has to emerge that recognises that the struggle of council employees, as employees with short-term sectional interests, is a component of the class struggle for socialism (because it is a struggle that rests on the power of people organised as employees), and that the struggle to make redundant through deprofessionalisation some of those employees is also a component of the class struggle for socialism (because it is a struggle that rests on a vision of different reciprocal social relations).[31]

Despite the growing maturity of socialist welfare politics and the fact that in practice – 'on the ground' (particularly in many of the local authority 'socialist' experiments) – there has already begun a fusing of efforts between a critical Fabianism and a realistic Marxism, we should remain cautious. The right is acutely aware of what Ralph Miliband's quote above reminds us – that it is basically from the power and confidence of the working class that a more humane and caring society will grow. The power of the traditionally understood British working class has been dramatically eroded in recent years, and the forces of reaction are not yet satiated. Some hope for cautious optimism is possible, though, even here. The fightback against the cuts has released a tremendous sense of responsibility about the future amongst public service workers; and the defeat of the miners' strike in 1985 – a historic defeat for the traditionally conceived British working class – released a tremendous surge of energy from the women of the mining communities. As Lorraine Bowler told 10,000 women from mining areas all over Britain at the first 'women against pit closures' demonstration in Barnsley in May 1984:

> We cannot allow this government to decimate our industry and our communities. Is this what we want for our kids? In this country we are not just separated as a class. We are separated as men and women. We as women have not often been encouraged to be involved in trade unions and organising. *Organisation has always been seen as an area belonging to men. We are seen to be the domesticated element of a family.* This for too many years has been the role expected of us. I have seen change coming for years and the last few years have seen it at its best.[32]

There is also a great deal of evidence that the labour movement has, albeit slowly, begun to recognise the deeply ingrained racism – individual, institutional and structural – in British society, in its welfare services and, not least important, in itself. The struggles here are, and will be, especially painful and protracted. The Labour Party leadership's crass arguments against the organisation of black sections is a case in point. But such actions should not be simply allowed to refuel our anger and revolutionary ardour. Many British socialists influenced by Marxist theory are more than aware of the deep legacies of imperialism in the British social structure; we should hardly be surprised by our constant detection of it. The British welfare state is far from a shining beacon of socialist achievement; it is riddled with liberal and conservative values and practices. But, in our opinion, more and more people are in a position to be persuaded of both that and the fact that, even in its mid 1970s form, it is eminently preferable to the egoistic ravages of the market.

The key question is how the labour movement can adjust its practices to create a popular movement for social change. Of course, it is relatively easy to see that arguments for a socialist welfare society could be enormously popular: demands for effective and comprehensive nursery facilities; for privileging social need over economic cost; for adequate housing and pensions; and so on. It is also, though, quite evident that many of the barriers to the effective popularisation of such ideas lie in the institutional nature of the labour movement itself, such as the jealous and ultimately self-defeating demand of many male trade unionists for a continuation of an adequate, so-called 'family' wage. The movement is plagued by intense sectoralism, racism and sexism. In Sheffield there are over forty full-time trade union officials – of whom three are women and none is black. The movement in the city has still not properly adjusted to the traumatic and rapid deindustrialisation of the late 1970s and early 1980s – a loss of jobs in manufacturing industries alone of 45,000 between 1979 and 1983. The drop in membership of the Amalgamated Union of Engineering Workers has been of the order of 30 per cent since 1979.[33] The single largest union branch in the city – much to the chagrin of the tradition-alist trade union structure – is that of the National and Local Government Officers Association, representing the city council's own employees. These developments, whilst deeply depressing, should not blind us to the real blockages that the traditional organisation of the British trade union movement has placed on the development of effective mobilisations and strategies for a socialist society.

In saying this we are not merely hurling the rather lame concept of 'labourism' at the British working-class movement. For this term is all too often used simply to depict an 'absence' (i.e. of a revolutionary British party) rather than provide any helpful assessment of a presence. The reality is that the labour movement has fought many heroic struggles for betterment and social citizenship. It has done so, though, with a *grossly restricted vision*. The central problem facing socialists is how to broaden that vision and how to prevent further divisions, demoralisations and the partial political marginalisation of the broad coalition of socio-political forces that supported and sustained earlier phases of welfare expansion.[34] We should not just dismiss the forms and nature of those earlier struggles – as in essence do so many on the left – but we should be painfully aware of their limitations. Ironically, the twin crises of British socialism and the British welfare state might just lead, in the medium to long term, to the beginnings of precisely the type of political, theoretical and or-ganisational changes necessary for the eventual achievement of a welfare socialist society.

## Notes

1  J. Westergaard, 'The withering away of class: a contemporary myth', in P. Anderson and R. Blackburn (eds), *Towards Socialism* (Fontana, 1965) p. 110.
2  D. Selbourne, *Against Socialist Illusion – a radical argument* (Merlin Press, 1985), p. 39.
3  Quoted in ibid., p. 42.
4  R. Samuel, 'The lost world of British communism', *New Left Review*, 154 (Nov./Dec.), 1985, p. 8.
5  See G. Dalley, 'Ideologies of care', *Critical Social Policy* 8 (Autumn), 1983, pp. 72–82.
6  See G. Stedman-Jones, 'Paternalism revisited', *Marxism Today*, July 1985, pp. 25–8.
7  Selbourne, *Against Socialist Illusion*, p. 14.
8  A. Gorz, 'Reform and revolution', in R. Miliband and J. Saville (eds), *Socialist Register, 1968* (Merlin, 1968), p. 112.
9  Quoted in Selbourne, *Against Socialist Illusion*, p. 34.

10  CSE London Working Group, *The Alternative Economic Strategy* (CSE Books, 1980), chapters 8 and 9.

11  D. Coates, 'Labourism and the transition to socialism', *New Left Review*, 129 (Sep./Oct.), 1981, pp. 3–22.

12  For more systematic accounts of the ideas of the new Conservatism, see N. Bosanquet, *After the New Right* (Heinemann, 1983); R. Mishra, *The Welfare State in Crisis: social thought and social change* (Wheatsheaf Books, 1984); M. Loney, *The Politics of Greed: the new right and the welfare state* (Pluto Press, 1986).

13  S. Hall and M. Jacques (eds), *The Politics of Thatcherism* (Lawrence and Wishart/ Marxism Today*, 1983).

14  P. Corrigan, 'Popular consciousness and social democracy', *Marxism Today*, December 1978.

15  R. Mishra, 'The left and the welfare state: a critical analysis', *Critical Social Policy*, 15 (Spring), 1986, p. 7.

16  B. Deacon, 'Strategies for welfare: East and West Europe', *Critical Social Policy*, 14 (Winter), 1985, pp. 4–26.

17  Mishra, *The Crisis*, 1984.

18  B. Deacon, *Social Policy and Socialism* (Pluto Press, 1983), p. 42.

19  See A. Walker, *Social Planning – a strategy for socialist welfare* (Basil Blackwell, 1984).

20  See M. Boddy and C. Fudge (eds), *Local Socialism? – Labour councils and new left alternatives* (Macmillan, 1984).

21  Deacon, 'Strategies', p. 12.

22  For a highly prophetic article written on this subject see S. Jacobs, 'The sale of council houses: does it matter?', *Critical Social Policy*, 1(2), 1981, pp. 35–53.

23  R. Plant, 'The very idea of a welfare state', in P. Bean, J. Ferris and D. Whynes (eds), *In Defence of Welfare* (Tavistock, 1985), p. 13.

24  R. Miliband, 'The new revisionism in Britain', *New Left Review*, 150 (Mar./Apr.), 1985, p. 12.

25  Quoted in F. Mount, 'First principles: a view from the right', *Marxism Today*, July 1985, p. 24.

26  See R. Lawrence, 'Voluntary action: a stalking horse for the right?', *Critical Social Policy*, 2 (3), 1983, pp. 14–30.

27  See J. Finch, 'Community care: developing non-sexist alternatives', *Critical Social Policy*, 9 (Spring), 1984, pp. 6–18.

28  L. Trotsky, *Where is Britain Going?*, p. 105, quoted in Selbourne, *Against Socialist Illusion*, p. 37.

29  L. Doyal and I. Gough, 'A theory of human needs', *Critical Social Policy* 10 (Summer), 1984.

30  Deacon, 'Strategies', p. 10.

31  Ibid., p. 10.

32  Quoted in S. Rowbotham, 'What do women want? Women-centred values and the world as it is', *Feminist Review*, 20 (Summer), 1985, p. 66.

33  See D. Child and M. Paddon, 'Sheffield: steelyard blues', *Marxism Today*, July 1984, for an interesting discussion of this period.

34  See G. Therborn and J. Roebroek, 'The irreversible welfare state: its recent maturation, its encounter with the economic crisis and its future prospects', *International Journal of Health Services*, 16 (3), 1986, pp. 319–38.

# Index

Abel-Smith, Brian, 65, 72, 74
Abrams, Mark, 51
Adamson, Olivia, 187
*Alternative Economic Strategy*, 219
Althusser, L., 124, 125, 185, 186
Altvater, E., 129, 131
Anderson, Perry, 60, 66, 68, 69, 114
Asquith, Sir George, 34–5
Atlee government, 40, 48

Bacon, R., 83
Bank of England, nationalization of, 40
Barker, M., 104
Barrett, Michelle, 127, 188–90
Beales, Harold, 45
Bell, D. 5, 7, 47, 48
Belloc, Hilaire, 90
Ben-Tovim, G., 192
Benington, John, 179–80
Bentham, Jeremy, 66
Beresford, Peter, 177–9
Bernstein, Eduard, 9, 14–15, 17, 20, 24,
    25, 28, 33
Bevan, Aneurin, 40–1, 42
Beveridge report, 74, 103–4
Bew, P., 186
*Beyond the Fragments*, 146
Black Report, 73
Blunkett, David, 178–9
Booth, Charles, 34, 72, 74
Bosanquet, N., 73, 74, 178
bourgeoisie, 23, 25
Bowlby, John, 105
Bowler, Lorraine, 225
Boyd-Carpenter, 64
Brenner, J., 188–9
Bridges, L., 182, 183–4
Britain, realism and welfare, 1, 164–6
Bullock, P., 116

Campbell, Bea, 153
Campbell, T., 109
capitalism: accommodating, 107–11; and
    the ideology of affluence, 56; Marx on,
    17, 20–6; welfare state, 151–9
Carchedi, C., 200
Carlyle, Thomas, 12
*Case Con*, 68
Cawson, Alan, 184, 194–8
civil society, rediscovering, 191–2
class locations, 199–202
class objectives, predestined, 116–18
class struggle, 199–205
Claudin, F., 112
Cloward, R.A., 143, 166
Coates, D., 85, 219
Cochrane, Allan, 198
Cockburn, C., 101
Cohen, Stan, 105, 173
Cole, G.D.H., 12, 13, 18–19, 22, 24, 28,
    67, 77, 78, 79, 80, 90, 91, 177
collectivism, 3, 28–30, 35
collectivism, Fabian: and the post-war
    settlement, 39–44; and the welfare
    state, 38–59
communism, 12–13, 111–14
*Communist Manifesto*, see *Manifesto of
    the Communist Party*
Comte, Auguste, 26, 31–2
concepts, sensitising, 185–92
Conrad, P., 105–6
Conservatism, new, 97–8, 165–6
Conservative Party, 1, 42–3, 89–90
constitutional action, socialism and, 80–5
control, social, 105–7
Coote, Anna, 153
Corrigan, Paul, 209, 221
Cox, A., 182, 183, 184
CPAG, 73

Crick, Bernard, 13, 54
*Critical Social Policy (CSP)*, 1, 174–5
Croft, Suzy, 177–9
Crosland, Tony, 45–6, 52, 64, 77–8, 81–2
Crossman, Richard, 65, 177
Crouch, Colin, 79
CSE State Group, 135
cultural revolution, 61–3
culture, poverty of English intellectual, 65–7
Cutler, A., 185–6

Dahrendorf, Ralf, 46, 126
Dale, J., 146
Dalton, Hugh, 40
Darwinism, 29–30
Deacon, Bob, 148–52, 221–2, 224
determination, 185–7
Dickens, Charles, 12
Donnison, D., 4, 64–5
Donzelot, Jacques, 189, 207–9
Doyal, Len, 151, 223
Duke, Vic, 204
Dunleavy, R., 196, 204

economic, and the political, 20–6
economic reductionism, 122–5
*Economist, The*, 41, 61
Education Bill (1944), 40
Egdell, Stephen, 204
Elster, J., 129
Eltis, W., 83
*Encounter*, 54
Engels, Friedrich, 13, 14, 16–17, 21, 23, 27, 110, 123, 166
English intellectual culture, poverty of, 65–7
Esping-Anderson, Gøsta, 95, 153, 154–7, 160
establishment politics, compromises of, 64–5

*Fabian Essays*, 15, 19
Fabian social criticism, 70–2
Fabian Society, 9, 11, 18–19, 25, 30, 39
Fabianism: British, and the welfare state, 1, 9–93; criticism and crisis, 89–93; dismissing the tradition?, 176–80; exorcising, 67–70; legacies, 11–37;

Fabianism *cont.*
    limited economic focus, 175; and Marxism, 11–14
Fellowship of the New Life, 18
feminism, 146, 153, 187–91
Ferge, Zsuzsa, 145
Field, Frank, 73, 74, 79
Foster, P., 146
Foster-Carter, A., 120
Foucault, Michel, 106, 206–7, 208
Fourier, Charles, 16
Friedman, Milton, 217
Fromm, Erich, 12
functionalist forms of analysis, 125–8
fundamentalism: origins of Marxist, 111–14; politics of, 114–22; theoretical excesses of, 122–8

Gabriel, J., 192
Gaitskell, Hugh, 41
Gamble, Andrew, 82
George, Lloyd, 35
George, V., 49, 122
German Social Democratic Party, 9
Giddens, A., 18, 23
Gilmour, Ian, 164
Ginsburg, Norman, 100, 135, 164
Gladstone, F., 178
Glyn, A., 115, 143
Golding, P., 103
Goldthorpe, John, 73, 78
Gordon, C., 207
Gorz, André, 218
Gough, Ian, 101, 133–4, 135, 143, 151, 196, 223
Gramsci, Antonio, 102, 123
Green, Geoff, 178–9
*Grundrisse*, 21
Gunter, Ray, 83
Gurnah, Ahmed, 205

Habermas, Jürgen, 130
Hadley, R., 177–8
Hall, Stuart, 165, 220–1
Hallas, Duncan, 114
Halmos, Paul, 51
Halsey, A.H., 72, 73
Hammonds, 50
Harrington, T., 193–4
Harris, L., 135–7, 144

Harris, Nigel, 38, 49
Hartmann, Heidi, 187
Hatch, S., 177–8
Hawthorne, G., 76
Hayek, Friedrich August von, 97
Heald, D., 180
Himmelstrand, Ulf, 151, 153, 159–60, 162–3
Hindess, B., 185, 206
Hinton, James, 69
Hirst, P., 185, 206, 208
history, verdict of, 32–5
Hobhouse, L.T., 20, 25
Hobsbawm, Eric, 25, 30, 33, 55–6
Hodges, J., 189
Hodgson, G., 115
Howell, David, 42, 52–3
Hussain, A., 189

ideological state apparatuses (ISAs), 102
ideology: end of, 7, 44–8, 52; and Marxist conception of welfare state, 6, 101–5
ideology of affluence, the new left and the, 52–6
*In and Against the State (IAATS)*, 97, 145–8
Industrial Injuries Act, 40
*Inequality in Health* (Black report), 73
Institute of Economic Affairs, 89–90
intervention, modes of, 195–6

Jones, C., 132
*Journal of Social Policy*, 49

Katsenellenboigen, A., 120
Kautsky, Karl, 22, 28
Kennedy, John F., 43, 52
Kincaid, Jim, 82–3
Korpi, Walter, 153, 160–1
Korsch, Karl, 22

labour, reproduction of relations, 101
Labour Party, British, 1, 9, 38–9, 65, 199, 217–19
Labour Representation Committee, 35
Laclau, E., 203
Laski, H.J., 54
Lavers, G., 41
Lawn, M., 202
Le Grand, J., 73
Lea, John, 174

Lee, Phil, 95–227
Lenin, V.I., 28, 110, 118–19, 123
Leninism, 112–13
*Let Us Face the Future* (Labour Manifesto), 40
Lewis, Gordon, 80–1
Lewis, R., 41
Liberal governments, 35
Liberty and Property Defence League, 35
Lipset, S.M., 5, 47, 48
London School of Economics, 9, 65
Loney, M., 183
Lukács, Georg, 22
Luxemburg, Rosa, 95, 109

McBriar, A., 28
McDonnell, Kevin, 209–10
McIntosh, Mary, 190
MacIntyre, Alasdair, 53–4
McKay, D., 182, 183, 184
MacKenzie, Jeanne, 30–1
MacKenzie, Norman, 30–1
Malthus, Thomas, 120
Mandel, Ernest, 96
*Manifesto of the Communist Party*, 13, 14, 16, 22–3, 24
Mannheim, Karl, 6, 7, 18
Manning, N., 122
Mao Tse-tung, 123
Marcuse, Herbert, 61, 68
Marshall, Alfred, 34
Marshall, T.H., 45, 51
Marx, Karl, 11, 12–13, 22, 26–7, 199
Marxism: 46–7, 69–70; and Fabianism, 11–14; legacies, 11–37; and welfare, 95–227; welfare and politics of social policy, 142–70
Marxist fundamentalism, 100–41: origins of, 111–14
Marxist theory, and welfare, 100–7: and political realism, 171–215
Massey, Doreen, 99, 216
Master and Servant Laws, repeal of, 32
Maude, A., 41
Middleton, S., 103
Miliband, Ralph, 55, 129, 222–3, 224
Mill, James, 66
Mill, John Stuart, 217
Mills, C. Wright, 6, 55
Mishra, Ramesh, 27, 67, 109, 221
Morris, William, 13

Müller, W., 129, 130
Murray, Robin, 175–6

Nairn, Tom, 66, 67, 68, 69
National Assistance Act, 40
National Deviancy Conference, 68
National Health Service Act, 40
National Insurance Act, 40
Neususs, C., 129, 130
*New Criminology, The*, 174
*New Fabian Essays*, 177
new left, and ideology of affluence, 52–6
*New Left Review*, 52–3, 55, 60, 66, 69
Novak, T., 132
Nove, Alec, 171–3

O'Connor, J., 100–1, 122, 128, 192–3, 197
Offe, Claus, 107–8, 130, 158–9, 163, 193–4, 154
Orwell, George, 54
Owen, Robert, 16
Ozga, J., 202

Panich, L., 117
Parkin, Frank, 70
Parsons, Talcott, 126
Petty, William, 72
Pickvance, C., 194
Pimlott, B., 177
Pinker, Robert, 3, 5, 7
Piven, F.F., 143, 166
Plant, Raymond, 81
Polanyi, Michael, 50
policy analysis, towards a critical, 180–5
policy formation, the state and, 192–9
political, and the economic, 20–6
political achievable, the, 171–6
politics: prefigurative, 145–53; realistic, 153–9; of social policy, 142–70; traditional Marxist, 144–5
Pontusson, Jonas, 160–3
Poor Law Reform Act (1834), 32
Popper, Karl, 4
post-war settlement, Fabian collectivism and, 39–44
Postgate, R., 67
Poulantzas, Nicos, 103, 118, 119–20, 129, 130, 200
power, a new view of ?, 206–9
Prior, Mike, 204
proletariat, 23–4; *see also* working class, English
Proudhon, Pierre Joseph, 13, 17

Purdy, Dave, 204

Raban, Colin, 9–93
racism, 104, 183–4, 192, 205
racism awareness training (RAT), 204–5
Ramas, M., 188–9
*Rank and File Teacher*, 68
Rawls, John, 81, 219
realism: political, Marxist theory, welfare and, 171–215; and transition to socialism, 159–64; welfare and Britain, 164–6
reductionism, economic, 122–5
Redundancy Payments Act (1965), 84
reform: impossibility of, 114–16; and revolution, 14–15
reproduction of labour and social relations, 101
revisionism, Fabian, and the welfare state, 2, 9–93, 95
revolution: cultural, 61–3; reform and, 14–15; vanguardism and the frontal assault theory of, 118–20
Robbins, Lord, 41
Rose, Hilary, 65, 177
Rowntree, B., 41
Rowntree, Seebohm, 72, 74
Russian Revolution, 14, 56, 112–14

Saint-Simon, Claude Henri, 16, 26, 31, 44, 46
Samuel, Raphael, 217–18
Sartre, Jean-Paul, 171
Saunders, Peter, 194–8
Saville, J., 135
Scargill, Arthur, 223
Scarman report, 104
Schneider, J., 105–6
Sedgwick, Peter, 75, 79–80
Segal, Lynne, 216
Selbourne, David, 217
Shaw, George Bernard, 9, 14–15, 28, 80
Shils, Edward, 46, 48–9, 54–5
Silburn, R., 85
Simeys, 51
Sivanandan, A., 205
Smart, Barry, 208
social administration, 2–6, 49–52, 64–6
social control, 105–7
social criticism, Fabian, 70–2
Social Democratic Federation, 11
Social Democratic Party, Swedish, 161, 164

social policy: analysis – the middle range, 180–5; the politics of, 142–70; towards a critical, 60–88
social relations, reproduction of, 101
social scientist, 51
socialism, 148–52, 157: and constitutional action, 80–5; the crisis of, 216–20; different from Marxism, 13–35; inadequacies of Fabian, 1, 9–93; realism and the transition to, 159–64; scientific and utopian, 16–20; the state and transition to, 26–32
socialist society, simplistic vision of, 120–2
Society of the Fabian Parliamentary League, 29
Spencer, Herbert, 20, 30, 48
Stalin, Joseph, 30, 113
state: the fragmented?, 194–9; functions of, 100–1; policy formation, 192–9; revisited, 128–32; and transition to socialism, 26–32
Stedman Jones, Gareth, 66, 106
Stephens, J.D., 160, 161, 162
Sumner, C., 117
Supplementary Benefits Commission, 84
Sutcliffe, R., 115, 143
Swedish Federation of Trade Unions, 163–4

Tawney, Richard, 13, 67, 73, 76, 79, 80, 90, 177
Taylor, Ian, 174
Taylor-Gooby, Peter, 49, 64, 65–6, 67, 69, 70
teacher, class location of a, 199–202
Ten Hours Bill (1847), 27
Thatcher, Margaret, 87, 89
Thatcherism, 165, 174, 220–1
Therborn, Goran, 142, 153, 157–8, 160
third way?, 216–26
Thompson, Dorothy, 135
Thompson, E.P., 53, 55, 56, 60, 68, 133, 171, 185
Titmuss, Richard, 64, 72, 73, 74, 76, 78, 177
Townsend, Peter, 65, 72, 73, 74, 76, 77, 78, 83
Toynbee, A.J., 50
Trotsky, Leon, 113–14, 114–16

*Unpopular Education*, 84, 192

Urry, John, 191–2, 203
utopianism, 4–8, 16–20, 120–22

vanguardism, and frontal assault theory of revolution, 118–20

Wainwright, Hilary, 216
Walker, Alan, 145, 221
Wallas, Graham, 19
Webb, Beatrice, 9, 30–2
Webb, Sidney, 9, 19, 25, 28–30, 30–2, 79–80
Webbs, 19, 33, 50, 66, 72, 73, 82, 177
Weber, Henri, 119
Weeks, Jeffrey, 18
welfare: the crisis of, 220–6; Marxism and, 95–227; Marxist theory and, 100–7: and political realism, 171–215; realism and Britain, 164–6; social division of, 72–8
welfare pluralism, 177–80, 217–19, 222–226
welfare reforms, status of, 132–7
welfare state: Fabian collectivism and, 38–59; Fabian revisionism and, 9–93; 'Liberal/Conservative' versus 'socialist' stratification in, 154–6; mandarins of the, 48–52; the unhelpful, 107–11
welfare statism, limitations of, 78–80
welfare studies, pathology of, 63–70
Wells, H.G., 9, 34
Westergaard, John, 125, 216–17
Wickham, G., 206
Wilding, Paul, 7, 49, 202
Williams, Raymond, 39
Wilson, Colin, 53
Wilson, Elizabeth, 105, 133, 134
Wilson, Harold, 39, 44, 52
Winnicott, D.W., 105
women's oppression, accounting for, 187–91
Woodcock, George, 62
working-class, English, 60; *see also* proletariat
Wright, Anthony, 90, 176–7
Wright, E.O., 133, 200–1

Yaffe, D., 116
Young, Jock, 173–4
Young Turks, 61–3

*Zycie Gospodarcze*, 120–1